Strugglers, Stragglers and Seekers:

daily devotions
for the rest of us

by Peggy Haymes

west summit publishing
inform. inspire. encourage.

www.HeartCallings.com

West Summit Publishing
1959 Peace Haven Road, Box 117
Winston-Salem, NC 27106

ISBN 978-0-9996281-0-2

Dedicated to the memory of my father

Joseph A. Haymes, Jr.

who believed the purpose of our lives
was to love God and love people
and who lived accordingly

Introduction to the Second Edition

All books take on lives of their own, but I've been humbled, pleased, and astounded by the life this one has lived. Portions have beeen translated into Norwegian and into Japanese in order for readers to share them with others. People who read it and used it for their daily devotion time have continued to re-read it and use it year after year.

I wrote this book with the hope that you might find in it permission to ask questions and reconsider old stories in the service of nurturing a faith that is more deeply and truly your own. I hoped that those of you with hurting hearts might find some measure of balm and those of you grown too complacent might be a bit jarred.

The nun who led a retreat center where we hold workshops used to greet participants with the wish that they would receive in those days whatever gift they needed at that time in their lives. I hold out the same wish and prayer for you who read this book.

There are no substantive changes in this Second Edition - I've cleaned up a few places that missed proofreading eyes first time around, and corrected some web information that's grown out of date.

Good journeys!

Peggy Haymes
November, 2017

Introduction

It seemed like such a good idea at the time.

I was spending a frustrating time in a bookstore looking for a daily devotional book to give as a gift. I felt a little like Goldilocks with the three bears.

My friend already had that one. That one was too conservative. That other one left me flat. As I vainly searched an idea was born. Why not write a book of daily devotions?

I'd spent ten years as editor of *Reflections* daily devotional guide and loved writing devotions for each issue. Why not do an entire book of them?

I'm afraid to figure out how many years ago that was. During the writing of this I moved back to my hometown. During the writing of this I've been a member of two different churches in two different towns (and you'll just have to guess which one it is when I write about "my church.")

A lot of things got in the way. Little things, like allowing all other work to crowd out this work. Big things, like accidents and illnesses and saying good-bye to all manner of people and things in all manner of ways. I kept fretting over all of these interruptions and detours.

Finally I got it.

This is where our spirituality happens. Getting away from it all is nice but for most of us for most of the time we have to practice our faith in the muck and mess of life or it doesn't get practiced at all.

So here it is, to be read in the muck and mess and glory and joy of your lives as they unfold through these days. The writing of it has felt like a gift to me. It is my hope that in some way it will be gift to you as well.

Good journeys!

Peggy Haymes
Winston-Salem, NC   January, 2013

January 1
Psalm 103:6-14

 I leaned my head back as far as I could without toppling over, looking straight up. In the desert air, the moonless night was clear and crisp and deep as eternity. I'd never seen such space, packed with thousands upon thousands of stars.

We slowly climbed the mountain in the pre-dawn chill, sitting upon the rocky summit as the horizon filled with the brilliant reds of sunrise. Mountains and desert and sky seemed to go on and on forever. I'd never experienced such vastness before. The psalmist says that God's love is that vast, that huge.

But I cannot take in anything so big. It's too much for me. And so the psalmist puts it into terms that are a little closer to home. A loving father has compassion for his child. He cradles the infant in arms that are secure and safe and loving. He pulls the frightened child into his lap and holds the child close. As much as any earthly parent has compassion for their children, so much more does God have compassion for us.

It's the first day of a brand new year. At some point in the next 12 months, you'll probably mess up. Maybe in a small way, maybe big. If you do, remember the vastness of God's mercy. It's there for you, too. In the coming year, you may experience hurt or struggle. If so, remember the tender depth of God's compassion for you.

I say these things not to depress you on New Year's Day but to give you freedom. Go out and live the biggest and the best life you can. Shoot for the best, because if you fall, God will be there to help you get back up. Live joyfully and freely because you know this love will not desert you.

Live fully and live well these days because you are not alone.

January 2
Luke 2:36-38

Unlike Simeon, Anna wasn't waiting for anything. As far as we're told, she didn't show up at the Temple every day hoping that this would be the day. She didn't scan the new faces wondering if this was the one. She was at the temple that day because that's what she did.

She showed up. She prayed. She fasted. She worshiped.

We don't know what drove her. Was she looking for something holy to fill a hole in her heart left so many years ago? Was it a safe place for a widow to pass her days? Was she driven by a deep hunger for God and a deep joy in God's presence?

We don't know. All we know is that she showed up. And on this day, she had the good sense to see what was before her.

We'd do well to learn from Anna. It's a temptation to base our showing up on whether or not some special attraction is worth our investment. "Oh, I don't know that we need to go to church today. There's nothing special happening."

But here's the rub - we never know when that something - or someone - unexpected is going to show up. In our worship. In our private prayers. We show up because that's what we do and suddenly we realize that God is here, too.

You're only half listening to (or preaching) a sermon when suddenly there's a word that is so much for you that it's as if it floats across the air on yellow highlights. You show up to pray because it's what you do and suddenly, like an old Polaroid picture developing before your eyes, the answer to a dilemma comes into focus. You show up at the soup kitchen because it's your monthly turn and out of the blue you realize that it's been Jesus standing there before you all along, disguised in a dirty old army jacket and four day stubble.

Anna showed up. She kept her eyes open. And she paid attention as the Spirit tapped her on the shoulder.

May we be as wise.

January 3
Jeremiah 1:1-10

Lately there's been something of a backlash against the so-called self-esteem movement. Commentators have warned against the dangers of telling all of our children that they're special. One day a newspaper columnist even attacked Mr. Rogers for being the source of much that was wrong in our culture today.

As a whole, I think these commentators have gotten it all wrong. The problem isn't in telling children that they're special. It's in not setting boundaries for them, establishing and enforcing clear consequences for poor choices. Children thrive when they have structure. Teaching choices and consequences has nothing to do with self-esteem except that children develop a healthy sense of self-esteem as they learn to choose wisely – and to discover that they can make mistakes, learn from them and still be loved.

I disagree with those people who say that we shouldn't tell our children that they're special because I think they are. I think we ALL are. I believe that God's word to Jeremiah is God's word to every one of us, "Before you were even born, I knew you." If we are uniquely created by God, if we were loved by God even before our birth, how can we not be just a little special?

Here's the difference that the columnists miss. Believing that we are beloved in God's eyes isn't an invitation to become divas and divos (is that the masculine form of diva?) It isn't license to expect the world to cater to us, to act expecting no consequences. Instead, God's blessing comes with a calling. "I knew you even as you were taking shape. And I have a work for you to do, a life for you to live."

Maybe, like Jeremiah, you are called to do a big thing. Or maybe, like countless other saints, you are called to live an ordinary life that is extraordinary in the lives you touch and the love you share.

Today, live as if it were true. Listen for God's whisper of love and embrace God's invitation for life – your own, unique life.

January 4
Philippians 2:12-14

I never knew quite what to do with this verse. I knew I was once saved, always saved. I knew that it was a gift of grace and not my own doing. So what was all of this business about working out my salvation?

While I'd never claim to edit Paul, maybe things would be clearer if he'd added one simple word: of. "Work out *of* your salvation…"

We cannot know what God's gift to us means in one day. Not even in one moment of baptism. (Maybe not even in one lifetime.)

We have to work it out for ourselves, day after day after day. What does it mean to be held by God? What does it mean to walk through this world knowing that you are so loved by God that God would stop at nothing to embrace you? How does following Christ affect the way that you work and how you relate to other people? What does it mean to be a citizen of a country and of the world... and of God's kingdom?

Any answer we could give in this one moment would be incredibly partial: this is what I know right now. Because today or tomorrow or next month something will come that shapes and expands and influences and challenges that definition.

I never got the fear and trembling part either. After all, isn't Jesus' word to us, "don't be so scared?" But maybe in this case fear and trembling means taking it seriously. These are important questions. It is important to be thoughtful and reflective. It is important to treat the questions seriously. When one of my professors was questioned on his view of scripture, he said, "I take it seriously enough that I have devoted my entire life to the study of it."

While I don't think we all have to get PhDs in biblical studies, there is something about taking it seriously enough that we bring the very best of our minds and our hearts and our souls to the endeavor.

There are no simple black and white checklists for what it means to live as a brother or sister of Christ. The best that we have is a life that calls us to keep working it out.

January 5
Deuteronomy 30:11-14

We'd staffed a lot of workshops together, so it was only natural that we should have some running jokes. One of those was, "Wait, there's a harder way."

"Wait, there's a harder way." I wonder if God thinks that on occasion as we struggle and strive. "I'm going to follow God," we say with every fiber of our being clenched tight. I used to feel that way about God's will for my life. It was going to be hard. It was going to be obscure. It was going to be something I really didn't like, like eating mustard greens.

Imagine my surprise to hear God saying, "Look — it's right here. As close as your breath, as close as the beating of your heart. You don't have to go on a quest to find it. You just have to open yourself to it." Imagine my surprise when God's calling in my own life turned out to include the things I really love to do, things that at times even feel easy to me. (I used to believe that if I enjoyed it, it couldn't possibly be what God wanted me to do!)

God gave the children of Israel a library full of laws to guide their living together and living with God. But the giving of the law is summed up with these words: "Look — it's right here."

The next time you feel like you have to go on a far-off quest to be connected with God's Spirit or to seek God's guidance, stop. Stop and take a breath. And then another one. And listen for the word that is in your mouth and in your heart.

January 6
Deuteronomy 30:15-20

"I have set before you life and death, blessings and curses. Choose life…"

Not to sound like a middle schooler, but… well, like duh. I mean, unless you're horribly depressed, you're going to choose life. Right?

Right?

Well, maybe not. You see, there are a hundred different ways of choosing death over life, and not just the obvious ones. There are lots of ways to die while you still live. You can close off your heart. It still beats, but nothing gets past the steel walls around it. You don't get hurt, but you never love. You can talk yourself out of your dreams and give up on the foolishness of hope. You can go through the motions of life, getting lots of stuff but never stopping to ask what it all means and what it means for you. You can decide that you're too broken, too sinful, too old, too whatever for God's grace to actually apply to you.

Choosing life means choosing to live. Sometimes that means dealing with whatever gets in the way of being fully alive, whether it's a change on the inside or the outside. Sometimes that means choosing to trust God for this one day, even though you cannot possibly see where all of this is going or how things can possibly work out. Sometimes it means taking a risk to share your gifts with the world or your heart with one other person. Sometimes it means believing, despite what they said or despite what you've done, that God loves you too.

You have a choice. Choose life.

January 7
Mark 6:1-6

I was talking with an older minister about working in churches. The people of my home church were very affirming of me and eager to bless my gifts. Someone had asked me if I'd ever consider returning home to a staff position there. "You know, Peggy," my friend said. "It's awfully hard to be minister to the people who used to change your diapers."

I think Jesus knew just what he meant. He started preaching in his home synagogue, and the people were amazed at the wisdom and eloquence of this young man. Instead of beaming with pride and delight, they started making fun of him. "Just who does he think he is?" they grumbled to one another. "We knew his daddy. We knew him when he was a little kid." In the south, that's known as getting above your raisin', and it's a very big no-no.

But here's the really astounding thing: Jesus couldn't do much while he was there. Miracles were in short supply. Healings were few and far between. Their unwillingness to accept Jesus as he was and for who he was limited his power. They weren't open to receive and so he couldn't give.

Some days, when it seems as if no prayer is answered, I wonder if it's not so much that God isn't giving, but that I'm not open to receiving. Maybe deep down I think it's impossible. Or maybe I think my prayer can only be answered one way, and so I don't see God's gift that's sitting on the doorstep.

It's a humbling and a troubling thought to think that we could be hindering God's work in this world.

God, use me. And if you can't use me, help me to get out of the way.

January 8
Hebrews 13:1-6

Yesterday we ordained two new deacons in my church. As I stood in line for the laying on of hands, I looked around me. Somehow, whether it's for the Lord's Supper or an ordination, the church looks different when we're all making our way down to the front. I see the matriarch, known for her bright hats, infectious sense of humor and deep faith. I see the teenagers who not so very long ago were children. I see the people I've cried with and prayed with and laughed with. I see people who, by their words or their actions or both, have taught me a great deal about what is means to be a faithful follower of Christ.

It never fails that as I stand in line or as I sit in the choir loft watching other people in line, I am moved by such deep love for these people. Sometimes I even get misty-eyed. And here's the truth – I know that at least some of them love me as well. I know it from their hugs. I know it from the way that they kid with me. I know it from the way they have always been there for me when I needed them.

"Let mutual love continue," he wrote. There is such a deep hunger in this world for such love. If you experience such love in your own community, give thanks to God. If your community seems to do everything except love one another, ask God how you might begin to be love there (knowing that it's not all up to you.) And if you're going it alone right now, ask God for the gift of community whether it's a circle of five people or a church of 500. Let mutual love continue, for it is the sustenance of our souls.

January 9
John 10:11-18

Being sheep isn't an exclusive club.

Oh, you might think so. All the sheep hanging out here. All that stuff about us sheep knowing the shepherd and the shepherd not being willing to lose even one sheep.

Israel thought it was a pretty exclusive club, and with some justification. There was that whole Chosen People deal. And then all of that stuff about being the sheep of God's pasture.

They had every right to believe that they were the one true sheep. Every so often a prophet or two would try to tell them differently, but it never quite stuck.

So now here's Jesus talking to the disciples, a bunch of Jewish guys who had every right to think they were the super chosen ones. As Jews, they were part of God's chosen people. As Jesus' disciples, they believed they were Gods chosen people who were following God's chosen Messiah. It doesn't get any more special and privileged than that.

But then Jesus slips in this one statement:

"I have other sheep, sheep not of this fold; I must bring them in also."

Of course, he was talking about us, the non-Jewish folks.

Except now we're on the inside. Were the ones who have the name of God's people. We're the ones who talk about the good shepherd.

I wonder if Jesus was talking to us right now if he'd say the same thing. I have other sheep, you know. I have to go and get them as well.

I don't know. I do know that whenever we get too clever about drawing lines between who is in and who is out God has a way of going along with a big old eraser, erasing them, drawing circles bigger than we'd ever imagined.

So maybe we do well to concentrate on our own sheep-ness - hanging with the flock, listening for the shepherd's voice. And if he appears to call some folks we didn't expect, well that's just the way he is.

January 10
Joel 2:25-27

As a counselor, I often work with people who were hurt in some way as children. Some of them were beaten; some of them were sexually abused. Some of them were beaten down by emotional abuse that bruised their souls just as surely as a punch would've bruised their bodies. As they heal, one of the things they experience is profound grief.

The grief may be for the safe father or mother that they never experienced. The grief may be for their childhood, for the one they had and the one they never got to have. As they heal, they also grieve for the ways that those wounds affected their adult lives – the opportunities they never took advantage of, the relationships they never let form, all of the times that their wounds kept them from dancing and moving ahead.

It makes me think of this passage from Joel. "I will repay you for all the years the locusts have eaten." There's no way, of course, that those years can officially be replaced. We cannot go back and have our high school prom again. We cannot go back and re-live that first marriage, even though now we see all of the wrong turns we took. And that's not what this passage promises.

What this passage promises is that the locusts are not the end of the story. After they have moved on, there can be life again. It is my delight to watch my clients heal, to see them reclaim those years for themselves. Even though it's later than they would have liked, their souls still learn how to dance.

You may have had a few locust years yourself. Trust in this promise of God's future – your future. Even if you're limping now, you may yet dance.

January 11
Psalm 32

Every so often a client will start telling me a story.. a story about something that happened to them or a story about something they did or both. They don't look much at me while they speak and sometimes they hardly breathe.

Sometimes they've been planning for weeks or days to tell me and sometimes it's a surprise to them - they don't know they are going to tell me until the words start coming out. Sometimes it's a story that no one else on this earth has ever heard. Afterwards they finally meet my eyes and say with surprise, "I feel such a relief."

That's they way it is when we carry secrets. Their heaviness increases in direct proportion to our feelings about not being able to share them.

Sometimes, like with my clients, the secrets are about the ways in which we've been hurt. But sometimes the secrets are about the hurt we've inflicted upon others. Or the ways in which we've hurt ourselves by failing to live up to our own values.

We think that if we don't look at them they'll go away.

But they don't. Instead they creep into our rooms at night and steal our sleep. They make our blood pressure just a little higher and our days just a little more off. Foolishly, we think we can hide our secrets even from God.

We cannot be whole and we cannot be wholly ourselves until we are honest. Not in the explaining things away kind of way. "Well, you know everybody was doing it." "Boys will be boys." I didn't mean to hurt them."

No, being honest with our secrets before God begins with owning our part in the sin. "I was wrong." "I shouldn't have said that." I shouldn't have done that." "I made a mistake."

It is the paradox that by owning ours sins, we are finally able to be rid of them. We create a channel through which God's forgiveness can flow. We can move forward to doing better and being better.

What are you trying to hide from God today? Is there a secret lying heavy on your shoulders? Maybe it's not a big deal to anyone else but it is to you. Or maybe it would be a big deal.

Trust God. Trust God enough to tell your secrets. Trust God enough to own your sin. And trust God enough to receive forgiveness.

January 12
Isaiah 43:16-21

"How's it going?"

"Oh, you know. Same old, same old."

Same old, same old. We know it well, don't we? Same old routine… doing the laundry, going to class… attending the meeting… checking the kids' homework… unloading the dishwasher.

Same old, same old. We know it even in our spiritual life. We'll sit through the same service (because someone's BOUND to complain if they make any changes.) If we grew up in a church, we hear the same stories we've heard a hundred times. If the stories are new, we're still left with the same old question of what difference it could possibly make to us.

Same old, same old. We know all about God. We just might not be sure of what God has to do with our day in and day out routines. There doesn't seem to be much room for that same old, same old spiritual stuff in our days.

But then God whispers in our ears, a voice trembling with excitement and glee. "I'm getting ready to do something so radical and new," God says, "it's going to be like having lifeguards in the desert. Where there was dry, there will be water. Where there was grief, there will be healing. Where there was suffering, there will be joy.

"And where the song of your life was nothing but the same old, same old, there will be a dance so new you'll blink your eyes with wonder. Even in the day in and day out-ness of it, you will be surprised by me. You will trip all over my spirit and be caught off guard by my ways."

God, give me the grace to see the new thing you are doing in my life. Grace my life with holy surprise.

January 13
Matthew 11:28-30

They look away and go to a place deep inside themselves. Taking a deep breath, they begin to tell their story. Their words are halting and fragile because it's a story that mostly stays locked away. A story they're scared to tell and a story that they're scared to be heard. The scars from an alcoholic parent or abusive past that keeps them feeling defective and broken. The secret addictions to gambling or food or porn that they cannot live with but fear they cannot live without. The marriage that looks so perfect on the outside but feels so dead on the inside. The pain or worry that never quite goes away. The waves of debt that are slowly drowning them. The demands of caring for the very young or the very old or the very sick.

As a minister and counselor, it's holy ground for me when people begin to share their stories – their real stories, not the official, authorized biographies. It's holy ground because in the acknowledgment of the burden is the opening for relief. Relief doesn't always come in having the burden taken away, but rather in knowing that we do not bear it alone.

So here's Jesus. He knows something about heavy loads, having had to carry his own cross when he was already weak, broken and worn out. You can be honest with him about whatever your own burden is without having to worry about what he will think or how you will look. There is no secret so shameful that he cannot hear. There is no burden so heavy that he will not take it on. There is no story of your life or mine that will make him do less than love us.

"Come on," Jesus says. "I'm here."

What are you waiting for?

January 14
Mark 5:25-34

Okay, pop quiz. Where's the miracle in this story?

You eagerly raise your hand… hey, I know this one! When the woman touched Jesus' clothes, she was healed.

Yes, that is indeed a miracle, but it's not the first miracle in this story. The first miracle is that the woman reached out, trusting that something good could happen.

Think about it. She'd gone from doctor to doctor for twelve long years, with absolutely no success. Nobody could cure her. Nobody could say, "Here is what to do in order to be well." How long would you keep trying? How many people would you see before you just gave up? When someone told you about the latest cure that worked for their cousin's sister-in-law, you might give it a shot. But would there be a part of you that thought, why bother? When everyone else had written you off as a hopeless case, could you keep going?

For whatever reason, this woman held onto the stubborn faith that healing was possible. Because of that, she was able to seek Jesus out, to reach out to him, and then, to be healed.

Are there places in your life where such stubborn faith is needed? Are you discouraged about something – or someone? Are you facing a situation that seems to have no answer, no possibility for resolution? Is there a place in your life that seems beyond the hope of healing?

If so, remember this woman. Let her inspire you to have the courage and the faith to reach out one more time, to seek Jesus out and ask for his help.

The truth of the matter is that healing doesn't always look like we thought it would look, and it doesn't always come on the timetables we've established. But reach out anyway, grab hold of God, and see what surprising things may come.

January 15
Romans 8:1-11

Jesus saw a woman
    condemned for her sin
    stones of judgment about to rain
        upon body and bone.

His compassion a shield
    he sheltered her until
    the angry mob drifted away.

"Does no one condemn you?" he asked of her
    and the emptiness of silence was the answer.
    "Neither do I," he said
    and she started to breathe again.

We gather up our own stones
    handing them to others to throw at us
    or even trying
    to bounce them off ourselves
        for we are sinners.
        We have sinned.
        We have screwed up.
        We have done wrong.
        We have fallen short.
            We've hurt other people.
            We've hurt ourselves.
            We've hurt this world.

In any language, we're guilty.

But he stands before us
    and gently pries the stone
    from our hands
    and sends the others away.

"Let it go," he says.
        "I don't condemn you.
        I love you."

Go your way, he says.
And leave this behind.
Go your way.
Go *my* way.

January 16
Matthew 9:14-17

The point, of course, wasn't about wineskins. Or even wine.

The point was that what Jesus was about wasn't just some upgrade to a previous version. While his roots were in what had come before, he was also doing something radically different. He wasn't just patching up the old religion.

The scary part is that he wants to do the same thing with us.

He doesn't want to just patch us up, upgrade us into new and improved versions of our old selves. He wants to make us into new creations. New, as in something that's never been before.

Jesus wants to do a radical makeover on us. This is not just slapping a few coats of paint on a couple of walls and calling it a day. This is putting a whole new structure in.

What Jesus proposes to do with us and in us and for us is to shape every aspect of our lives. The decisions we make. How we live in this world. How we live with each other. How we live with ourselves. This new thing means that Jesus wants to have his fingerprints all over our lives.

I can't tell you what that will look like for you today. Maybe you'll be called to speak out. Maybe you'll be called to sit in silence. Maybe you'll be called to embrace something. And maybe you'll be called to give something up, let something go or give something away. Maybe you'll be called to live with open heart and open eyes.

The one thing I know for sure is that this faith of ours is about creating something new.

The scary thing is that Jesus wants to make of us and of this world a new creation. The lovely thing is that as we allow him, we find our true beauty and our true life.

Anyone for new wineskins?

January 17
Isaiah 49:14-18

Play practice was over and everyone scattered. I waited just inside the door of the now dark, downtown church for my mom to come and pick me up. The adult in charge thought all the kids had gone so he'd left as well. As I looked out on the shadowy and deserted streets, I heard all kinds of noises in the old building. It seemed that I'd been forgotten.

I finally found a phone (this was in the days long before cell phones) and called my mom. She thought someone else was bringing me home. That person thought I'd already left. To my great relief, my mom pulled up to the church not so many minutes later.

Feeling forgotten was like feeling like I was in kind of a limbo. But there are worse ways of being forgotten than being forgotten at the church. It's that feeling of feeling utterly alone; as if the world has forgotten about you and that you matter. You may be physically alone. Or you may be surrounded by people and yet even more deeply alone. Sometimes in those dark nights of the soul it feels as if even God has forgotten about you.

Isaiah's audience knew that feeling. They'd lost homes and work and families and friends. They'd lost their country. What made it even worse was that they were sure it wouldn't happen because they were God's chosen people. But happen it did, and God's beautiful temple was in ruins. Their lives were in ruins.

Have you ever felt like your life was in ruins - or maybe just coming apart at the seams? Ever feel like your faith is nowhere near as sure and self-assured as it once was and things seem to be crumbling a bit?

If so, come on up here and stand beside Israel. God has a word for both of you.

God lifts up your chin and looks you in the eye. "Forget about you?" Can a woman forget about a child she's nursing?

Even if such a thing were possible, I couldn't forget you. Your name is tattooed on the palm of my hands. Every time I lift a hand, your name is there. You are impossible to forget."

So if you ever doubt it, if you ever feel like maybe, just maybe God's forgotten all about you because you can't see much evidence of God working in your life, take heart.

Take into your heart these words of love. "I cannot forget you," says God. "I cannot *not* love you."

January 18
Romans 8:12-17

In her book, *Writing to Change the World,* Mary Pipher tells the story of walking along in a market in Burma. Poor people were selling this trinket and that piece of junk. She watched as a teenager was taken by soldiers, beaten and then thrown into a truck while his mother screamed. Pipher realized that what she was seeing was a people completely without hope.

One man squatted in the gutter selling children's Magic Slates. He looked at Pipher then scrawled on the slate, showing it to her. "Freedom from fear." It was the motto of Aung San Suu Kyi, a western exile who'd returned to Burma to work for democracy and who was under house arrest. The man looked into Pipher's eyes, smiled and then erased the words he'd written.

Freedom from fear. Most of us won't know the kind of fear that permeated that man's daily life. But most of us know something about fear.

It's the fear that creeps into the space in-between the test and the test result. It's the endless game of what-if that keeps us awake at night. It's the fear of not having enough or of not being good enough or of having to face living our lives without that person whom we thought would be in our lives forever.

We weren't meant to live, Paul says, with the cringing fear of a slave. We weren't meant to live in fear at all. In fear is slavery but in the Spirit of God there is freedom. There is freedom that come what may - even if the test results are the worst they can be - we do not face these days alone. There is freedom that God will provide for us, maybe not in the way we order and usually not in the ways in which we expect, but God provides nonetheless. It is the freedom that we don't have to measure ourselves by some arbitrary standard of what is good enough or successful enough or beautiful enough. We are God's children, and we can live in the full freedom of being ourselves - our wonderful quirky, goofy selves.

There is a very fine saying: What would you do if you knew you could not fail? Today mend it just a bit. Today consider: What could you do - and who could you be - if you had no fear?

January 19
John 14:25-31

Peace is a choice.

I know, it usually doesn't feel that way. So often it feels like our inner peace is dependent upon our outer circumstances. When I'm out of debt, I can be at peace. When my children are successfully launched into their adult lives. When my health clears up. When I get a job.

Actually, we don't have to wait for any of these things. We can choose peace. Right here. Right now. No matter what our circumstances.

Etty Hillseum was a young woman growing into adulthood in Europe as Hitler's shadow began spreading. As a Jew, her life became more and more limited. She couldn't visit certain parks or ride her bike on certain streets. Finally she was taken away to one of the camps.

As you read the collection of her letters and her journal you see the most extraordinary thing happen. As her life grows smaller, her spirit grows larger. From behind the barbed wire she writes of walking with joy in her step. She writes that although the Nazis have seemingly taken everything from her, they can never take her ability to pray.

Kind of makes that traffic jam that was stealing your peace seem not so big now, doesn't it?

Jesus said that he was giving us a different kind of peace. It's not a peace like the world gives, fragile and dependent upon the circumstances of our lives. This peace is rock solid, available for anyone who chooses it.

Peace is a choice. It's not always an easy one, but it is a choice. Instead of worry, I choose peace. Instead of frustration, I choose peace. Instead of despair, I choose peace. Instead of second-guessing, I choose peace.

Jesus is offering peace to you now. What will you choose?

January 20
Psalm 6

When they call to make an appointment, they tell me that they're grieving. The loss of a parent. A spouse. A child. A friend. Sometimes when they come for the first appointment the tears are just beneath the surface. And sometimes they come spilling out as soon as they sit down. As they grab for a tissue, many of them apologize. "I don't know why I'm such a mess," they say.

I tell them that I do. And they're not a mess. They are grieving. Grieving is hard.

And messy.

Even when we know better in our heads, many of us carry around the unspoken expectation that we shouldn't struggle. We shouldn't feel down. We shouldn't ever be discouraged. We shouldn't be sad. After all, if you're happy and you know it, clap your hands, right?

Right?

That's one of the reasons why I love the psalms. They are such a good and honest tonic for such foolishness. Not only do the writers have the courage to name the realities of their conditions, they are trusting enough to bring them to God. There's no pretending in the psalms, no "being fine" when one's soul is weighted down or one's heart is breaking.

Only when we correctly name where we are can we start to find the way through. Otherwise, it's like trying to find directions to San Francisco with a starting place of New York when you are anywhere other than New York.

Start with where you are. Be brave enough to bring that to God in language as honest as you can bear.

God can certainly hear it.

And God can walk with you through it.

January 21
Mark 9:38-41

There's always someone
    someone who wants to draw the line
    between us and them.
Someone who's quick to point out
    what "they" are doing
    why "they are wrong"
    what's the matter with "them."
There's always someone
    who is quick to decide
    they alone know the truth,
    they alone know what is right and holy and just.
"Those people are not like us....
How dare they speak of God!"

God, forgive me when I become
one of the line drawing people,
    more concerned with keeping the club pure
    than wrapping the world in your love.
God, forgive me
    when I am so eager to stand in judgment
    of those line drawing people
    that I become one of them as well.

God, teach me to live,
    to see,
    to speak
    and to love
        in the flow of your heart.

January 22
Judges 6:36-40

It's called "laying out a fleece" and it comes from this story. Gideon wasn't sure he could trust God's promise to deliver Israel from her enemies so he devised a way of making sure.

Spreading a fleece out over the floor before he went to bed, he asked God to cover the wool with dew during the night while keeping the floor dry. That would be the proof he needed that God was truly with him and leading him.

Sure enough, the next morning the floor was dry but the fleece was sopping wet. Still, Gideon had just a smidgen of doubt. "Now don't be angry, God, he said, "but could you just show me one more time?" This time, he asked for the reverse result. Sure enough, the next morning the fleece was dry but the rest of the floor was covered with dew.

Through the years I've heard people talk about "laying out a fleece" in ways that don't seem especially helpful to me. "If God means for me to get this job, then I'll hit every green light and won't be late for the interview." Sometimes it feels like treating God like a magic eight ball, shaking things up and then turning them over for the answer. "It is doubtful."

Maybe we've missed the point with all of our questions about whether or not it's an act of faith to ask God to put up or shut up. Maybe the point is that Gideon went as far as his faith would allow him, and then he asked for help.

I'm not sure that God responds to manipulation. I do believe that God hears and honors our honest cries for help. "I'm confused, God, and don't know which way to turn. Give me some kind of sign, God, so I'll know the way."

Have the courage and the trust to go to the limits of your faith. But when those limits come up sooner than you think they should, don't waste your time beating yourself up. Just ask for help. You never know when a fleece might become a bridge to an even more deeply trusting faith.

January 23
John 11:17-36

They were hanging out, doing all of the useless feeling things you do when a beloved friend has lost a loved one. Mary's brother Lazarus was gone and they were doing what they could do for her.

Without saying anything, she left. What could they do but follow her? If she was going to the tomb to weep, well then they'd go with her. Of course she was going to weep for what else does one do in the shadow of death?

And indeed she wept. But soon the weeping turned into a gasp. If there were tears they were now tears of joy, joy for the farewell turned welcome. And some of those bystanders were never the same.

Sometimes we think we know the order of things. It's the way things have always been. It's what should be logically expected. And sometimes we are right. But then there are those other days...

Expecting mourning, we walk right into dancing. The dreams we thought were dead and buried suddenly have a pulse. The joyful life we thought we beyond our grasp is suddenly as close as our breath.

The miracle was for Lazarus but not just Lazarus. The miracle was for his sisters Mary and Martha but not just for them. The miracle was for a group of mourners who got raised up by the witnessing of it.

And not just them.

The miracle is for us as well. We are reminded again that God is in the business of bringing light where we only see dark, of bringing hope where we only see despair, of bringing life where we're resigned to mourn death.

Today and not just for today, allow yourself to be surprised by God.

January 24
Psalm 100

In other psalms of praise God is praised for bringing forth creation or bringing Israel out of bondage. In today's psalm the call to praise is basic and fundamental.

Praise God because we belong to God. God made us and God claims us. And that's enough reason for praise for one day.

God made you. You may want to quibble about the size of your ears or of your thighs but leave that for another day. Today remember the incredible wonders your body performs a thousand times a day. We've spent hundreds of years studying the human body and are still chasing its mysteries. And that's the skin you live in every single day.

God made you and God claims you. If you so choose you can walk around in a T-shirt that says God's Family Reunion and you'd be telling the truth. That's what happens every Sunday or Tuesday or whenever God's people gather. No matter how healthy or crazy your own parents were, you ultimately belong to God.

Sing your praise even if that means joyful singing that is also yet a terrible noise. Speak your praise even if the words are jumbled, even if they sometimes come slow, wrapped up in the stuff of all in your life that doesn't feel terribly praiseworthy. Write your praise, for as the words flow down our arm they become real and take on a life of their own.

Breathe your praise. Breathe it in and breathe it out.

For God made us and claims us and my word, what an amazing thing that is.

Today, praise God.

January 25
Deuteronomy 6:10-18

Remind us, O God,
that we always forever
   live in partnership.
We offer the work of our hands
    and the sweat of our brow
    and the best of our minds
       but always there is more.
Always standing on the shoulders
of those who paved the way.
    Those who opened doors.
    Those who dreamed dreams.
Always there is more...
    You who gives life to our dreams
    Who gives strength to our working
    Who makes a way we do not yet see
    Who works in ways
      we can neither explain nor define
      but we know to be true
        deep in the mystery of our souls.

Remind us, God
that we always forever
   live in partnership.
Remind us
   lest our thanksgiving be thoughtless
   and our gratitude be half-hearted.

January 26
Matthew 12:33-37

As I write this I'm listening to some of the anthems we're working on in choir (a nice advantage of the internet.) Listening to them online reinforces what we do in rehearsal. As I listen to this piece I remember how impossible it seemed to me the first time we sang it in rehearsal. I was lost half the time and when I wasn't lost I was singing the wrong notes. Each time we rehearse it the anthem becomes a little more familiar to me.

By the time we sing it on Sunday morning, I want to know it by heart. I don't mean that I won't need any music, although that's nice when it happens. I mean that I know it in my heart. It feels like second nature to me. I know what I need to sing (mostly) and singing in worship becomes part of the flow.

It's not such a bad picture for our spiritual lives. Day in and day out we rehearse. We open ourselves up to learning the song of God's Spirit. In less poetic language, we keep trying to learn about God and learn about ourselves... and who we are as God's children. We keep trying to tune our lives so that our living is in harmony with the grace of the gospel.

We read scripture. We read other books that inspire us, challenge us, comfort us. We talk with fellow pilgrims. We gather together with them to talk together about our journeys and learn from each other. We join in worship, listening for God through prayers and litanies, sermons and anthems... and sometimes the acolyte in scuffed basketball shoes. It is a lifelong journey and a daily task.

But we do not lose heart tending to our spirit, for this inner world becomes the soil for the fruits of our lives.

January 27
Habakkuk 3:17-19

Sometimes stubbornness is a virtue.

Those of you with stubborn two year olds may be wondering about my judgment at this point, but bear with me. I'm talking about the kind of stubbornness I've seen in my clients, the stubbornness that is determined that whoever or whatever told them that they were no good or that their lives did not matter will be proven wrong. Even if they do not believe it themselves in that moment, they keep showing up and working on their healing on the off chance that such stubborn hope is true. Sometimes stubbornness is what helps us survive.

Habakkuk speaks of a different kind of stubbornness. Even though there is seemingly no reason to give thanks and praise to God, he will praise God anyway. Such stubbornness refuses to give up the hope that hope is yet coming, that a day of bounty and fruitfulness and all good things will yet come again.

Even though the fig tree does not blossom, God is still my strength. Even though I don't get the job. Even though the love of my life has still moved away. Even though life looks nothing like I hoped it would or even though it might be, even so yet will I praise God.

This is a prayer to be howled into the wind of the storms. This is a prayer to be whispered through clenched teeth. This is a prayer of a stubborn soul who believes that the grace and mercy of God is greater than any situation in which we find ourselves.

Do you need such a prayer today? Perhaps you've prayed it yourself at times. If all this talk seems strange to you right now just tuck it away. I suspect one day will come when you remember it and understand it.

And if you are there now, howl it at the storm and let it echo in the emptiness. Yet will I rejoice. God is my strength.

God lifts me up.

January 28
1 Corinthians 12:4-13

I like to write. If you haven't already realized that, I think you'll catch on pretty quickly if you keep reading. When I was a teenager we had a mission education group for girls that was loosely modeled on the Scouts - you did activities and passed steps. The pinnacle was achieving Queen Regent in Service status that came with a gold cape and a spiffy pin to go with the crown and scepter you'd already earned. All over the American south women have scepters stashed away in closets.

But I digress. Since I love to write, I always looked for those tasks in the step that started with "Write a..." Write a poem. Write a letter to missionary. I was all over those tasks. They were easy for me.

Still are. The minister of music asks me for a litany for a service and I am all over that. It comes easily to me. It's not such a big deal... at least to me.

You know what does impress me? The people who can crunch numbers. I'm in awe of them. The church treasurers and church budget creators.

And I think that's kind of the point Paul was trying to make to the people at Corinth. We all have different kinds of gifts and the body of Christ needs all of them. Some of them are obvious,

like teaching a class or singing in the choir or playing the piano or cooking up dinner on Wednesday night.

Other kinds of gifts sometimes slip by unrecognized... the gift of rocking a baby in safe, loving arms, the gifts of encouragement, the gift of asking the right questions, the kinds of questions that make a community step back and listen again for the calling of God... the gift of organizing and getting things done, the gift of growing good food for hungry folks whose bodies and souls need more than just canned goods.

You have gifts. The work of Christ and the body of Christ need those gifts. The needs of this world are too real and too big for us to keep pretending that who we are and what we have to offer doesn't matter.

January 29
John 4:46-54

Trust.

There's no desperate like the desperation of a parent with a sick child. Stroll through the halls of any children's hospital and you'll see them... parents who have given up everything else in their lives for the sake of healing and holding onto their child.

A Gentile military officer knew the feeling. His son was dying and if there was any chance that this Jewish preacher could heal him; well, he wasn't above begging. He begs long enough and hard enough that Jesus tells him to go on, his son will live. And so the official goes on his way. And so the boy recovers.

This story is woven through with trust on the part of this nameless official. First, he trusted enough to ask. He trusted enough to beg.

Maybe it was his last and only hope. Maybe it was the last ditch, we've got nothing to lose effort. Still, he sought Jesus out and begged him for a miracle.

I don't know about you but I know that I sometimes talk myself out of being so bold. It'll never work. It's too much to ask. I shouldn't bother. I never even get around to asking God... for anything.

The official trusted enough to come to Jesus and he trusted enough to leave him. It's all okay, Jesus said and on that basis alone, the official went back home. He didn't insist that Jesus come with him. He didn't set up a Skype session so he could make sure before he left. Jesus said that it was all okay and he trusted that it would be.

I don't know about you but I know that sometimes I want reassurance and warranties and proof that it will all work out. And Jesus doesn't give us that.

He just tells us to go, to go in the direction of our love. We cannot see right away what God is doing in our worlds and sometimes it takes more time than we'd like. But Jesus says for us to go on, and if we trust him, we do just that.

Are you able to trust today?

January 30
Luke 5:1-11

Put out into the deep, Jesus said.
Let down your nets into deep waters.

Ah, but Jesus I live in a world made busy and shallow
        by our unceasing creations of distractions
We make fun of
    the shallow lives of others
        yet invest the coins of our hours
    watching them
    reading about them
    following them.
The shallows are comfortable, Jesus.
We know what's there.
We stay in the shallows reading what we've always read,
        thinking only what requires no thought,
    asking only questions we already have answers for,
        living the way we've always lived.
No doubt. No deeps.

Yet when morning comes
    we're more empty than full.

Put down into the deep, Jesus said. Let down into the deep
waters.

Good Lord, give me courage
    to live deep.

January 31
Acts 9:36-43

When my aunt died, the family gathered at her house after the funeral to eat together and be together. Among the dishes crowding the table were some of the recipes for which she was known, including her justly famous chocolate pie. Sharing in the recipes she used to love to make seemed a fitting way to honor her memory.

Dorcas was known for her sewing. And when she died people were bereft. When Paul showed up they crowded around, showing him the clothes that she'd made for them.

Just by reading the text today I feel like I know Dorcas. Don't you? She's the woman who crafts beautiful banners for worship. He's the guy building the ramps for whoever is in need. They're the people whose cakes you want to sample at the covered dish dinner and who always have a casserole in the freezer for a family in need. They're the people who quietly and humbly and gladly do what they do because they just love God and love God's people. We cannot imagine having church and doing church and being church without them. When they're gone from us we feel just a little bit lost. Dorcas' friends felt that way but thanks to Paul, their grief turned to joy.

We generally don't get that kind of blessing. So express your appreciation to the Dorcases in your life now, as you have the chance. More than that, learn from them.

Find your own place of serving and your own gifts to give. Let yourself humbly and gladly love God and love people through the work of your hands and the gift of your time and the sharing of yourself.

February 1
Proverbs 1:1-7

When was the last time you heard someone described as "wise"? We have lots of people who are clever and people who are smart. We have people who are eloquent and people who are quick with a quip. But what about wise?

When I think of wisdom, I think of someone who goes deep. Not necessarily someone who uses big word and important phrases, but someone who thinks deeply. Who is willing to ponder something, who is willing to look at things from more than one side. The wise person may not be the person with all of the answers. Indeed, the wise person may be the one asking the questions.

Proverbs reminds us that reverence for God is the beginning of our wisdom, its foundation. When we are grounded in God, we are grounded in God's spirit of justice and compassion. It allows us to open our eyes to see those who are invisible and to open our ears to those who have no voice. It enlarges our perspective to include more than just what's good for us.

Are you wise? Don't sell yourself short so quickly. Yes, you may be goofy and absent-minded and sometimes slow to get the point. But you may also be wise. Seeking God and God's way is the beginning of our wisdom.

Are you willing to seek God's spirit in your life today? Are you willing to start on the path to wisdom?

February 2
Acts 5:1-11

Let's be honest – there are just some stories in the Bible that aren't exactly suitable for children. Take today's text, for example.

Annanias and his wife Sapphira concoct a plan. They'll sell some property, but not let the church know how much they really made. They'll say it sold for a much lower price, act like they're giving generously from that smaller profit all the while pocketing the difference. When husband and wife are individually confronted with their deception, they are literally scared to death.

Now do you want to be the one giving children the pictures to carry in their little heads of people hauling dead bodies out of the church? I didn't think so.

Besides, in our privacy valuing culture, we don't think it's anybody else's business what we make and what we give. So what do we do with this story?

For all of its strange and unsettling details, the truth of this story is this: deception kills us. Maybe not as directly as Annanias and Sapphira, but the cost of living our lies is paid for with the stuff of our life. We can never be completely present in the moment if we are always having to make sure that our walls of deception are being maintained properly. We can never know the full freedom and joy of life in God's Spirit if we're always having to keep that Spirit at arm's length lest a confrontation become too uncomfortable.

Whether it's cheating on your spouse, your taxes, your business partner… or even cheating yourself out of the life that God desires for you, there is a heavy price to pay.

Today ask for the courage to seek the truth.

February 3
Luke 3:7-14

He didn't ask them to follow him or even to go looking for the guy who was coming after him. He didn't tell them to quit their jobs or leave their families.

Tax collectors and soldiers were about the sorriest lot possible, at least as far as the Jewish folks were concerned. Both were reminders that Israel was an occupied country. Both were well known for taking advantage of their power.

When they came to John asking to be baptized and asking how to live their lives after they came up out of the water, John basically said the same thing to both groups. Act with integrity and honesty. Do not take advantage of people.

Back in the days when I was planning Bible School, one year we introduced youth to different laypeople in the church. For me, it was one of the most interesting youth Bible Schools we did. For one thing, we traveled to different workplaces, seeing members of our church in their "natural habitat." More than that, these people shared with us how their faith impacted their work.

A nurse talked about working with grace and compassion. A news photographer talked about the tension between getting the pictures his job required and being sensitive to the pain of the people whom he was shooting. A lawyer talked about making career choices based on what was best for his family, not necessarily what created the biggest bank account.

Sometimes Jesus calls us out from where we are. Many other times Jesus calls us to follow him in the midst of our lives. And sometimes, that's the more challenging task.

What would John say to you today?

February 4
I Peter 3:8-17

We have a choice.

We may not like the choice. It may not seem like a fair choice. But we have a choice.

When someone does something bad to us, we can choose to plot our revenge. Or we can choose a different path. Someone says something hurtful to us. We can choose to focus on hurting them back, hurting them just as badly if not more. Or we can choose a different path.

The choice is the thing. Choosing doesn't mean we roll over and play dead. A former supervisor of mine used to talk about the favorite song of some Christians:

Just as I am without one plea,
Come wipe your muddy boots on me.

But in-between doormat and revenge, there is another choice. A choice that if someone hurts us, we may tell them so instead of automatically lashing out against them. If there is evil, we may confront it without stooping to its level. That was the genius of the work of Dr. Martin Luther King Jr. — he didn't try to fight injustice with more injustice.

It can be a hard thing, to make such a choice. After all, it feels so good to hurt them back… Well, at least for that moment. But then the acid of our words begins burning our own selves. Heaping abuse on those who have abused us only leaves us feeling trapped by all that stuff.

Today you'll have a chance to practice – maybe in a big thing or maybe in small. Today exercise your own freedom of choice. In so doing, you may find that the blessing isn't in coming out on top. The blessing is in the knowing that no one can make you sink to the bottom.

February 5
Romans 1:8-17

Now may the grace of God the Father, shed abroad in our hearts through Jesus Christ his son, made personal and powerful in our lives through the Holy Spirit the comforter, be with you one and all through the days, 'till we meet again.

That was the benediction (give or take a word or two) my childhood pastor offered nearly every Sunday for twelve years. It became so familiar that I typed it here without having to think about it. It was automatic.

There was a comfort in the familiarity. Some people liked it because they could time putting on their coats in order to make a quick getaway and beat the Methodists to the cafeteria. But the real danger in such familiarity is that we miss the point of it. We assume we know it so we stop hearing it.

For those of us who grew up around church stuff today's text carries such a danger. I am not ashamed of the gospel, Paul writes, for it is power to the Jew and to the Greek.

To the Jew and to the Greek. We're old hands when it comes to such divides. We're such old hands that we forget how radical it is.

Think about the deepest division you can. Those that seem to be unbridgeable divides. Democrat and Republican. Gay and straight. Immigrant and long time citizen. "Churched" and "spiritual but not religious." Employed and jobless. Resident and homeless. Conservative and liberal or moderate and fundamentalist. (There is even a divide in how to make the labels.)

God in Christ spans all of these divides. All of them. There is not a single person in a single group for whom God didn't become flesh, sharing the suffering that they suffer and dying the death they face.

Think of the face of the person who seems your enemy... or whom your kind of people call enemy. Look at them closely, for that is who God loves. And you too.

February 6
John 6:16-21

It is I, don't be afraid.

Lord, there are so many scary things in this world;
     sometimes it's hard to keep track of them all.
Giant things, like global warming
     and drug resistant diseases and mad cows
     and virus-laden mosquitoes...
          and nuclear weapons.

It is I, don't be afraid.

Big things, like crime in my community
     and whether or not there will be layoffs
          at the biggest employer in my town.

It is I, don't be afraid.

Things no one knows are keeping me awake at night,
     like will my kid get through high school
     and what should I do about that lump I think I felt.

It is I, don't be afraid.

I'll be in the boat with you.
I may not always still the waters,
    but I'll be with you
    and together we'll make the journey.

You will reach your destination.
You are not alone.
Don't be afraid.

February 7
Deuteronomy 6:20-25

It was one of my favorite parts of Christmas.

On Christmas Day, after we'd made the trek to my mother's mother's house and had sufficient food we'd go to my father's mother's for more food. That was good but not the best part. For me, one of the best parts was sitting by the fire in the old farmhouse after dinner, sitting with parents and aunts and uncles and a smattering of cousins. My aunts and uncles and my parents would tell the stories from when they were young. Stories of their adventures. Stories of people whom I felt like I knew just because I'd heard their names so much.

From these stories I learned more about who these people were. And I learned more about who I was. I was a Haymes, kin to a line of people who treasured good music and good books and who had a creative streak that ran wide and deep.

When your kids ask, "What is all of this religious stuff about," Moses tells the children of Israel, don't give them a theological treatise. Tell them the story. "We were slaves in Egypt. God led us out. God led us through the wilderness. God freed us."

What's your story? What's the story of God in your life? It doesn't have to be the Guidepost version of challenge, rescue and spiritual truth. It can have some loose ends.

One of the important pieces of Christian community is the sharing of our stories. Unfortunately, in many churches we can get so task oriented that we leave no time and space for story telling.

Have you shared your story? Start with your family, or a friend. Make a space in your church life for sharing stories.

February 8
2 Corinthians 4:1-2

Therefore, having wild success, we do not lose heart.
Wait, that isn't how it goes? Oh, okay....
Therefore, getting good press in the paper, we do not lose heart...
It doesn't say that either? Oh, okay...
Therefore, getting a proclamation from the mayor, we do not lose heart...
Not that either? Oh, okay... I've got it now.
Therefore, finally shutting up that person who's been against us all along, we don't lose heart...
What do you mean, that's not what Paul wrote?

Therefore, having this ministry by the mercy of God, we do not lose heart...

That's it? You mean, it's not really about us?

Good people all over the world are working day by day to live out the ministry to which God has called them. Maybe you're one of them. Probably you're one of them. It may or may not have the official tag of ministry but it's ministry all the same.

Sometimes such ministry is hard. Often it's difficult, and often the labor is long before any fruits can be glimpsed. The work of seed planting can be discouraging at times.

Therefore we take Paul's words to heart. We hold on and keep going because this ministry is the grace and gift and calling of God.

When you feel discouraged, remember. It's not all up to you and it's not all about you. We have this ministry, this work, this task, this dream by the grace of God. And in this God we find strength for yet another day.

February 9
Psalm 1

He glanced around my front yard, its tall trees beginning to come into full leaf. "You know these big trees" he said, "take up a lot of water."

It didn't surprise me. Mowing the lawn, I'd stumble over roots stretching over my yard, sometimes popping through the soil far from the tree itself. The roots grow far and deep, pulling up the moisture that will go to the leaves on the branches that tower over my house. In times of drought, the trees compete with the grass for the little bit of moisture that remains.

The psalmist used the image of a tree planted on the river's edge. Always and forever, there is water flowing, water flowing by and water flowing into the roots and trunks and branches and leaves.

God's spirit is such a stream, flowing through our lives. Sometimes we don't realize it. We pave it over with distractions; we try to put our roots elsewhere only to find ourselves coming up empty and dry. All the while God is inviting us to come and have a good, long soak.

Let yourself soak in God today. Even if it's only for five minutes, let yourself relax into the grace-full waters of the Spirit, breathing in the deep love God has for you. Let your heart find its true rhythm that wants, that needs, that is yearning to love God back.

It doesn't have to be hard or complicated. Take a few minutes to think on the things God has done for you. Take a few minutes to think on the things God might have you do.

Let yourself soak in God.

February 10
Jeremiah 7:1-15

When I was a teenager I saw the original "Poseidon Adventure." In the movie, a cruise ship is hit by a rogue wave on New Year's Eve, overturning it. In the main ballroom where many of the passengers had been celebrating, the ship's purser assures them everything will be all right. All they have to do is stay in place and someone will come to rescue them. Of course, everything isn't all right. They are in mortal danger and only the ones who risk ignoring his orders have a chance to be saved.

I thought about that scene as I read today's text. There were a lot of false prophets/blind pursers in Jeremiah's time. They told the people they'd be safe because this was God's temple and nothing could happen to it. Jeremiah told them they were trusting in the wrong thing. The temple of the Lord would not save them from the consequences of living lives of injustice.

What do you do when someone tells you something you don't want to hear? Do you immediately discount it? Do you argue with them? Do you get angry and walk away? Do you change doctors? If it's your ministers, do you start working to get rid of them?

Is God trying to tell you something that you don't want to hear? Have you been holding on too tightly and giving in too-small doses? Is the prejudice you'd be ashamed to admit popping up? Or maybe you yourself are the one you are not treating with justice, kindness and mercy.

God, give us the grace to hear the words we need to hear... even if they are not always the words we want to hear.

February 11
Deuteronomy 8:1-10

In the midst of the big challenges they forgot about the small miracles. Through all those years with no Macy's in sight, their clothes didn't wear out. With all of those miles through all of that wilderness... sand and rock and whatnot... their feet didn't swell. It seems like such a small thing when compared to facing down Pharaoh or escaping from an army. The lack of puffy feet doesn't seem quite as dramatic as locusts and other assorted plagues.

Except when your clothes are in tatters and there's no way to get new. Except when your feet are so sore every step is both challenging and cruel. In such times such small things loom quite large.

Sometimes we miss the story of God's provision in our own stories because we think it has to be worthy of a Hollywood extravaganza. The sick being healed. The lost being found. The escape from the house just before the tree fell on it.

We're so busy looking for the Pharaoh and his plagues that we miss all of the care that was here. We had what we needed. We were able to go to where we needed to be. Physically. Spiritually.

And even if we're not yet in the Promised Land we're not back where we were. I know... some days that doesn't feel like near enough. Some days we just want to be there already.

Even on those days, especially on those days, take a step. And another. And another. And as you're stepping, give thanks for your spirit that finds a way to keep walking. As you're stepping, give thanks for a God who does not forget you even in small things and baby steps.

February 12
Isaiah 51:1-3

Recently I spent some time with my aunt, the widow of my father's brother. Of my father's family she is the last remaining from her generation. Part of the gift that she gives to me is the sharing of her stories.

She tells me stories of the adventures that my father and brother shared growing up. As much as I begged, my father never got around to putting those stories to paper so I hang onto every story she tells.

But her stories don't stop there. She's one of the family members who has done a lot of genealogical research on my grandfather's and grandmother's families. She tells me their stories as well. Some of them are of mostly historical interest, like the ancestor who fought at Gettysburg.

There are others, however, that seem to be part of the threads of the fabric of my own life. The teachers. The artists and musicians and creative sorts. The entrepreneur before there was ever such a word.

Look to the rock from which you were hewn, the Lord says through Isaiah and he wasn't talking about the stuff of ancestry. com. Look to the people whose stories are a part of your own fabric of faith. Abraham and Sarah.

They're our people too, reminding us that our faith unfolds as we leave our places of comfort to follow God's wild and outrageous call. Remember the stories of those who came before you, Abraham and Sarah and Jeremiah and Ruth and Mary and Joseph and Peter and Paul and Mary and Martha. They're all in your family tree, and mine too. More than we can name and more than we know.

They're your people. Learn from their courage and learn from their fear. We are, all of us, woven together in this grace-blessed fabric of love.

February 13
Matthew 11:1-6

Once John had been so sure. "Behold the lamb of God," he'd cried out upon seeing Jesus. He trembled to baptize him, knowing he was turning the cosmic order of things upside down.

But things look different when you're languishing in prison. Was John expecting a different sort of Christ? Were the stories he was hearing about Jesus not measuring up to the messiah he thought he was preparing the way for? Or did the prison cell just seem too far removed from a crowded riverbank and heaven breaking through?

"Are you the guy or should I keep looking?"

Jesus could have answered in different ways. He could have become angry with John. He could have written him off. After all, if he didn't believe after all this time it was his own fault. He could have ignored the question. He could have sent back a detailed theological treatise demonstrating how he was exactly the right one.

Instead he tells the messengers, "You tell John what you're seeing and hearing. Blind have sight and the deaf can hear. The lame are dancing a jig. The dead are living. The poor have good news for the first time in their lives."

Not the number of people who were following him. Not the number of people who'd been converted to his way. Not the rich young rulers and Pharisees and Roman officers he was hobnobbing with. No, this was the message: The people who had nothing now have everything.

What if they cane bursting into our churches, if they interrupted our private devotional times? What if they wanted to know, "Are you followers of Christ or should we look for others?" What would we say?

What would we say?

February 14
Song of Solomon 8:6-7; 5:10-16

A friend was charged with the task of writing a commentary that included the Song of Solomon. Throughout the years commentators, trying to justify the inclusion of this book in our Bible, have sought to read it as an allegory of God's love for us. "The more I study it," my friend said with a sigh, "the more I realize it's just about sex."

It doesn't take much reading to realize that this is no etheric, spiritual love. This is physical. The two lovers admire each other's bodies and desire them.

So why should such a book be in our holy scripture (other than being an avenue to entice seventh grade boys to read their Bibles)? What were they thinking?

I can't answer that question, but I can say that I am glad that it is here. The Song of Solomon reminds us that our sexuality is a gift from God. It is more than a way to continue the human race. It is a source of pleasure, of satisfaction, of connection and expression. It goes far beyond our narrow definitions of sexuality to include wonderful experiences of sensuality... the smell of a spring rain, the taste of a ripe strawberry, the touch of a soft blanket.

Today give God thanks for the gift of our sexuality and sensuality. Too many people have received negative messages (like, "Sex is awful and dirty and you should save it for the one you love.") Instead, let us encourage healthy discussions about healthy sexuality in our own faith communities.

February 15
1 Corinthians 13

And this is love… Not feeling so hot herself, she nonetheless gets up to change the sheets and comfort the sick child, yet again. The staff meeting tomorrow, the car that needs to be fixed, the fight with her best friend fades into the background. The one thing, the only thing that matters is this little one who needs to be soothed and cared for.

And this is love…. She stopped recognizing him a long time ago, the slate of the memories of their life together long ago wiped clean. He is a kind stranger, sometimes welcomed with warmth and sometimes greeted with wrath. Yet patiently he comes to see her, week after week, sometimes bringing the flowers that she does not remember were her favorite.

And this is love… She swallows hard before she speaks, knowing that her words may change everything. Being honest may mean losing a long and wonderful friendship. Still, she speaks the truth about addiction, about her unwillingness to look the other way, her unwillingness even to be a friend if that friend continues to kill herself slowly.

And this is love… He does more than show up Sunday after Sunday to teach the preschoolers; he opens his heart to them, even and especially the ones who don't fit in. She thinks the homeless people ought to have more than a sandwich, so she cooks a good, hot, home style meal. As she serves them, she looks each one in the eye and sees the child of God in front of her. He goes to the hospital to sit by the bedside, even though it is a fearful thing to bear witness to such pain.

And this is love…

May we live as people of such love.

February 16
Galatians 5:13-15

Noted marriage and couples counselor Harville Hendrix has a question that I've found to be useful in all kinds of relationships. "What's more important to you – being right or being in this relationship?" In light of Paul's instructions to the Galatians in today's text, the question could be modified, "What's more important? Having your own way or having this relationship?'

Whether they're romantic couples or close friends or members of a group whom you may or may not like, relationships are messy. I think it's one of the appeals of solitary spirituality. Frankly, on some days it's a lot easier to love God if you never have to deal with God's people.

People come to churches seeking community, but community is messy. What do you mean, you want me to help in the nursery? I've done my part. It's somebody else's turn now. I don't see why that's in the budget - it doesn't help me. Did you hear about so and so ....?

Community means speaking the truth in love. Community also means not speaking when our words will do nothing but hurt (no matter how good it may feel to us in the moment.) Community means allowing ourselves to be inconvenienced for the sake of love without being doormats for the sake of looking saintly. Community means talking to a person with whom we have a disagreement, instead of just talking about them.

Community is messy and it's hard work, no matter how small or large the group. But it is precisely this work that opens the door for possibility and miracles. In such communities, hearts may be connected in ways far deeper than anyone dreamed was possible. Far greater dreams can be dreamed together, and not only dreamed but also birthed among us. Sheer fun is deepened into delight and pure joy.

In Christ, you are set free. In Christ, you are bound by love. Both things are true.

February 17
Psalm 96:1-6

Who knows how it became his favorite song? However it happened, his mom often overheard her three year old son singing to himself, "Gimmie that old time religion…"

Interesting that the psalmist doesn't say, "Give me that old time religion." The psalmist says, "Sing to the Lord a new song…" Throughout the psalms, and indeed throughout scripture, there is a creative tension between remembering the stories of old and singing a new song.

In remembering the stories of old, we tell again the tales of God's working in our lives and in our world. But we are not limited – God is not limited to those old stories. God is always doing a new thing.

As God's people, we cheat ourselves if we forget our history, and we deprive our children if we do not tell it to them. For me, one of the most enjoyable things about our church's centennial celebration was discovering the stories of God's working in its history. Our children need to know the stories of Abraham and Sarah… and mom and dad. But we try to limit God if we think past ways are the only ways in which God works. In our churches and in our own lives of faith, we need to hold our history with one hand while opening the other hand to God's surprising future.

Today, you may appreciate that old time religion, but also sing to God a new song. If you are very brave, you may open yourselves to the new song that God wants to sing through you.

February 18
Genesis 6:11-22

On the front of the greeting card is a picture of the Noah's ark beginning to float away. In the foreground two dinosaurs cling to a rock, one of them saying to the other, "That was today?"

We love the story of Noah's ark. It's a great story for the kids. We sing about the floody, floody and have fun picturing the chaos of two of everything being cooped up in a boat. Coming to it as an adult, however, it gets a little more problematic.

What do you do with a God who gets so disgusted with how creation is turning out that wiping things clean and starting over seems to be the best plan? What's the message for a devotional thought?

Let's face it, if any of us started building an ark, announcing that it was God's command we'd either be taken to the nearest mental health facility or overwhelmed and overrun by the end-of-the-world people who knew they were right.

So maybe the message, maybe one message for us today is this. What we do matters. How we live matters. Regardless of what everyone else is doing, regardless of what everyone tells us we should do, how we live our lives is a matter between ourselves and God and it matters. Noah (who frankly, later turned out to be not such a perfect saint himself) was just living his life as he saw fit, and God saw his faithfulness.

I doubt God is going to ask any of us to save creation (although I wouldn't completely rule it out, God liking to surprise us with the unexpected and everything.). God does ask us to love justice, do mercy and walk humbly with God.

Who knows? That might be just as radical as building an ark.

February 19
Luke 4:1-12

Temptation doesn't always come dressed in a red suit, horns on its head, carrying a pitchfork. Sometimes it comes in the guise of a really wonderful end justifying some not quite wonderful means.

It really doesn't matter how we get there because there *is so good and so important and will make such a difference.*

Sometimes it means trading show for substance, especially if the show will attract big crowds.

We want to give the people what they want to hear so they'll keep coming back.

Sometimes the temptation is just being less than God created us to be... not using a talent with which God graced you... settling for less than the joy God has given you... playing it safe or playing it scared. Listening to what everyone else thinks you should do as a way of avoiding God's calling for you. Becoming so busy that we can avoid actually doing anything. Not caring for the body God has given you or not using the mind God has entrusted to you.

Today, take some time to think about the temptations with your name on them. Go beyond the chocolate dessert or box of popcorn at the movies. Go deeper and name the temptations that draw you away from God's path and God's dream and God's demand in your life.

Be courageous enough to name them then trusting enough to name them to God. Then ask for God's help in facing them.

February 20
Mark 5:1-20

Reflections of a Modern Day Legion
Ashamed and embarrassed,
    I do not want the exiled parts of myself
        to be discovered,
        to be seen.
I try to pretend they do not exist,
    But they keep breaking free,
        crying out in the night,
        leaving me bruised and broken.
The small places in my heart.
The secret prejudice that I hide behind my inclusive smile,
    The secret addiction,
    Even the doubts and depression and deep darkness
        that I hide beneath my words of faith.
    The secrets themselves that keep me chained.

Jesus,
I don't feel worthy to be in your presence.
I need you to go away
    lest you see all that I am,
    lest you see all that I hide.
        Go away, for I am Legion.
But you do not flee…
You tell me that you want to take away
those things that do not belong to me,
you want to heal those hurts
that do not define me.
You want to bring me home.
You want the exile to end…
        Jesus, help me trust you that it can be true.

February 21
2 Corinthians 6:1-10

I can only control what I do. I cannot control what other people will think about me or believe about me. If they choose to think the worst I can make my case but I cannot compel them to think differently. My clients often spend a lot of time learning these truths.

Paul seems to have understood this. In this passage to the church at Corinth, he details the way people have completely missed the point about who they are and what they are about. Treated as imposters and yet absolutely real. As unknowns and yet they are very well known. People keep trying to push them into boxes that do not fit.

Paul's response to this is to remain absolutely clear about his mission. His work is to preach the gospel of Christ. His task is to live with integrity and love. Those are the things under his power.

What about you? Are you choosing to exercise the power that is yours to have, the power to chose how you will live and speak and love? Are you seeking to follow the way of Christ or are you trying to garner votes in the popularity contest? When all changes around you, are you able to stay true to yourself and God's calling in your life?

Tough questions. It takes a lifetime to answer them. At the same time, there's nothing to prevent us from starting today.

February 22
Matthew 13:44-52

The View

They paid good money for an ocean front house...
    the wide Atlantic spread out before them...
    the never-ending
    ever-changing
    parade of people
            walking
            running
            playing
        in front of them.
And yet there they sit
    in their beach chairs
    on the driveway
    watching cars drive slowly up and down.

How many times do I do it, God?
How many times
    do I trade my birthright of wonder
    for a mess of ordinary?
How many times
    do I turn away
    from the rare and beautiful moment
    for the sake of the cut-rate,
    common
    available any time
    kind of day?
God, don't let me settle for passing cars
    when I can have wonder.

from *heart prayers 2* © 2010 by Peggy Haymes. used with permission.

February 23
Ruth 1:1-14

The book of Ruth is the story of a widow whose two sons die, leaving her with only her daughters-in-law for family. Some of you know how hard it is to be a single parent or to be suddenly left alone when a spouse dies. Multiply that by about a million times and you'll come close to how hard and desperate things were for Ruth. There was no promise that she could even survive. Therefore, she sent her daughters-in-law off to find another husband, another lifeline.

Ruth is the kind of story that we usually don't hear. Oh, we may tell more stories about women and their experience. But it's very easy to distance ourselves from the stories of the people who are on the margins. The immigrant working in the field. The teenager using food stamps to buy food for her kid. The developmentally disabled. The old woman shuffling through the grocery store. It's much easier to apply labels. It's much easier to write them off. It's much easier to keep them on the margins where we do not have to be bothered and do not have to be troubled. It's easier not to see the human being.

The story of Ruth reminds us that for God, there are no margins. Every person on the planet is smack dab in the middle of God's love. They are important to God. God knows their name and cares about their lives.

The next time you feel tempted to write someone off, to see a label and nothing else remember the story of Ruth. Maybe you'll listen to their story. Or maybe, at the very least, you'll offer them the respect of truly looking in their eyes, person to person.

February 24
Ruth 1:15-22

The arrival of anyone new was sure to cause a stir, but two women traveling alone were sure to raise questions. Some of the older women shielded their eyes from the glare, looking, wondering. There was something familiar about the older woman and yet something so strange. She seemed a shadow of a self they had known long ago. It looked like Naomi, but her once sparkling eyes were empty. She moved as one who had no life and no light left in her life. When she spoke, her words had an edge.

"Yes, I'm Naomi, but don't call me that. Call me bitter (Mara), because that's what I've gotten from God."

As I once heard Nancy Hastings Sehested say in a women's retreat she led for our church, sometimes we go through a Mara time, a time of bitterness. We've tried to be faithful but success hasn't come. Sometimes the bitterness comes hand in hand with deep grief. Sometimes it comes along with envy and jealousy. Sometimes it's no more substantial than the most elaborate pity party. But sometimes it is hard–earned.

Naomi didn't try to pretend things weren't as bad as they were. She didn't put a happy smile on her face and talk with the confidence she didn't own. She was empty and she was desperate. And she was honest.

But this isn't the end of her story. Her bitterness does not keep her from walking through the doors that God will open. Naomi is bitter. And Naomi is faithful. Both may be true.

When you face a time of more demand that you think you can bear in a day, remember Naomi. Be honest about where you are. And be open, for God may not be done working in your life.

February 25
Ruth 2:1-13

God demanded a certain inefficiency. Harvesters were commanded not to pick the fields clean but to leave some around the edges so that the poor could come and glean food for themselves. Ruth goes out to gather food for her and her mother-in-law.

She winds up in the field of Boaz, a relative of her late father-in-law. She catches his eye, and he does some checking.

He winds up telling her to come to his field and no other, promising that she will be safe here.

Ruth asks why he should go out of his way for her, a foreigner. He replies that he has heard of her great kindness to her mother-in-law, and kindness is being repaid with kindness.

Ruth didn't choose to remain with Naomi in hopes of earning some reward. I have no evidence that she had any shred of a thought about bringing good karma into her life. She did it because it was the right thing to do. She did it because it was what love called her to do.

It is not an algebraic formula, if I do x then I will receive y. But there is something that happens when we chose out of love, when we do something just because it is the right thing to do. In our choices, we are opening doors that we do not yet see. They may be doors that are opening for us. Quite frankly, they may be doors that will open for someone else. But in our choosing we create one more avenue for God's working in the world.

Ruth's choice to stay with Naomi was in many respects foolhardy and dangerous. She had no prospects for marriage in going along with her and the life of a woman alone wasn't a good life. But somewhere in her bones, it was something she knew she had to do. As the story plays out, it was a choice that made all of the difference.

Today as you make choices great and small, listen to your heart. Listen to the stirring of God's spirit in your heart, then choose with faith. Such choices may make all the difference.

February 26
Ruth 4:13-18

Be honest. Outside of the movie theaters or a Nicholas Sparks novel, who saw this one coming? If you've grown up hearing this story you may miss the surprise of it. In a few short chapters we've gone from death to birth, from bitterness to joy, from grief to celebration, from emptiness to full, from poverty to provision.

On that day when Ruth decided to glean the fields, to glean this particular field, she had no way of knowing how that one decision would change her life. And not only her life but Naomi's and Moab's lives as well.

We often do not know the full meaning of events in our lives until much later. We see only this one scene and not the whole story. When I was hit by a car, I thought it was a very bad thing. It's still not my favorite moment in my life.

And yet it gave me much unexpected time with my mom in what turned out to be the last year of her life. Sitting in a wheelchair, I vowed to go for my dream of running a road race. Which led me to a training program. Which led me finally (after a lifetime of failing) to becoming a runner and even completing triathlons. Even better, it introduced me to a circle of friends whom I now cannot imagine not knowing. While the injury brought pain and disruption, in the long run it has also brought appreciation, laughter and joy.

I don't think God orchestrates such events in order to bring these gifts into our lives. I do think that the testimony of Ruth's story... and ours... is that God never stops working in our lives. Even when things seem horribly off course and out of kilter. Even when everything seems terribly wrong, God is still there, working behind the scenes, doing that redemptive thing over and over again.

And in the end, we may yet be surprised.

February 27
Luke 5:29-39

We are only one generation from the tax collectors. And one generation from the Pharisees. That's one of the tricky things about this business of following Jesus.

Reading a story like this, I know which characters with whom I want to identify. It's obvious that the tax collectors are the good guys. They're the people whom Jesus is defending. And maybe I'm not so far from them.

After all, I have certainly had my moments of being less than faithful, of living less than the life that Jesus has called me to live. If tax collectors are the ones designated as sinners, then hand me my IRS employee badge.

The only problem is that I'm afraid I may be more kin to the Pharisees than what I'd like to admit. After all, they were the religious leaders. As I write, I'm looking at my ordination certificate. I almost literally grew up in the church. At the girls' mission group camp in seventh grade I even won the "Joy in Jesus Award." (I generally don't like to brag about that as it seems to be a little counter to the whole spirit of the thing, but I share in the interest of full disclosure.) The point is that I've always been on the inside of the church.

So I guess maybe I have a foot in each camp. Maybe you do, too. So this text speaks to me both of hope and humility. There is hope for the tax collector in me. Jesus is still looking for me, and not in a bad way. He still wants to make room for me at the table, even when I am feeling my most unlovable, even when I have failed miserably in this whole business of being faithful.

But there is also humility for the Pharisee in me. I may have been in Sunday School since before I was born but that doesn't mean that I know it all. I don't even know all that scripture means to say to me. Whenever I start drawing the lines declaring who is in and who is out in God's camp, it is the humility to remember that God is coming behind me with a great big eraser.

We are always just one generation away from tax collector and Pharisee. And sometimes not even that much.

February 28
Isaiah 40:25-31

When I was ordained, this was one of the texts that I chose to be read. I chose it because I've always loved it. I love the imagery of it – running and not being weary, soaring like an eagle. If I'd known how long I'd have to wait before I was called to begin that ministry I might have reconsidered my choice of texts.

But maybe it was the perfect text after all. For the prophet promises that when we grow weak or weary, God will renew our strength and lift us up.

Lots of things in this life leave us weary. Dealing with the same issue or the same problems (or the same arguments in our relationships) leaves us weary. Looking for answers that seemingly never come leaves us weary. Sitting hour after hour in a hospital room or making trip after trip to the nursing home leaves us weary. Watching our loved ones suffer and knowing there's not a blessed thing we can do to take the suffering away leaves us weary. Fighting for a cause where it's hard to see success leaves us weary. When it seems to us that we take two steps forward only to take five back makes us weary.

What wearies you? Whatever it is, take heart. If you listen closely, you may hear them in the distance, the beating of eagles' wings. They will lift you up. Listen closely and you may feel it, the rush of God's Spirit blowing through. It will give you the second wind – or the fourth.

February 29 (as needed)
Acts 17:22-34

Paul stood in front of the Aeropagus and said, "Athenians, boy have you got it all wrong. You have completely missed the boat and you've got the fast track to hell."

Well, that's not exactly what the text says. Instead, we see that Paul started from a common place. He searches for God. They search for God. The only difference is that Paul has a better idea of just who this God is – and how we are connected.

In the end, some found the idea of resurrection of the dead too preposterous to be entertained. Others were intrigued. And some became believers.

For some of you, "evangelism" may make you think of cheap tracts illustrating a Roman road or warning of hell. For others it means browbeating those who are different. But evangelism just means sharing good news. I think that means sharing in a way that is indeed good news.

Perhaps the very beginning is just being able to talk about faith. More than talking, being able to listen as other people talk about what they have and what they're missing, then being able to talk about the role of faith in your own life. I believe that one of the gifts of Christian community is giving us a chance to talk with each other about faith so that when the opportunity comes to talk with those outside of the church, it will not be such a foreign task.

These days, as I listen to people talk about the "Christian God" they don't follow, I find myself agreeing with them. I wouldn't follow the God they described either. But the listening then becomes the starting point for the sharing of my own experience.

Today, ask God for the grace to speak... But first, to listen.

March 1
Jonah 2:1-10

She was all of maybe six or seven, and was engaged in a head butting match with her father. He asked. She refused. He reminded her of consequences. She pouted. She finally wound up standing behind a bedroom door, saying, "I'd come out if my daddy would give me a kiss but I know he won't." He gave her a kiss on the top of her head and an explanation as to why things were so and the nature of consequences that come with disobedience. All was resolved without any more fireworks.

Jonah was a little like that little girl. He was bound and determined not to do what God asked him to do. So determined that he took the next ship in the opposite direction of where God wanted him to go. So determined that he wound up being thrown overboard by frightened sailors. So determined that he wound up in the belly of the fish, where suddenly he has a newly discovered interest in talking with God.

Sometimes we wind up in the belly of the fish as well. Sometimes it happens just because it's where life brings us; it's what life brings to us. But sometimes, many times, it's of our own doing. God calls us to one direction and we go the other way.

We're afraid that it's too hard or too inconvenient or that we might have to care about people we'd rather condemn. So we go our own way and wind up in the belly of the fish.

The belly can look like a lot of things. Sometimes it manifests as a depression that sucks the joy and life out of our lives. Sometimes it looks like frustration where nothing we do seems to go right or be right. Or sometimes it looks like an aching emptiness - on the surface we are wildly successful but inside it makes no difference.

Jonah had the courage to call out from the belly of the fish to this God whom he'd been avoiding. God's grace is big enough to hear him and deliver him and give him a second chance.

If you're in the belly right now, especially if it's by your own doing, it may seem like there's no point in calling out to God. You messed up. You didn't pay attention to God then, why should God listen to you now? But the good news is that God doesn't have the same scorekeeper that we do. Call out to God - you might just get vomited out.

March 2
Jonah 2:1-10

This is not the prayer we expect. Throughout this story, Jonah is petulant, resistant and hardly the shining faith. Yet here he is, still in the middle of the crisis and in the gut of a fish offering not a cry for help but a prayer of thanksgiving.

There are two ways to pray such a prayer, I think. The first is as a form of holy denial. When I was a student intern I met with a family in the ER. The husband and dad had been helping a neighbor. Something went wrong, and something so simple turned out to be deadly. As I met with them, the family smiled and reassured me as to how God was going to use this for a wonderful work and they had to give thanks. While that may be true, there is usually a hard journey through grief, anger and sadness to get to that place. Giving premature thanks can be a way of trying to fool ourselves into thinking that the situation isn't as awful as it really is.

But there is another way to pray such a prayer. It is thanksgiving as hope. It is the sentiment often expressed by psalmists: "Hope in God for I shall yet again praise him." It is the prayer that says, "I do not know how my world will be whole again. I do not know how my life will be right. But I trust that God can hold even this and can heal even this and can keep working even in such circumstances."

We need not deny that we've found ourselves in the fish's belly without a clue as to how to find our way out. We don't have to pretend that the pit isn't deep or dark. And yet, we also do not have to pretend that God does not see us, even here, and that God does not stop loving us, even now.

March 3
Jonah 3:1-10

He was perhaps the most reluctant prophet in history. After trying to run away from God and being unsuccessful, Jonah finally buckles down and does what God has asked him to do. He goes to the city of Ninevah and warns them of their coming destruction. I wonder if he looked at his feet like a thirteen year old, mumbling that God was going to judge them and stuff. I get the feeling that actually, once he got into it, Jonah was full of energy along with the fire and brimstone. "You people are so toast!"

Whatever he did, it worked. From the king on down, the people heard what he was saying and believed it, repenting on the spot.

Which just goes to show you that God can use just about anybody. Which includes you and me. Not exactly a saint? Guess what – God can still use you. Avoided God? Guess what – God can still use you? Afraid? Not really convinced you have anything to offer? Pretty convinced that what you have to offer isn't good enough? Check, check and check. God can still use you.

What's your excuse? Jonah can trump it. He doesn't like the people God is sending him to and he doesn't want the mission to succeed. And yet God still uses him.

What's your excuse? It really doesn't matter because this isn't about us succeeding because of our will and energy and skill. It's about God working through us.

What's your excuse? Confess it to God then move on. There's work to be done.

March 4
Jonah 4:1-11

Sadly, it's not clear that Jonah ever gets it. He pitches a fit when his mission is successful. "I knew this was going to happen God because you are just way too merciful. I just might as well die." The teenage drama queen had nothing on Jonah.

He goes outside the city to sit and pout. God makes a vine to grow to give him shade and Jonah is happy for the relief. But the next day the vine shrivels up, and once again, Jonah could just die. "I have every right to be angry," Jonah said. "My shade is gone and I might as well die." Jonah was not what we therapists would call a resilient personality.

God tells Jonah that he's missing the point. He makes the life of the plant a life and death matter for himself while not caring about the lives of all of the people and all of God's creatures in the city he has just left.

Outside of teenage drama queens, I don't know of many people who are as good at throwing pity parties as Jonah. But I think we might be equally gifted in missing the point. We get passionate about the injustice of our team losing the game because of (what we perceive to be) a bad call. But the fact that some of God's children in our own city are going hungry hardly raises an eyebrow. We get all energized over the fact that they changed the time of Sunday worship but we never pay attention to the people sitting by themselves in worship, looking very lost.

We can laugh at Jonah because, let's face it, he's an absurd character. But let us also look in the mirror. There may be more resemblance than we'd like to admit.

March 5
Luke 18:1-8

Sometimes, God, it's easy to lose heart.
    We prayed for her healing
    but she died anyway.
    We prayed for his safety
    but the plane brought his body home.
    We prayed for the job
    but it went to someone else.
    We prayed for our marriage
    but now we're divorced.
    We prayed for peace
    but wars drag on.
Sometimes, God, it's easy to lose heart.

Grant us the grace to keep praying without ceasing
Trusting that
    we do not always recognize the answers that come.
Trusting that
    even when the answers are truly wrong
    and bad things happen
    and injustice wins yet again,
    by our prayers we are kept close to your heart.

And there we may find strength
    and comfort
    and grace enough for this day and the next.
    More than that, we cannot ask.

March 6
John 1:35-42

God and Google

God, it's all well and good
    to see this master plan for my life.
I'm grateful to know
    and to feel in my bones
    where I'm headed.
But here's the thing...
Even Google gives me
    turn by turn instructions
    and I can see the pictures of the places
    and where I will go
    to the left or to the right.
And even Google
    tells me exactly
    how long it will take
    for me to get there.

God, don't you think
    you need to upgrade your technology?
I know, God,
    part of the faith
    comes in walking the journey,
    not just in getting there.
Teach me patience
    and wisdom
    and courage
    for taking just the next step.

March 7
Isaiah 43:1-7

I'd been away from home for three weeks after being hit by a car, in the hospital first and then recuperating at my parents' house. During that time, my next door neighbors were keeping my dog, Oakley. I was going home that day. Just for a brief visit, but home nonetheless. But first I wanted to stop by my neighbor's yard to see my dog.

Using my crutches, I managed to get to the low wall at the edge of their driveway. They let Oakley out in the fenced yard, and it didn't take but a minute for Oakely to spot me. Her whole body wagged as she tried to poke her nose through the chain link fence to get to me. She was overcome by the sheer, overwhelming joy of seeing me again.

Would it be sacrilegious to suggest that God loves us like that? Sometimes when we talk about God's love for us it's in hushed, theological tones echoing with fragile stained glass. Or it's shallow and syrupy sweet. But today's text is a different picture.

It's been set to music and is one of my favorite anthems, and so it feels to me like it should always be sung. God's love is strong enough to hold you up in the middle of the tsunami, to keep you safe in the middle of the California brushfire. The words themselves sing, singing of God's care for us that comes straight from the heart of God's love.

God loves us - God loves you and God loves me - with a no-holds barred kind of love. God loves us not for what we've done but just because we've showed up. God's love would go to the ends of the earth for us and indeed, has already been to hell and back. God dances in place with the sheer, overwhelming joy of loving you. Of loving me.

You are deeply, fiercely, completely and without reservation, loved. Now go and live accordingly.

March 8
Colossians 1:3-10

What does it mean to live a life worthy of the Lord? Paul gives some hints: bearing fruit in good works and growing in the knowledge of God. Part of both of those things, I think, is the need to reflect upon our lives.

It's easy to fall into the habit of running without thought. It's the next cry, the next tug on our sleeve, the next memo from the boss, the next squeaky wheel needing some grease. But in order to grow into the people whom God created us to be, to live the lives that God has called us to live we need times to step back, to reflect.

I once heard a woman on NPR say, "All of those people talking on their cell phones all of the time... when do they have time to listen to themselves?" And it's true that there's no shortage of distractions available. Talking on the phone, playing games on the phone, surfing the internet on the phone, texting other people on the phone, listening to music (sometimes on the phone!). But it's not just for the technological among us. There are televisions that can play constantly and car radios and the radios that play inside our heads that broadcast all kinds of nonsense.

The church has a long history of retreat ministry, a time in which we pull away from our distractions to listen to God and to listen to our lives. I highly recommend it. But even if you are not able to do that, there are still a thousand opportunities to stop, listen and reflect on how you are living your life and where your life is taking you and how and where God fits into all of this. In your car, put down the phone and turn off the radio. Take a walk or a run or a bike ride. Let yourself sit one evening without a television to distract you.

Finding the time doesn't have to be hard. Sometimes the hard part is doing the listening.

March 9
Matthew 9:35-38

God,
let me look upon the crowds with eyes of compassion.

It's too easy
    to look with fear
    or with judgment
    or with apathy.
I keep my heart safe.
I keep my life neat.

But if I see with compassionate eyes...
    my heart may break
        with the sight of their pain
    my soul might be stirred
        with the depth of their need.
I might have to change the way I think about them.
I might have to change what I think...
    And I might have to change what I do.

God,
    give me the courage
    of compassion.

March 10
Ezekiel 37:1-10

There have been times when I could have sworn I was preaching to a valley full of dry bones. (Let me hasten to say I'm not speaking of any of *your* churches.) I say something that I know is at least mildly funny and no one cracks a smile. I preach with all of the passion and power and conviction I can muster. This is important stuff we're talking about, stuff that makes a difference in our lives. But I see no flickers of recognition in the eyes staring back at me. And after the service I receive only polite, limp handshakes from people who mutter "Nice talk" as they are already looking past me. Just a valley of dry bones.

In Ezekiel's case, the bones were symbols of the exiles. They were without strength and without power and without hope of ever bringing their nation Israel back to life. But the wind blows and pulls them together. And the wind blows and restores muscle and sinew and power. In Hebrew, the word for "wind" and God's Spirit are the same, so Ezekiel couldn't help but get the point. God's Spirit brings life, life even when things seem as dead as a landscape full of picked over bones.

What in your life seems dead right now? Is it a relationship? Or maybe even your relationship with God? Or your work? Or day after day-ness of your life? Is there a place in your life that feels dead, dry and picked over?

Ask God in. Ask God's Spirit to blow through that place, to blow on those dead bones. The Spirit blows where it will and it may very well blow you to a place you did not anticipate. The breath of God's spirit may lead you to new life but in that leading you may have to give up holding onto some old bones.

Stand in your bones, and be very brave. For the wind will come and bones may yet dance.

March 11
Psalm 22

Sometimes my clients will complain to me that they shouldn't be feeling the sadness that they feel over the loss(es) in their lives. They shouldn't be frustrated with the struggles they've been facing. They shouldn't be experiencing any after effects of the very terrible traumas they endured.

I nod my head that I understand and grunt compassionately. And then ask them how in the world, out of the entire human race, they managed to be exempt. After all, they wouldn't begrudge any one else in the world the very same feelings.

Part of the suffering in our lives comes to us unbidden, a consequence of the things that happen and don't happen in this life. Drivers run red lights and plow their cars into us. Jobs are eliminated. No matter how deeply we love them, the people whom we love die anyway.

Part of the suffering in our lives is our own creation as we weave out stories about how things should be. How we should – or shouldn't – be feeling. It's not enough to face some hard thing. Many of us make that hard thing infinitely harder by measuring ourselves against some impossible and mythical expectation.

It's not just that this psalm is in the Bible. I find comfort and reassurance that of all of the Hebrew scriptures, these are the words that came to Jesus as he was dying. "My God, why have you forsaken me?!" Along with the bitter wine he was offered, Jesus had the bitter taste of despair in his mouth.

So why should we expect that we should never be bothered with such feelings?

Today as you pray, pray whatever is the honest word of your heart.

March 12
Acts 12:12-17

I'm glad this passage is in the New Testament if for no other reason than comic relief. Peter has been miraculously sprung from prison, and he immediately finds the others. Hearing his knocking, Rhoda goes to the door. Hearing his voice, she is so overcome by joy that she forgets to let him in. She has an argument with the others as to whether or not it's really him, while Peter still stands outside, knocking. I don't think that's what Jesus had in mind when he said, "Behold, I stand at the door and knock."

I'm glad this text was included because it was such a goofy thing to do. It's like looking for your glasses that are on top of your head. It's like driving off with your coffee cup still on top of your car. It's making a great dish for Thanksgiving dinner and then forgetting to put it on the table. It's goofy.

I know I've done goofy things - how about you? We are blessed when we can laugh at ourselves with gentleness and grace. God's unconditional love means we don't have to be perfect (whew!). It means that we can laugh at ourselves when we do something goofy and forgive ourselves when we make a mistake. We're not going to lose God's love because of it.

We're not told of how Rhoda reacted when she learned that she'd left Peter standing outside. I hope that she rolled her eyes and smited herself on her forehead and laughed at herself, saying, "I can't believe I did that!"

In fact, I think she probably did something exactly like that. For that's what we do when we are overcome by joy.

March 13
Matthew 7:7-11

Sometimes we learn more by what isn't said. "Ask, and it shall be given to you," Jesus tells us. What he doesn't say (but we often imply) is that it will be given in exactly the same form as our asking. Thank God.

I don't know about you but I'm old enough to appreciate not having received some of the things for which I prayed. If God had done everything that I asked I would have missed out on some unasked for but infinitely better gifts.

Ask, and it is given... but God's not a short order cook. We open up our hearts and ask and keep on asking. (The verb forms used here indicate a continual process: keep asking.) God hears our prayer and answers the heart of it, not the form of it. God answers the heart of our prayers, our soul deep desire to live fully, to be all we were created to be, to walk in joy, to hold God's hand when the way gets scary.

Ask and keep on asking. Ask as a way of embodying our trust in God. We may trust that God will not shame us for asking, even if that for which we ask is less than noble. God will not disinterestedly dispense asnwers like a gumdrop machine. Ask and trust that God is continually working with us, working in us and working for us that our lives may bear fruit and that we may truly lives as God's sons and daughters. We ask for bread trusting that God will not come back with a stone.

More than that, God may indeed come back not just with bread but also with life itself.

Take and eat. Trust and keep on asking.

March 14
Romans 12:1-2

Long ago and in a world far away, a world in which kids did not yet spring from the womb with a backpack full of books attached to their backs, I asked my mom to get me a strap to hold my books. I was in junior high and some of my friends had rubber straps with a hook on the end. Wrapping the strap around the books made it easier to carry them.

I came home from school one day and my mom proudly showed me what she'd bought. It wasn't the strap I'd asked for but one that was a little better. It had handles so that I could carry my books under my arm or by the handle. I hate to admit that I was a little less than grateful. The real point wasn't the best way to carry my books. The point was being just like my friends.

"Don't be shaped by this world," Paul writes, but it's hard not to want to fit in. We want to be like our friends, our coworkers, the beautiful people on the entertainment channel. It's hard to swim against the grain.

Until it isn't.

Be transformed, Paul says, and transformation isn't something we make happen by the strength of our effort. It is something we allow. It's something we open the door to, take the first steps toward, step into the river and allow ourselves to be carried. When we are transformed it is, paradoxically, coming home to the place we knew all along. We'd just forgotten it along the way. Transformation doesn't turn us into something alien but into something more human. Something that is us.

Today, open the door to God's transformation in your life.

March 15
Psalm 56

She didn't say anything. She didn't fix things or suggest ways for me to make my life better. She just sat with me as I cried. She didn't tell me it was all going to be better. She let me pour out how awful it felt in that moment. She handed me a tissue, and she let me cry. And in some mysterious way there was something so comforting, so healing in not being alone in that moment. She didn't do anything. She did everything.

Hard times are hard times. Whether you weep with sadness for the grief of what you've lost or for the shame of what eats at your soul, hard times are hard times. Whether you stay awake all night anxious with fears about the future or you cannot sleep for the memories of the past, hard times are hard times. They get a little easier, however, when you know you are not alone.

"You have kept count of my tossings; put my tears in your bottle." Hard times are hard times, but it lightens the load a little to know that we are not alone. God is so intimately involved in our lives that a single restless night doesn't escape notice. God catches every tear we weep.

I hope that your life is flowing smoothly and joyfully when you read this. If so, tuck these words away for the time when the night seems just a little darker and the dark seems just a little deeper. And if you find yourself facing hard times now, wrap yourself in them like wrapping up in a quilt on a cold winter's night. Not a single restless night goes unnoticed. Not a single tear falls uncaught. God is there.

March 16
Matthew 14:13-21

If Jesus ever needed to get away, now was the time. He'd just gotten the news that his cousin John was dead. Not only that but that his death was a beheading done at the whim and wish of an offended woman. Who could blame him for wanting some time to himself?

But the crowds didn't know that. They only knew that he was their hope for healing so they followed his boat along on shore, greeting him when he landed. This time Jesus didn't turn away, couldn't turn away. For the rest of the day he healed their sick.

At the end of the day the disciples asked him to send the crowds away so that they could find something to eat. (This was a highway exit with no McDonald's, Burger King or even a Sheetz.) Jesus replied the crowds didn't need to go anywhere. The disciples could feed them. The disciples said the little bit of food they had wasn't nearly enough but Jesus asked for it anyway. At the end of it all turns out there was, as we say in the south, a gracious plenty.

This story sounds familiar because I've heard it my whole life. But why does it feel so familiar?

Maybe because it keeps happening. I keep wanting to send people away. What I have isn't nearly enough. Not enough food. Not enough money. Not enough time. Not enough energy. Not enough ability.

But Jesus keeps saying, "Give me what you've got."

Is it enough? Is it really enough? It doesn't seem like it to me. Funny thing is, when I let go of my doubts and offer what I have, no matter how puny and inadequate it seems, Jesus finds a way to do more with it than I could have dreamed.

So, what do you have? Jesus says, "Bring it to me."

March 17
Luke 8:22-25

Maybe the disciples have been getting a bad rap all of these years... at least for this story. Here's the scene:

They are in the boat sailing across the lake. Jesus takes a nap. While he's sleeping, the winds increase until the waves are breaking over the side of the boat and the boat starts filling up with water. Things are getting a bit dicey, so they wake Jesus up and in a panic tell him they're about to sink. Jesus stretches, rubs his eyes and tells the wind to cut out all of this foolishness.

Wouldn't you have said, "Hey, we need to wake up Jesus"? What should they have done? Just let him sleep through it? Wasn't waking him up something of an act of faith that maybe he could do something? Or maybe they just wanted to give him the heads up so that he could start planning what to do once he hit the water. Seriously... wouldn't you have done the same thing? I suspect I would.

Jesus gives them a good talking to, but only after he has calmed the wind and stilled the waves. So maybe this is the lesson for us.

In a perfect world, I have enough faith. In my imagination, when life gets stormy and it feels like I'm about to go under, I calmly turn to Jesus, knowing that he will come through for me.

The only problem is that I don't live in that world. Sometimes, like the disciples, I'm so full of fear I can't see straight. Sometimes I can't imagine how I'll ever get out of this perfectly fine mess I've gotten into. Sometimes the best I can do is to shout at Jesus to wake up.

He may need to give me a good talking to about my lack of faith. But that will come after the storm has passed and my fear is but a memory.

So, if you're in a storm, reach out and call out. If you can do it with great faith, give thanks. And if you can't, call out anyway. He'll help you sort it out later.

March 18
Genesis 25:27-34

Only later did he realize what a bad bargain he'd made. In the moment, all he could think of was how hungry he was, how it felt as if he would collapse from sheer starvation if he did not get something in his belly right away. If he died from hunger, a birthright would be of no good use to him. Only later did he realize what a bad bargain he'd made.

Only later did she realize what a bad bargain she'd made. She'd chosen convenience over commitment, the path of least resistance over the path God might have wanted her to follow. All she could think about was how safe it all was, how she didn't have to risk failing or falling or being uncomfortable or not knowing what the next step was going to be. Only later did she realize that she'd traded away the chance to make a difference for a great big bowl of not having to be bothered. Only later did she realize what a poor bargain she'd made.

Only later did he realize what a bad bargain he'd made. Working later and later, drinking more and more, it seemed like a good plan to keep outrunning those pesky demons. He could be successful and be the life of the party and not have to feel anything. Only later did he realize that he'd traded the love of his family and the possibilities of his friendships for a big bowl of empty.

God, we don't even realize how many times a day we have a chance to make the bargain. May we choose wisely and in faith.

March 19
John 8:1-11

Some people are easy targets. Take this woman, for example. She'd been caught in the act of adultery. (Never mind that the act of adultery implies two people.) But Jesus wasn't about going after the easy target. Sure, stone her, he told the gathered crowd. Whoever has never sinned can start. The sound of disgruntled mumbling mixed in with the soft thud of stones being dropped to the earth. One by one they drifted away.

Some people are easy targets. The person whose transgression gets splashed across the pages of the newspaper, whose face pops up on the evening news. The person caught in sexual sin. The alcoholic who smashes his car... and maybe smashes someone else. The parents who beat their children.

We can all agree on their sin and we can all point our fingers at them. What a disgrace they are. What monsters they are. We bring them to Jesus expecting blood and he just lifts their chin, looks them in the eye... and sees a person. He tells us to go ahead and judge them harshly, but only if we ourselves have never sinned.

The point for us may not be what sentence the judge needs to hand out or our speculation about whether or not the marriage will last. The point is that we are all sinners. Yes, some sin carries a greater weight – or at least I believe so – because some sins wound not only ourselves but other people as well. We may become angry when we see innocent people harmed. We may become frustrated with the waste of life and opportunity.

But we dare not write them off for in one way or another, we all belong to the same tribe. We are, all of us, sinners. All of us need to hear the words of Jesus, "Go on your way, and sin no more."

March 20
Mark 8:22-26

Of all the healing stories, this is one of my favorites. I love it because Jesus didn't make it happen all on the first try.

The disciples were used to the routine by now. A blind man comes to Jesus, Jesus spits a bit and lays his hands on the blind  guy's eyes, and presto! He sees. So this story is rolling right along until Jesus asks the guy how he's doing. "Well," the guy says, "I can see people walking around but they look like trees."

I can imagine the disciples shooting secret glances at each other, trying not to let Jesus see the raised eyebrows and concerned looks. What was up? Was he losing it? This had never happened before. Unperturbed, Jesus just lays his hands on him again and the guy walks away with twenty-twenty vision.

It's neither a news flash nor a particularly profound statement to say that we live in an instant world. I thought it was a joke the first time I saw the box of quick cooking pasta – was ten minutes too long to wait?

But spiritual formation and spiritual journeys and living the life of faith is a much longer journey. Sometimes we make progress but it's still a little foggy, a little fuzzy. Change doesn't happen overnight.

Like the blind man, may we have the patience not to give up when things don't happen right away. May we have the faith not to walk away but to keep hanging around.

March 21
Acts 5:33-42

I've been in more business meetings than I care to remember…
Churches I've been a part of, groups I've volunteered with,
established organizations and just emerging, not quite formed
ones. In all of these meetings one of the things that I've observed
is how necessary it is to have a Gamaliel and how very blessed
we are when we have one in our midst.

The Jewish leaders wanted to kill Peter and John. They
wouldn't shut up about Jesus and they wouldn't stay shut up
in prison. The leaders were enraged and decided that death was
the only proper way to deal with the upstarts. Make them an
example and nip this thing in the bud.

Then Gamaliel stood to speak. He reminded them of another
religious leader whose movement had died out quickly and
quietly. Then he puts forth a wise and courageous position.
"If this is not of God, then nothing will come of it. But if it is
and we oppose it, we will be left on the wrong side of things.
We'll be going against God." It was wise counsel. But it was
also courageous for it acknowledged that they knew only in
part. What if they were wrong and God was behind this Jesus
movement all along?

The Gamaliels among us seldom say the most in a meeting.
They are seldom the first to speak, preferring to listen to the
debate before adding their perspective. But when they do speak,
everyone listens. What they say seems so patently obvious after
they've said it that everyone mentally slaps their foreheads for
not thinking of it first.

Are you a Gamaliel? Perhaps someone needs you to be. Ask
God for such wisdom and such courage.

March 22
Hebrews 12:12-17

I'd always wanted to be a runner but I'd failed every time I tried it. When I was unable to walk after my accident I gave myself the goal of finishing a road race. Now I was in a training program to get me ready to do just that. Although I was doing run/walk intervals that were designed for people who had not been active, it was hard. I'd only been walking again for a couple of months when I started. Some days I thought I wouldn't be able to finish that day's practice. I was tired and I was limping but I kept focusing on the one thing I could control. Take one more step. Just take one more step.

The book of Hebrews was written to a group of people who were tired and limping. Things weren't going as they thought they would. This Christian life was much harder than what they'd signed up for, or so they thought. They were thinking about giving up. So the writer of Hebrews encourages them.

Make your limping legs strong. Resolve the arguments that are cutting the legs out from under your community. Foster the peace that is your strength. Get moving with the things that you can do.

I suspect we all hit upon those times and places when it feels like too much, when we want to throw up our hands and say, "I didn't sign up for this." You went to college and did everything right. You didn't plan on being unemployed. You married a healthy spouse. You didn't plan on illness that wiped away all of your plans. You decided to follow Jesus. You didn't plan on struggling.

Lift your drooping hands and make strong your weak knees. Or, if it is the best you can do, keep limping along as best you can. God is still walking beside you and will help you take that very next step. And sometimes that next step is all you can do and all you can see. And God will help you find the strength.

March 23
Mark 14:32-50

It had to have been one of the low points of Jesus' life, at least up until this point. He knows he's at the jumping off place, the place of no turning back. He doesn't want to face what he is about to face.

Jesus does the very human thing of asking some friends to be with him. He needs their support while he wrestles with the choices before him. He could very well die very soon. And he could very well die very painfully. Being the Son of God didn't exempt Jesus from physical suffering.

Jesus finally comes up for air and returns to his friends, only to find them asleep. Three times he leaves to pray and to struggle and three times he returns to find them sleeping. Finally he surrenders to what must be, and finally the one who will betray him finds him. One of his very own disciples will hand him over.

One of the gifts of the incarnation is that Jesus was in every way a human being as we are human beings. One of the realities of his crucifixion is that he walked the way of our lives even through the pain and the suffering and the dying. Being the Son of God didn't mean that all would go smoothly for him, that he'd never face disappointment.

It sneaks up on us, even when we know better. Without realizing it we find ourselves thinking that if we were faithful enough things would be easier or our friends wouldn't let us down or tough choices wouldn't be so tough. But it wasn't that way for Jesus? Why should it be for us?

Today take comfort in knowing that this dark night wasn't the final chapter in Jesus' life. This isn't the end of the story. Take comfort that God truly knows what you've been through because God has been there. And take hope and encouragement in knowing that God never stops working to bring light in the midst of darkness and new beginnings in the midst of endings.

March 24
Psalm 41

"Happy are those who consider the poor."

So how do you consider the poor? I know it's not such an easy question. Some years ago a church in town noticed a homeless man who frequented the park down the street from them. He became their cause. Out of, I think, a very loving spirit they started reaching  out to him, trying to make his life better. The only problem was, he didn't want anything different. As much as the church wanted to help him, he didn't want what they had to offer. He was fine with his park bench.

So how do you consider the poor? For myself, I have to begin by checking my assumptions at the door. There is no monolithic "poor person."

She might be a welfare mom having too many babies with too many baby daddies. But it's the only life she knows how to live – and the only way she knows how to feel loved. He might be that homeless guy at the shelter but he used to be a responsible neighbor before he lost his job and his insurance and had the big health crisis. She might be a former straight A student but now she's hiding behind a wall you're not going to penetrate because her addiction is more important to her now than her life. That young kid at the back of the soup kitchen line is just as terrified as he looks. He's just here because his dad kicked him out for being gay.

She's from a neighborhood most good folks don't drive through. She's never known what it was like to live in a place where hope could be had for the taking. And he has that look of determination in his eyes – no matter how hard the road, no matter how high the obstacles he's going to find a way out.

And that doesn't even count the working poor – the people who tally up your groceries or clean your offices.

God, help me to pay attention to the people I'd rather not see. Give me the courage to do what I can and to speak what I must. If I'm giving food for the soup kitchen or building a house for Habitat or involving myself in the political decisions of my country, help me to consider the poor.

March 25
John 15:1-11

"Abide in me," Jesus said. And here's the thing about that abide business – it doesn't sound like something I can do once and check off my list.

"Abide in Christ. Done. Next thing."

No, it sounds like something that I have to live into, day after day, week after week, hour after hour. Hang out with him, make my dwelling place with him. Live with him.

Jesus isn't like an energy drink that you can guzzle for a quick burst of efficiency. Jesus said that we bear fruit as we are willing to live with him, day after day.

So how do we do that?

The answer will be different for each of us. For some, it means taking that long solitary walk every day during which you talk to God and you listen for God talking to you. For some it's singing in a choir, learning the music and making the music and listening to God in the midst of it all. For some it means sitting down with a fellow pilgrim every week or so to talk about your lives and to talk about how God is moving in your lives. For some it comes as you read scripture and let is soak in, letting it lead you.

You have to find your own way, but this much is true for all of us. Apart from our connection with Christ, we cannot do all we dream of doing nor all that God calls us to do.

How are you hanging out with Jesus?

March 26
Genesis 27:30-40

It was done. The terrible thing was done.

Isaac had duped his father into giving him the blessing that was reserved for his brother. It was a blessing that could not be retracted or changed. The blessing now belonged to Isaac.

Esau comes home and fixes his dad dinner, blissfully unaware of what's taken place. He serves him up some stew and asks that Jacob's blessing be given to him. Jacob's old heart nearly stops. If this is Easu, then who received the blessing?

Esau's anguished cries are heart wrenching. "Please – bless me. You have to find a blessing for me." But it's not possible. What's done is done. The only blessing Jacob has left to give is a backhanded one at best.

This, of course, isn't the end of the story. There will be more to come. But we do well not to gloss over this scene, not to mute Esau's terrible cries. Although our customs are different we still have in each of us a fierce need for a blessing.

If we are lucky, we receive that blessing from our parents. Or from teachers or church leaders. Someone blesses who we are. If we have not been as fortunate, we may spend a lifetime searching for that blessing.

Think about the people in your life who may need your blessing. If you have children, they certainly need one. It doesn't matter if they didn't turn out anything like you thought they would – they still need the blessing of your unconditional love. If you don't have children, there are still people in your life in need of blessing. Yours may be the only one they ever get.

They need the blessing of knowing that they are valued and valuable children of God. They need the blessing of someone who sees beyond the labels that cover them and can see their true selves. They need the blessing of having someone believe in them.

Today ask God to show you who in your life is crying out for a blessing.

March 27
Luke 19:11-27

Jesus,
When will I learn?

When I make my choices
    driven by fear
    my hands cramp up
            from holding on too tightly.
My life gets smaller
    and smaller
    and I have less and less to show
            for my day and my hours.

Teach me, Jesus,
    how to trust.
How to act in faith
    knowing that even my doing
    will be blessed
    as my heart opens
    and my spirit grows wide.

Let me not pull back out of fear
    but step forth in faith.
            Beginning today.

March 28
Exodus 3:1-12

Who am I to do such a thing?

It was an understandable question as Moses stood next to the barbecuing bush. He was a fugitive, carving out a life on the lam in the wilderness. Who was he to challenge Pharaoh?

Who am I to do such a thing? I've not had God nudge me towards anything quite so grand as taking on a ruler and freeing a people, but I know the question. Am I letting you peek behind the curtain too much if I admit that I've had the same question while writing this book? Who am I to think that my words could have something to offer you, not once in a while but every day of the year? It seems utterly foolish.

But as Paul reminded us, God often likes to use precisely the foolish things of this world. A fugitive who never won a public speaking award. A solitary writer banging out words on a laptop. A soccer mom who normally wouldn't dream of going before the city council except this cause seems to have her name on it. A retiree who sits in chairs two sizes too small in order to eat lunch with a kid who was a stranger before he became a buddy.

Who am I to do such a thing? For most of us it's a perfectly logical question, and for most of us it's exactly the wrong question. It's not about who we are; it's about who God is. Moses on his own power would have been an abject failure. Moses allowing God to work through him led a people to freedom.

Who is God to do such a thing? Ah now, that's a question that springs not from fear but from wonder.

March 29
Exodus 4:1-17

If you've never heard Ken Medema's song, *Moses,* then you've missed a treat. It's one of those kinds of anthems that always gives me chill bumps, no matter how many times I sing it.

In this re-telling of the story of Moses by the burning bush, Medema uses the image of the rod as those things that we have to be willing to let go of and to let God have in order to follow the path God has for us. They are the security blankets we hold instead of holding onto God's hand.

What are you holding onto? In my work, I see people who sometimes have been holding onto hurts. The pain is very real but it is time to do the work of healing and move on to life. I see people who are holding onto old, outdated images of themselves that frankly were never very true to start with. I see people who are holding onto fear because it's the most familiar companion they have.

To go along with the 2010 soccer World Cup, Nike created a commercial with the theme, "Write your own story." Well, God wants to write a story for us, with us but first we have to let go. We have to let go of our old stories about being somehow less than a beloved child of God and our old stories about not being good enough. We have to let go of our old stories about small things not mattering and ministry only looking one way.

What are you holding onto?

It's time to let it go.

March 30
Exodus 5:1-9

Sometimes, God, I feel like I'm just being told
    to make more bricks with less straw.
        There's more to do,
            but no more hours in the day.
        There's more to bear,
            but no more strength in my heart.

I cry out, Lord,
    for help,
    for relief,
    for escape
        but the only answer that comes is
        more
        more
        more.
        Oh God.
        Sometimes I get so tired.

Give me strength, Lord, to do what must be done today.
    Multiply my meager straw,
        my scarce hours,
        my fading strength.
Hold me up and lift me up
    until the day comes
    that you lead me out
    and I wander into that land
        of freedom and ease.

March 31
Exodus 5:10-22

They weren't off to such a great start. Moses and Aaron gird up their loins and go to see Pharaoh, offering him the perfectly reasonable option of setting his slaves free. "Hmmm..." said Pharaoh, picking at a fingernail. "I don't know this god you are talking about. Never heard of him. Not so sure about that one. But it does seem quite evident to me that you and your people have way too much time on your hands. With all of this extra time you should be able to make extra bricks quite nicely."

Far from being welcomed as heroes, Moses and Aaron are met with complaints from the people (a nice bit of foreshadowing!) "Look what you've done," they say. "Not only are we not free but now we have an impossible quota to fill. What kind of leader are you?" The text doesn't record this, but I think I can hear Moses muttering something to the effect that this isn't what he signed up for.

Leadership can be hard, especially when you wind up with egg all over your face. You plan the big fund raiser and barely make enough to cover expenses. You convince the church that a new service is the way to go, and no one shows up. You're excited about doing the good deed of mowing the grass of a shut-in but not only is he not grateful, he complains that you cut it too short (or left it to long) and do you really call that edging? You plan an experience of spiritual growth for the kids that rapidly degenerates into a water balloon fight which is the only thing they'll report back to the church about their trip.

Sometimes it's not what we signed up for. But it's not the end of Moses' story and it's not the end of ours. Take a deep breath, regroup... but don't count on calling down plagues on anyone's head.

April 1
Exodus 13:17-22

Throughout the exodus experience the people mumble and grumble and complain to Moses because they're not taking the fast track to the Promised Land. The wilderness was the long, hard way around. Yet in today's text we get a fascinating peek into the reasons why they were led this way.

The direct route took them through the land of Philistines. God feared that these all too recent slaves would be spooked by the prospects of having to fight a war on their way and would want to flee back to Egypt. So God led them the longer way, taking them around the roadblock.

Following my graduation from seminary I served a church in an interim capacity and was crushed when it was not possible to continue full time. (When I arrived they were already in the process of calling someone.) I was especially crushed because I'd been out of seminary for seven months and had no prospects for a ministry position.

Just a couple of months later a pastor called me about an associate position at their church. They wound up calling me, and between the time I spent on staff and the time I spent there as a non-staff member, I spent twenty-four of twenty-six years with them. Now I cannot imagine not knowing these people, can't imagine not being blessed by the friends I made there and not being challenged by the journey I walked there. I thought God's purposes were being thwarted. Later I realized that like Israel, I just didn't have all of the information.

We see in part. When you feel like life has led you to a long detour, perhaps even a dead end, remember this text. Perhaps God is leading you in ways you cannot yet see.

April 2
Psalm 19

One of the things that I enjoyed about being around my father is that he was an artist. I always enjoyed watching him paint and draw and I certainly enjoy getting to hang his pictures in my home and office. But mostly I enjoyed getting to see the world through his artist eyes.

We stood on the golf tee together and did the usual golfer talk about which club to use and where we wanted our golf balls to land. And then he pointed out the beauty of the winter light and how the winter Bermuda grass gently changed color over the hillside like the shades of a horse's coat. Riding together to the beach he pointed out the beauty of the clouds, their form and their color and their ever-changing wonder. He pointed out a full moon and didn't just stop there. He talked of how fascinating it was that such a place existed.

Seeing the world through his artist eyes meant seeing the small details that are too easy to miss in our business-like days. Seeing the world through his artist eyes of faith meant being amazed over and over again at such a creative, artist God.

Today, try to look at the world with those same kinds of eyes. See the extraordinary colors of the birds. Take note of the tiny flower. If your stars are not obscured by streetlights, walk out into the evening and look straight up into infinity. Take notice of the endless variety of faces around you.

See the world.

And give thanks to the One who created it.

April 3
Luke 17:11-19

I fully expected to walk out of the hospital. I thought I'd have a really good story to tell about having been hit by a car and having nothing more than a few scrapes to show for it. That is, until the doctor came to my bedside to tell me I wouldn't be walking for a while.

In that moment, I knew I had to make a choice, the only choice left to me. At that point, there was little I could do for myself except this one thing. I had to decide how I was going to think about this, on what I would focus. I decided that the coming months of healing might go more easily if I focused on gratitude.

The reality was that I did have a lot for which to be grateful. I wasn't killed. I didn't have a head injury. I didn't even have a broken collarbone, which would have made life in a wheelchair infinitely more difficult. Thank you, God.

The following months were filled with more challenge than I'd dreamed, not only my healing but the deaths of people very close to me. I had times of sadness and grief and anger and frustration. But in the end I always came back to gratitude. Thank you, God.

Gratitude is much more powerful than we know. It can change our attitudes and change our lives.

Today, practice gratitude. Actively look for those things for which you are grateful. They may be very easy to see. Or you may have to look hard. But even one small thing is a beginning.

Practice gratitude.

April 4
Matthew 4:1-11

There's a saying in 12 step programs that goes something like, "Never get too hungry, too angry, too lonely or too tired." Program leaders know that when you get in those positions it's much harder to resist temptation.

After his baptism, Jesus went into the wilderness. While we're not told directly what he did besides fasting, I don't think that it's too much of a stretch to think that he was preparing himself for his ministry. Surely he was praying. Probably he was seeking a vision for his work.

Sometimes temptation comes when, like Jesus, we're hungry. He was physically hungry, and that can bring its own temptations. But deeper temptations come when we are spiritually famished. When we don't take good care of ourselves it's easy to being to let things slide or to wander into places we normally wouldn't go, emotionally or physically. One of the things that I learned early on in studying professional ethics is that one of the most ethical things I could do was to take good care of myself physically, emotionally and spiritually. If I did that, I was less likely to make a bad ethical choice.

At the same time, temptation can come when we are clear and strong. When we get a clear focus and vision for our lives, temptations come spilling out in all kinds of guises. It may be the temptation to cut corners, or to settle for less of a vision, something smaller and safer.

Jesus didn't pull an all-nighter to cram for his testing. He'd spent his life up to that point studying and learning and growing so that when the time came, he was ready.

May we do the same.

April 5
Psalm 90

Some days, God,
    I'm just empty and dry.
I know where I've screwed up
    and I know where I've fallen down
    and I know where I've fallen so completely short
        of your dreams for me,
        of your desires for me
        of what you ask of me.

I wouldn't have a prayer in this world,
    not the hope of a prayer,
    if it were not for your grace.
You have every right, God,
    to turn a deaf ear to my cries.
        God knows I've done the same to you.
And yet,
    you still beckon,
    you still wait,
    you still love.

On this day, God,
    may I make my dwelling place
    in your own wide heart.
And for this day,
    that is enough.

April 6
1 Samuel 17:1-18

Today's text is a study in contrasts. On the one hand, we have a giant of a man in Goliath. Not only big physically, he's big in bravado and intimidation. He offers a challenge to reduce the battle to just two men, offering to go mano a mano against anyone the army of Israel is willing to put up. Winner takes it all.

I suspect that when Goliath was issuing his challenge a lot of guys on the other side were looking down at their feet. Not only would going against Goliath probably mean getting really hurt and really killed, they could endanger everyone else.

On the other hand is David. While his brothers went off to battle, he's stuck at home taking care of the sheep. The only way he lands up at the battlefield is as a message boy. His father wants him to take some things to his brothers and, in return, bring home news of them. If they'd had Federal Express and e-mail back then he could have just stayed home.

Two different men from two different worlds. One of them is definitely the major player while the other one is just a bit player.

Or is he?

That's the thing about God stories. You have to pay attention because just when you know where they're going, they turn on you. The bit player becomes the hero. The sheep-keeper becomes the giant.

God can do it in our stories too, you know. Just when we think we're destined to stumble along the same path, God puts up a detour sign that takes us into places we didn't know were possible and wouldn't have missed for the world. Just when we think we know what our place is in this drama, God gives us a little nudge and pushes us forward.

Let yourself be open today to the ways in which God may be changing your own story.

April 7
1 Samuel 17:31-50

David knew what he needed, and what he needed to do.

He knew he needed to go up against Goliath, to take on his challenge. This wasn't just youthful bravado. While he might have been inexperienced when it came to armies, David was experienced at meeting danger and overcoming it. From his battle against the wild beasts, he knew he had skills for defending himself.

He knew what he needed to take with him. While Saul tried to outfit him with the latest and greatest in armor and weapons, David knew that wasn't what he really needed. He knew that he was better off using the one weapon with which he was familiar, a slingshot and some smooth stones. He knew that he needed to trade armored protection for agility. David knew what he knew and didn't let the authority of Saul or the critical importance of the occasion take him away from that knowledge.

Sometimes we lose sight of what we know. In our gut, we know that we need to do a certain thing or follow a certain path but we let others talk us out of it. We judge others to be so much more capable than we are in knowing these things, and we put down or minimize any wisdom we may have gained along the way. It may be the way someone tells you that you should pray or worship. It may be the way someone tells you that you should believe. Or it may be the way someone tried to talk you out of commitments and ministries and acts of service that you know in your bones have your name on them.

I don't think that God wants us to leap without looking and fly after any passing fancy. But, like David, we are called to appreciate our experience and gifts. We are to trust that we know what we know... we know what we need and what we need to do.

If we do, with God's help, we may then be off to slay a giant or two.

April 8
Mark 14:1-9

God,
let me live like this woman.
> Let me do what I can for you.
> Let me love you extravagantly.
> Let me not care
>> what others are thinking
>> let my mind be focused
>>> only on you.

God,
let me live like this woman.
> Let me do what I can for you.
> Let me not care if it makes any sense
>> or is pragmatic or prudent.
> Let me follow my heart
>> as it loves you wildly.

God,
let me live like this woman.
> Whatever I can do for you –
> Whether it is give to the poor
>> or comfort the sick
>> or teach the children
>> or prepare a body to be buried…
Let me do it with great love and great passion.

God,
let me live like this woman.
> Let me care that much.

April 9
1 Corinthians 1:10-25

They gathered together, armed with books and arguments,
    ready to debate.
I loved my books and loved my learning,
    but it wasn't enough.

And they gathered together with signs and wonders,
    enough to take my breath away.
I loved the awe of it and I was truly inspired by it,
    but it wasn't enough.

He sat slumped over in a corner, by himself.
The dust of the road hung heavy on him,
    not quite covering the bruised and the bleeding
    and the brokenness of him. And I was intrigued by him.
    Because it seemed to me that this crumpled man
        knew something of life,
        something of my life.
Knew something of the hurt
    of bones that ached
    and something of the hurt
        of friends who walked away
    and something of the hurt
        of feeling like even God had moved on.
He didn't try to convince me or wow me.
This man, he just loved me.
This man, this Jesus,
    he loved me to death.

And it was enough.

April 10
Matthew 12:9-14

When do I sit in judgment?

It's easy enough to condemn the Pharisees here. They were so wrapped up in their rules and regulations that they forgot to see the person. They forgot that the commandments were given as an avenue of God's grace, not as an end unto themselves. It's so easy to see here.

Maybe it's not so easy in my own life.

When do I miss the point? When do I short-circuit what God is doing in the world because I assume that I know that God wouldn't work that way? When do I get in the way of God because I won't step out of my comfort zone?

The Pharisees thought that the rules and regulations they received from God were the end of the conversation. Jesus came to tell them that they were just the beginning. God wasn't done working in the world and Jesus would break God's own commandments in order to do that work.

It's a tricky thing, because we all have a great gift for self-justification. (I used to make my pitch for anything I wanted my mom to get me by declaring, "But it's for school.") The ten commandments, as the bumper sticker says, are not the ten suggestions. But neither are they to be carved in stone in our own lives. God's compassion supersedes them.

So how do I keep the balance between being faithful to the demands of faith and knowing when to break those rules for the sake of God's children? How do I keep from kidding myself?

I think the answer is in relationship. As I focus on my relationship with God, some things become clearer and I hear God's call to compassion. But it's also important for me to have honest, open relationships with other Christians who can help me know when I'm just taking an easy way out and justifying it.

What about you?

April 11
Psalm 42

In today's text, it's easy to focus on the refrain, "Hope in God, for I shall yet again praise him" And indeed, it is a deep expression of faith. But today I'm just as interested in what comes before that.

The psalmist describes an aching for God, a bone-deep longing for God. I wonder how often we let ourselves feel our spiritual hunger that deeply.

Sometimes it happens on the heels of a great disruption in our lives. We lost someone we love very deeply, and we fear that our hearts will truly break. Sometimes it's because we feel stuck with no hope in sight. When I finished seminary, I had to wait a year before I was called to a church. Often during that year I walked into my job selling clothes wondering, "How long, O Lord?"

But I wonder if more times than not we cover over our spiritual hunger with distractions. We can literally eat our way past it – or drink our way. We can constantly entertain ourselves. We can stay very, very busy so that we don't have to listen to our longing. Even better, we can stay very, very busy at church, as if a full calendar automatically means a full soul.

What are you hungry for today? For what do you long? Do you long for a closer sense of God's presence in your life? Do you hunger for the ability to trust more or commit more deeply or even the ability to take the next step? Are you longing for direction for that next step?

Allow yourself to listen to your soul cries. They may be cries of delight today – or they may be cries of longing.

Listen. Just listen.

Then talk with God about them.

April 12
Acts 9:1-9

One of my seminary professors once jokingly told me that I wasn't going to have a very good testimony because I hadn't had enough riotous living to be saved from. After all, I'd grown up in church. I can't remember a time when I didn't know Jesus loved me and I loved him back. When I made a public profession of faith, it wasn't any great news; more of a letting folks know what had been going on for a long, long time.

I don't know if it's the same way now, but when I was growing up there was a certain preference given to those with dramatic testimonies. It was the people whom Jesus really saved, and saved good that we wanted to hear. The only problem was that for lot of us, it wasn't our stories.

How did you come to faith - or how are you coming to faith? For me it was growing up in a church, singing about God and Jesus. For Anne Lamott, it began with being lured into a church by its joy-filled gospel music. For one young man it was seeing a neighbor live a quiet, faith-filled life and then finding in a church the family he'd never known. For another person it was reading a book that finally connected all of the dots.

How did you come to faith – or how are you coming to faith? Our stories are as different as our fingerprints. Although they are all different, they are equally valid. It doesn't matter if your journey was different than mine; all that matters is that we are journeying.

Have you shared your story? It's always a wonderful experience for a class or a small group to take the time to listen to one another's stories of coming to faith, the "boring" ones as well as the dramatic ones.

How did you come to faith – and how are you coming to faith? Thank God for your own story, then ask God what new lessons you may learn from it.

April 13
Acts 9:10-19

Imagine that you're sitting around your house one day, minding your own business, just having a little prayer time with God. And God starts speaking to you.

Great! You'd been wanting direction for your life.

And God says, "Go down to such and such street, and in the house on the corner you're going to find a man named Osama Bin Laden. He's suffering from an illness, and you're going to bring healing to him."

No way, you think. Not after what's he's done. He's killed so many innocent people. But God keeps on talking.

"You're going to bring healing to him because I have great plans for him. I'm going to use him for my work."

What would you do?

Okay, that's a ridiculous comparison.

Okay, it's not completely ridiculous. When Paul first bursts onto the scene in the New Testament he's known as Saul, and he's dedicated to destroying this new Christian sect. He held the coats of the men who were busy killing Stephen for no other reason than Stephen was a follower of Christ. He approved of the killing. More than that, he took it as his mission to hunt down these heretics. If he was not actually killing them himself, he was carting them off to prison, which was no garden party.

The point is, Saul was, in capital letters, THE ENEMY. Sure, he'd had a powerful experience on the way to Damascus, but Annanias had yet to see proof of that. And yet, he went.

He trusted that the power of God that raised Jesus from the dead might be power enough to turn a fire breathing Christian hunter around. He trusted that he only need do what God had asked him to do. He risked radical obedience.

Chances are, none of us are going to be in such a dramatic situation. But God may ask us to see someone with new eyes, free of the distortion of reputation or prejudice. God may ask us to reach out to someone we'd rather push away.

May we run the risk of obedience.

April 14
Matthew 16:24-26

I just don't get it. Jesus said, "Take up your cross and follow me."

In my experience, crosses aren't just lying around. Most people have their crosses fall on them out of the sky, like the falling piano in the cartoon. The child who isn't as healthy as you expected or is more challenged than you'd hoped. The divorce or affair that blindsided you. The addiction that didn't go away once you were married. The doctor's visit that begins with the words, "I'm sorry..." Seems to me that it's not so much a matter of whether or not we'll pick our crosses as whether or not we'll try to throw them down.... If we could.

Of course, that's what we mean by crosses...something that's hard, that's a challenge, something we didn't know we'd signed up for. But maybe that's not what Jesus meant. For Jesus, taking up his cross meant single minded obedience to the will of God... come what may. It meant letting nothing keep him from that will, not suffering or humiliation or abandonment or death... Or even his very human desire to avoid all of the above.

"Wherever he leads I'll follow," the old hymn says, and following means obedience to the journey to which God has called you. It may mean leaving all that is familiar to strike out to a new place. Or it may mean finding ways of being faithful in the place in which you find yourself. It may mean keeping your heart on God even as your heart is breaking for the pain in your life. It may mean keeping your heart open to the world even though you know once you care you'll have to act. It means going beyond what is safe to what is vulnerable. Sometimes it means letting nothing keep us from a way that may be fraught with more pain than we'd dreamed and more demands than we thought we could bear... not even our human desire to avoid all of it.

It means loving God more fiercely than we love our ideas about how life ought to be. And it means trusting that in the end, we'll take up more than a cross. We'll find our very lives.

April 15
Genesis 32:22-32

Ironically enough, this perfectly fine mess all started with a blessing. As eldest son, Esau was due to receive his father's blessing. But mom Rebekah schemed and manipulated and got Jacob to play the part of his brother in order to receive a blessing from his blind father.

How strange it is now that Jacob is wrestling in the night with this strange visitor Jacob does not ask him for submission. Instead, he says, "I will not let you go until you bless me." Wasn't his father's blessing enough?

Or maybe it wasn't real enough. Jacob knew he'd been dishonest in gaining his father's blessing, which was why he was terrified by the thoughts of meeting up with his brother. Rebekah's scheming had given him the pathway to the first blessing. Maybe he wanted something honest. Maybe he wanted something that was real.

"I will not let go unless you bless me." Jacob had to fight for this blessing. He had to struggle and to wrestle and to hold on with fierce determination. He needed his blessing, the blessing that had his name on it and not the one originally intended for Esau.

We need the blessing with our name on it. Sometimes it means recognizing that what we had received as faith and counted as blessing no longer feels right or fits right or seems right to us. Sometimes it means realizing that what seems to be blessing for so many other people rings hollow for us; it does not have our name on it.

We need the blessing with our name on it, and sometimes we have to struggle through sleepless nights. Sometimes it means wrestling with the God who is suddenly not looking like or acting like the God we thought we knew. Sometimes it means recognizing that what you have called your life isn't the real and authentic life God has called you to live.

Where's your blessing? Are you willing to wrestle for it?

April 16
Genesis 33:1-11

Earlier in this story Esau is portrayed as something of a dolt, ready to trade away his blessing for the immediate satisfaction of a good meal. He is no match for the quick-witted scheming of his mother.

Today's text gives us quite a different picture. Jacob may have wrestled with the angel, but Esau has had some kind of transformation as well. The last we saw of him he was enraged at having been cheated, vowing vengeance on his brother.

That was the Esau that Jacob was terrified to meet on the road. Instead, a different man hugs him with great delight. "And who do we have here?" Esau asks as he takes in the sight of all of his nieces and nephews. When Jacob tries to give his brother his carefully planned gifts, Esau waves them off. "I've got plenty... but hey, look at you! How are you?"

I wish we had Esau's story. I wish we could know what made the difference for him. Did he also have a profound spiritual experience? Or was it gradual, a dawning on him that he missed his brother and no hurt was big enough to come between them? However it happened, Esau let go of the hurt and the grudge. Like the father welcoming the prodigal son, Esau welcomes back his prodigal brother.

We all have Esau's choice. Sometimes the hurt is a deep one, like your brother conspiring with your mother to cheat you out of what is rightfully yours. And sometimes it is petty but as troublesome as a pebble in your shoe. We all have a choice as to what to do with those hurts.

Too often religious people urge and quick and pain-free forgiveness, one that bypasses the actual work of healing. Such cheap grace seldom works. Some people have to struggle with realizing and acknowledging that they truly have been hurt. But after the realization and acknowledgement and work of healing, there comes a point in which we have to say, what now?

Some relationships may need to stay broken for any number of good reasons. But others may be restored if we are willing to have the courage and the grace of Esau, willing to let go of our grudges in order to embrace a brother, sister or friend.

What grudges are you holding onto?

April 17
Mark 10:13-16

One of the things that I love and appreciated about the churches I've been a member of is the place of children in them. When the children's choirs sing or tone chimes play, they aren't cute performers but rather worship leaders. Some of the most profound, moving and spiritually insightful statements have come from children. Some children regularly assist their parents as they help serve then monthly dinner at the homeless shelter. Whenever I had a chance to serve with those children, they always taught me something about seeing people with Jesus' eyes.

In the world of Jesus' day, there were a number of groups who had no right to expect respect; for example, women and children. They had no place, no standing. But Jesus pushed the religious leaders out of the way to say to these other folks, "Come on over here – your place is with me."

If you are busy raising children, allow yourself to think seriously about what they are learning about God from you – and your faith community. Allow yourself to be open to what they may be teaching you.

If you have no children or your children are all grown, then ask God to show you the places in your life where you might welcome children and share with them the possibilities of faith.

April 18
Jeremiah 8:8-13

The doctor shuffles a few papers, re-reads your test results and smiles reassuringly. "Everything is just fine," she says. "Go on and have a good time." Months later you are outraged to discover that you have cancer, cancer that has been there all of these months, cancer that should have been treated long ago.

Enraged, you storm back into the doctor's office. "Why didn't you tell me?" you demand. The doctor is seemingly puzzled by your anger. "Why, I didn't want to make you feel bad," she replies.

It's absurd, right? And yet it's precisely what the priests were doing in Jeremiah's time. They were telling the people what they wanted to hear and not what they needed to hear. They reassured the people that everything was okay and there was no need to change when everything most definitely was not okay.

It's a tough thing to be truth teller for we generally don't deal well with them. Honestly, did you ever get a good reaction when you said that the dress did indeed make her look fat? On a more serious note, we don't like people who tell us that we have to change or that everything's not coming up roses. Ministers have been known to lose their jobs for such and public officials have been voted out of office. Friendships have been lost.

This is not an invitation to bludgeon people over the head "for their own good." But each of us must look at our own lives to discover where we need to speak a tough word… and where we need to be open to hearing it.

April 19
Amos 2:6-8

Amos didn't mince words when it came to letting Israel know why God was angry with them. In short, they were exploiting people – the people who didn't have any power or any voice. The poor and the needy and the afflicted and even girls were simply objects to be used. Amos let them know that God wouldn't stand for that.

It's easy for us to stand on the sidelines and cheer Amos on. Lord, what a prophet. Until, that is, he turns his intense gaze to us. We don't know why we should be nervous. After all, we're not selling anyone into slavery because of their debts to us. We're not pushing anyone out of the way and have even known to hold the door open for someone in a wheelchair. Amos, you've got no beef with us.

Or maybe…

Part of Amos' message was that every child of God deserved to be treated like a child of God. Every one of God's children deserved to be treated with respect and dignity. Yeah, yeah, yeah… You already know all that stuff. But Lord, it's hard to do sometimes.

Maybe it's the old person whose memory isn't what it used to be. Or the young people whose style isn't what yours used to be. Or the person who disagrees with your politics and religion. Or the wait staff who's working as hard as they can, even if the kitchen is backed up and taking forever with your order. Or the people who clean your building. Or the mom who's paying for her groceries with food stamps. Or the person whose handicap makes it harder for them to express the brilliant thoughts they have. Or the person whose handicap means they will never be able to think the same thoughts that we take for granted.

With God, there are no optional people.
All God's children deserve to be treated like God's children.
And we are all God's children.

April 20
Luke 10:38-42

In talking with other women, I've found that they either love this text or hate it. The Marys of this world feel vindicated after years of being told (directly or indirectly) that they should take their noses out of the text books and into the cookbooks. They like being freed from the shackles of Martha-dom. And I understand. I was always the girl who wanted to be in the den watching football on Thanksgiving Day, not in the kitchen with the pots and pans. (Okay, not exactly the same thing as Jesus teaching, but you get the point.)

For the Marthas, it's not their favorite scripture. It feels like just one more place where their unappreciated work is devalued again. Somebody had to feed that crowd. Everybody always thinks dinner just happens by magic and nobody stops to think that maybe the cook would like the freedom of cooling her heels.

Because it's easy to take sides, it's easy to miss the point. Jesus didn't tell Martha that her care for them was wrong; he said she was anxious about all of the wrong things. The dishes could wait while she listened to him. They would do just fine with a peanut butter and jelly sandwich; she didn't have to spend all of her time in the kitchen making a feast. "You don't have to be anxious over all of those things," Jesus said.

I recently had a dear friend visiting me from Norway. Because I've been living at the corner of Too Much to Do and

Not Enough Time for a goodly while now, there was a lot I needed to do. Of course, it was the week of things going haywire at work so I had even less time.

It was her first visit to my house, and I wanted things to be perfect. "I can stay up all night," I thought to myself. I could clean the carpet in the wee hours of the morning. Maybe I could get that landscaping done before breakfast. Then I realized I was being anxious about many things when only one thing was needful. My house was clean. And we were going to have time together.

When she came, she raved about my house. Not about how perfect it was but about how welcome she felt. I was awake enough and rested enough to enjoy long hours of talking together – the most important gift.

Today ask God to help you be clear about what is needed for you. And ask God to help you let go of any anxiety about the rest.

April 21
Psalm 84

It was time.

I'd not been back to my former church since the last Sunday I served on staff there. This particular Sunday was the last Sunday before a new pastor came. It seemed to me to be the perfect time for one last visit. For closure. (Perhaps only a therapist could be that foolish.)

I sat down in a very unfamiliar place in a very familiar sanctuary, smiling at myself at the difference in view between sitting up front and sitting in the congregation. Soon I was literally and figuratively surrounded by people whom I loved. At some point in the service, I realized I was home. This was where I was supposed to be.

Shortly after the new pastor arrived we had lunch and had a conversation about how a former staff member might return as a member without causing any difficulty. Shortly after that I came back home and stayed for eighteen years.

If you are very blessed, you are a part of a part of God's people where you feel equally at home. Not perfect. Not always in agreement. But always the place to which you belong.

But I know that not everybody has such a blessing. I listen as people share their frustration of feeling like a fish out of water, feeling as if there's nowhere where they really belong, no feeling of home.

The truth is that no matter what your experience or mine, our best and truest place of belonging is always in God's heart. This presence is with us no matter if we are in the depths or flying high. In God's heart is always a place of welcome, no matter if we toe the theological line or if some think our beliefs to be odd or if we do not know what we believe.

No matter where you are today, no matter how you are, home is here. Stop. Take a deep breath. Then feel the soft quilt of love that surrounds you. Drink in the cool water of love that refreshes you. Breathe in the delight of God who delights in you.

April 22
John 13:1-17

In one short verse, John sums up the essence of servant leadership. Jesus knew where he had come from and where he was going. He knew who he was, and in that knowing he was free to pick up the towel and wash their feet.

It's when we know who we are that we can choose to be servants. Knowing who we are frees us from having to serve as a way of pleasing people and making them like us. That's not true servanthood. That's a bribe.

Knowing who we are frees us from having to have our contributions recognized and appreciated. It doesn't matter if we get the certificate or our picture in the paper. That's not true servanthood. That's an investment in pumping up our ego.

During the last few months of her life my mother's strength and stamina began declining and I began doing more for them. I organized their move into a retirement home and took carloads of books to be donated. I took dinner to them and brought them groceries. Finally, when she was too weak to get in and out of the tub, I brought my tub bench over and helped her bathe – a task she'd never wanted me to have to do but one I didn't mind doing.

Because I knew I was her daughter and she was my mother and I loved her and she loved me. It seemed to me that it was just what one does in such a situation.

Do you know whose you are? You're God's child. You've come from God and to God you will return, and in the in-between God is with you. So go now, pick up your own towel and hold it lightly.

April 23
Romans 5:1-4

The words roll along like stair steps…
> suffering produces endurance
> endurance produces character
> character produces hope.

If you read these words out of context, you might be tempted to say, "Not every time." After all, suffering doesn't always produce endurance. Sometimes it produces despair and bitterness.

But these words are in a context. Paul has been talking about God's great gift of grace. We don't have to do anything to deserve it. We don't have to do anything to earn it. All we need do is receive it. And once we are standing in grace these things do indeed become true.

We find endurance in suffering because we know we do not suffer alone. God is beside us, sometimes helping us bear the pain, sometimes giving relief but always giving us strength to bear that next moment, that next breath.

Endurance produces character not out of our own strength but because in our suffering, we have had to rely upon God. Such intimacy shapes us and changes us. Having endured what we once thought impossible to face, we cannot help but be changed.

And in the end, there is hope. Hope because we are yet still here. Hope because we have seen that no matter how dark the valley, we do not walk it alone. God's grace is our light and God's heart is our comfort.

Amen.

April 24
Hosea 11:1-12

If you ever start to doubt how deeply and tenderly God loves you, read these words from Hosea. God's children have been messing up time and time again, and God has every right to wash the divine hands of them. But God can't quite do it. God can't quite give up on them.

What tender images Hosea paints of this God… God is like the person who, when a baby is placed in their arms, instinctively lifts that baby up to their cheek. God cuddles us and holds us and feeds us, even when we do not recognize the source.

Sometimes we mess up. The accountability of our faith demands that we recognize and confess such sins. But it doesn't stop there.

God has every right to come storming into our lives, enraged and ready for blood. Instead, like a loving parent God says, "Come here. I won't give up on you. I still love you." Picture a mom or a dad, holding a child close, resting their head on top of the child's head, rubbing the baby's back. This is what God is waiting to do for us.

Do we get it? It's not about following rules, although knowing how much we are loved we cannot help but want to do well. It's not about checking off the naughty and nice list. It's not even about being good enough. It's about how very much God loves you.

No matter what you've done. No matter what you've failed to do. No matter what you've said or didn't say. No matter what you've achieved or how many times you've failed. God wants to hold you up, cheek to cheek and whispers in your ear.

"I love you.

Forever."

April 25
Acts 16:25-34

I expected to see a large truck rumbling down the road in front of my office. About the time I realized there was no truck I realized we were in the midst of an earthquake.

Now my friends in LA would have yawned their way through it, but for us East Coasters, it was a remarkable moment. We generally don't get earthquakes around these parts. Tornadoes, hurricanes, ice storms... Yes. Earthquakes, no.

At least, not physical ones. Like everyone else, we have our share of emotional and spiritual earthquakes.

Do you know the feeling? It can feel like everything is breaking open and in that moment the openness feels pretty good. It's opening up to new possibility and new future. But there are other times when the quake just seems to be knocking things off the shelf, breaking up what we'd thought we'd hold forever.

When we're in the midst of one of those quakes, it's easy to feel like it's a disaster and nothing else. But sometimes, as Paul and Silas found out, an earthquake can lead to freedom. It can shake us free from those things that are holding us back, that are keeping us imprisoned.

Are you game? Are you brave enough to allow God to come and shake up your world? Are you willing to let God break open some of those chains, to let God's Spirit blow down some of your walls?

Living through the quake can be a scary thing. But oh, the feeling of walking away from prison...

April 26
Matthew 6:25-34

Do not be anxious about your life...
Yeah, well, Jesus, that's easy for you to say.
Have you seen what the stock market's been doing?
Do not be anxious about your life...
It's just that you never had to deal with overseas competition for your job.
Do not be anxious for your life...
Have you even seen gas prices?
Do not be anxious for your life...
You never had kids, Jesus. You don't know what it's like trying to raise them these days.
Do not be anxious for your life...
Not to be a smart-aleck, Jesus, but it's a lot easier to say that when you can multiply bread and fish.

Do not be anxious for your life... not because everything is easy and struggle never comes. Do not be anxious, for the God who made you and loves you wholeheartedly and without

reservation will not forget about you. Do not let your anxiety block his working. Trust in the Love who made you and who delights in you and who dreams the best for you.
Trust for today.
Trust for this hour.
Trust for this moment.
Trust.

April 27
Deuteronomy 31:1-8.

Transitions are hard. We grow familiar with the old, and while there were things that disappointed us or frustrated us about the old, it was at least familiar. We knew what – or who – we were dealing with. When change comes we are suddenly back in a land of not knowing.

Israel was facing an unthinkable transition. For all of the griping and hard times they'd given Moses, he was also the only leader they'd ever known. He'd faced down Pharaoh and led them out of Egypt and out of slavery. He'd navigated their way through the sea. He was there to intercede with God on their behalf. He'd shepherded them through the wilderness and while there was too much wandering for their taste, the quail and the manna and the water did keep coming. What if they came this far only to have the new guy blow it?

Transitions are hard when you're the new guy, too. Imagine what Joshua must have felt and thought when Moses called him in and gave him the news. Joshua never saw a burning bush himself. Would he be able to lead the people through that final step?

To Joshua and to the people and to us, Moses says, "Be strong and of good courage. The Lord your God goes with you and he will not fail or forsake you."

Be strong and of good courage. God is still here, even if your landscape looks a little different. Even if your life looks very different. Be strong and of good courage. God will not fail you nor will God forsake you.

Even here.

Even now.

April 28
Luke 23:13-25

Maybe Barabbas was a hero. We think of him as a murderer and a low life and wonder how the people could have clamored for his release. But we're told that he was in prison for murder and insurrection, so maybe he was a hero to the people. Maybe the person he'd killed hadn't been one of them but had been one of the hated Romans. In such a case, in the minds of the people, Barabbas did nothing wrong.

In contrast, Herod and Pilate keep telling the people that Jesus has done nothing wrong. "As far as I can tell, he's innocent," Pilate declares but the people don't care. "Take him and give us Barabbas!" they shout.

Maybe they didn't care about this Jesus guy; they just wanted a chance to set Barabbas free. Or maybe they knew all about him and didn't think he was as innocent as Pilate said he was. In their minds, he was guilty. Guilty of shaking things up. He was guilty of disturbing the peace because he'd disturbed their peace that came with a safe, neat and unquestioned spiritual system. More than that, he showed no signs of leading a rebellion against Rome. What good was he?

Barabbas was their ticket to freedom. Or so they thought.

God, I guess not all blind people are named Bartimeus. When my priorities are misguided, heal me. When my assumptions are misled, heal me. When I miss seeing what you are doing in this world because of what I think you ought to do, heal my blindness.

Lest I be like the crowd. Lest I cry for Barabbas.

April 29
Genesis 31:43-50

When I was in college, a boyfriend gave me a "mizpah" necklace. Based on this text, it was two halves of a coin, inscribed with part of verse 49: "The lord watch between you and me, when we are absent from one another."

Which all sounds lovely and romantic... until you read the rest of this text. It was father-in-law Laban threatening his son-in-law that if he mistreated his wives in any way (including taking more wives), God would be watching. Somehow it doesn't seem quite so hearts and roses.

Remember, this is the same Laban who told Jacob that he needed to work for seven years in order to be able to marry the beautiful Rachel. After seven years, in the darkness of the wedding tent Laban substituted his other daughter Leah, the one known as the girl with weak eyes. In order to gain Rachel's hand. Jacob had to toil for another seven years. With his track record, Laban was one to be talking about mistreating people.

So what do we make of this text? Maybe the point – or one of the points – for us is that following God's path does not mean we will only be brought into contact with good and kindly souls. We may encounter people who are mean and people who are unreasonable. That does not mean that God is any less with us. Even when our path takes a detour, it does not mean God is any less with us. For all of Laban's meddling, one day Rachel and Jacob welcome to the world a baby boy named Joesph.

Today if you come into contact with a less than honest character, just remember Laban. And mutter "mizpah" under your breath.

April 30
Revelation 21:1-4

Some days, God,
    it seems as if there are more tears
    than my weary eyes can cry.
Friends who are suffering and friends who have died.
Teenagers who don't live to see graduation
    and babies who know only abuse and not love.
In any given newspaper
    in any given town
    on any given day,
    there is enough to break my heart.
    Not to mention the commercials with sad-eyed dogs
    and scared, battered kittens
            begging for a rescue,
            a chance
            a life.
So much suffering, God…
    even without going to the dark places of my own heart.
The hopes that have been stillborn
    or deemed too far gone.

God, I know you call us to joy but sometimes,
    just sometimes,
    all we can do is weep.
In such times remind us,
    there will better a day,
    there will better a time
    when you will wipe away our tears
    and we will cry them no more.

May 1
Matthew 20:17-28

Who knows what she was thinking. Maybe she was the original stage mom. Maybe she'd been pushing her boys James and John to ask for a promotion. Every time she brought the subject up, they looked down as they stubbed a toe in the dirt. "Aw, ma," they said. Maybe they promised they would but kept backing out so she decided she had to take things into her own hands.

Or maybe she'd been thinking about how much they'd all sacrificed for this gig, especially her. Instead of her boys staying home and making a good living and raising their families, they were off wondering the countryside. She'd given up not one but two sons to this cause. There should be some reward.

Or maybe, like any mother, she just wanted what was best for her boys.

As we tell this story, the momma of James and John usually comes out looking bad. We see her as power hungry, totally misunderstanding what Jesus was about. Then again, are we so different?

Maybe we're not asking to be Vice-President (or Vice-Messiah, as the case may be.) Still, we want to know what our return on investment is going to be.

There has been a trend for people to "church shop." Not in terms of seeking a community that's a good fit for them, a place where they can be welcomed, be challenged and find support for their own gifts and calling. No, the church shoppers just want to know what's in it for them.

Will you feed me? Will you provide activities for me and my family? Will you not ask me to do anything to help make these things happen?

We follow Jesus not because we have the best return on investment. We follow because it's the way that we have life.

May 2
Acts 28:23-31

Throughout the book of Acts we've been following Paul as he skips from one place to another and one challenge to another. Everywhere he turns there's some kind of impediment: shipwrecks, opposition, people who just plain don't get it. Finally, at the very end of the book of Acts we learn that he is able to preach the gospel without hindrance.

Except that tiny matter of not being able to go anywhere for two years because he's under house arrest. But for Paul, that doesn't matter. All that matters is that he can share the good news with anyone and everyone who comes his way.

So what gets in your way? What gets in your way of living a radical Christian life? It's been said – and said a lot these days – that the biggest obstacle to people following Jesus is the way in which many Christians are living. What keeps you from being the light, being the example that makes people say, "I want what she's having"? What hinders you?

Maybe it's fear. Fear of what people will think or say or do. Or fear of where such a path will lead. Or fear of failing if you even try. Or maybe it's just not practical... Or possible... At least that's what you tell yourself.

All of those things are probably true. But so what?

Today, consider what hinders you. And then, if you are very brave (or can pretend that you're brave), ask God to help you with those things.

May 3
Luke 11:1-8

We call this the Lord's Prayer, but that's really a misnomer. He gave it to us, so maybe it should be called the disciple's prayer. What part of this prayer resonates with you most deeply today?

While I pray all of it, at different times in my life I've focused on different parts of the prayer. If money is tight, I cling to the trust that God does provide what is needed for each day. When I've messed up, I lean into God's forgiveness. When someone has treated me badly, I remind myself of my responsibility to cultivate forgiveness in my own heart. When I am tempted, I am reminded that it's not God doing the leading. And sometimes I stop and stand amazed... at the way God has led me or the sunrise that graced the morning or the faces of the people whom I love and who love me. And I must thank and praise God for all that is holy.

Jesus gave this prayer to us as a model, and perhaps part of his teaching was that there is no part of our lives that is outside the bounds of our prayer. We pray for earthly things like bread. And we pray for spiritual things, like forgiveness. We ground the living of our lives in God's kingdom, where the last are first and where the greatest law is love.

What do you need to pray today? Do you need to ask for that daily bread, even and especially if you do not know how it will come? Does your soul need attention? Do you just need to sit in appreciation of how totally cool God's creation is?

Whatever you need to pray, pray it honestly. Whatever the conversation of your heart or the cry of your soul, offer it to God without fear.

Pray the Lord's Prayer in your own words.

And then trust in the God who hears.

May 4
Romans 8:18-25

One of the unfortunate legacies of previous generations of theologians was setting up creation in opposition to humankind. Instead of being caretakers and stewards of the Garden, we were to bend it into submission. It was ours to do with as we pleased.

The church stood by silently as we fouled our nests. Resources were there for our taking. One of the low points came when a cabinet member announced that we did not need to worry about conservation and being good stewards of the earth because Jesus was coming soon. (However, I get the image of Jesus coming back, taking one look around and saying, "I gave you such a nice place and look how you trashed it.")

Here in Romans Paul gives us the picture of redemption that includes creation itself. We're not the only ones freed from the bondage of death. Creation itself can rejoice in eternal life.

I believe that it is not God's intent that we live apart from creation (as if we ever could) but that we live as partners, thankful for what we receive, caring for what we have been given. Each of us has to decide how we do that.

Many churches have baskets at the doors of our sanctuary to collect the Sunday bulletin for recycling. Some people provide beautiful gardens in their yards that become habitats for birds and butterflies.

We need people in the midst of our faith communities to keep prodding us. We need to recognize that care for creation is a part of our spiritual disciplines. We need to spend time outside actually connecting with that creation whose care is in our hands. It is indeed a question of faith to ask, "How can I love the earth?"

So, how are you loving the earth?

May 5
Numbers 11:1-15

Teresa of Avila once cried out, "Lord, if this is how you treat your friends, no wonder you have so few of them." Moses would have understood.

In today's text, he reaches his limit. Not enough to get the people free of Pharaoh's control. Not enough to guide them though the sea. Not enough to make sure they have food and water, even in the desert. The people of Israel spend their time talking about the all they could eat bar in Egypt. "We had cucumbers. Remember how good they were? And the melons – so sweet and juicy. And the onions and garlic- not like this bland manna stuff."

Finally Moses explodes. "God, what did I ever do to you to deserve this? Are they my children? 'Cause they're acting like a bunch of spoiled brats. It's too much for one person. Just kill me now."

Then you know what God does? God gets some help for Moses. God instructs Moses to stop doing everything by himself and to line up some people to help carry the load.

Hmmm... Hitting the wall and reaching my limit. Spouting off at God. God suggesting that maybe I don't have to do everything by myself.

Nope – can't identify with this text at all.

How about you?

When you feel overwhelmed, you don't have to make nice and look good for God. Be honest. But be just as honest in your listening. God may actually have a way to make things better.

May 6
Numbers 11:26-30

So Moses has picked out seventy guys to help him share the burden. They go outside the camp and the spirit of God that came upon Moses came upon them as well. So far, so good. But then word got out that God's spirit was also upon two men who'd stayed behind in the camp.

A young man runs to Moses to tattle. "Eldad and Medad are prophesying. Make them stop!" And Joshua, hearing the news, chimes in. "Yes, make them stop."

Had Moses been tweeting at this point, he would've written: @Joshua. Smh (shaking my head.) As it was he told them that not only was this random outbreak of God's spirit not a bad thing, he wished it was upon every single person in the camp. It was presumptuous and just plain silly to think that God's Spirit could be confined to just a few people in just one place.

We still do it, you know. We still try to limit God's Spirit. Oh no, we think. God couldn't – or shouldn't – speak through that person – or those kinds of people.

Who makes you want to go and tattle? Who makes you want to tell God to cut it out and play by the rules? Who makes you uncomfortable?

It's a good thing to admit these things, even confess them. Because sooner or later that's exactly who God is going to bring into your life. That's exactly who God is going to use to speak to you.

Will you be able to hear?

May 7
Luke 24:13-27

You talk as you put up all of the leftover from all of the food that the Sunday School class brought. You talk about the service and how fine it was. You talk about the people showing up whom you didn't expect to see – and the ones who couldn't make it. If you're fortunate, you even play remember when and find some solace in unexpected laughter. The one thing you don't talk about is what life will be like now without that one person you couldn't imagine living without. Because right now you cannot imagine such a life.

You go through the box of stuff you brought home from the office. You go back over all of the days and weeks and months that led up to this day, going over them as meticulously as a coroner trying to find the cause of the end. The one thing you don't do is think about what you'll do tomorrow morning when you don't have a job to go to.

You don't even notice the stranger who's showed up at the kitchen door. You don't pay attention to the person who's now sitting next to you as you sort. Until he asks you what's going on. You can't believe he doesn't know, but you tell the story anyway.

Then he tells you a story about how God has a way. A way of making beginnings out of the surest of endings. A way of fostering light in the darkest of nights. A way of calling forth light where there has only been darkness and death.

And your heart is strangely warmed.

Whenever life takes to Emmaus, remember that you don't walk alone.

May 8
Luke 24:28-43

A hunk of bread. A piece of fish.

Such ordinary things. And yet in these things the Risen Christ is revealed to his disciples. He doesn't whip up a dozen miracles on the fly. He doesn't even multiply the bread and fish this time. He just sits down with them and eats.

It's how Jesus makes himself known to us. To be sure, sometimes it's through unmistakable events like storms made to hush up and blind people shopping for sunglasses and lame people signing up for dance lessons. We tell ourselves that things would be so different if he came to us like that. We'd know. We'd know for sure.

But now when it matters most, Jesus is the most casual about how he makes himself known. Tearing off a hunk of bread. Chewing some grilled fish.

Kind of makes me wonder how many times I've missed him. When I've gathered with family and friends (or friends who are family and family who are friends) around a dinner table, did I notice him pulling up a chair? When I sat on my patio with a fresh cup of coffee, listening to the birds and laughing at the squirrels, was he leaning up against the tree? Was he there behind the counter with the guy taking my order? Was he out there with the kids playing soccer? One of the lessons of the post resurrection stories is that you just never know where Jesus will show up. And what he'll be doing.

Jesus, as I go about my day and my week, may my eyes be opened as well.

May 9
Genesis 1:1-19

I have no idea of what the weather will be like when you read this, where you read this. There's a pretty good bet that in my neck of the woods spring will be plum busted out all over. In this part of the world the land loses its bashful southern decorum and breaks out in a riot of color. This past year temperature and rainfall and sun conspired to create prime conditions for a breath-taking spring. A number of neighbors have made it a point to stop and tell me how much they've enjoyed my flower-laden camellia bushes. (I smile and say "thank you" like I had anything at all to do with it.) My azaleas are covered in colors that are deep and rich and seem nearly to vibrate.

And God made all of this. And not only this. God made the rugged desert mountains, an ever-changing palate of light and shadow. God made the redwoods that reach up to heaven, stretching up taller than I can see. God made the iridescent lizard skittering across the stone wall. God made the small stream that winds its way through the woods and God made the powerful river cutting its way through a canyon.

God made the deep purple blue of a Colorado sky and the pastel colors of sunrise and the bold, extravagant colors of a sunset. God made the daisy and the rose and the sunflower and the snapdragon and the rosemary and the basil and the thyme... well, I could just go on and on.

Today thank God for the parts of nature that you enjoy. If you live in an urban area, you may find it in a window box, a park – or the breeze that flows over your skin.

Thank God, the wild and untamed and magnificent artist.

May 10
Genesis 1:20-31

As I write this, I'm at the beach. I run barefoot on the beach, feeling the pad of my foot meet the soft, firm sand. I hear the constant roar of the ocean (You know that thing never gets turned off?) and the punctuation of seagull cries. I feel the breeze on my skin and see the light dancing on the water.

At home I walk my dogs under a night sky, some nights seeing the stars with crystal clarity. I walk among my trees and touch them, feeling the rough bark and the aliveness of their trunks. Early morning runs have taught me about the ability to see in the darkness and to appreciate the blessed light of a full moon.

If you have your own chances to connect with creation give thanks. But far too many of us spend far too much time insulated and isolated. We leave our climate controlled houses to get in our climate controlled cars to drive to our climate controlled workplaces or churches or stores. The closest we get to nature is cleaning the bird droppings off of our windshields.

I was saddened to read the comments of a teacher who reported that if she let her preschoolers just go outside they had no idea of what to do with themselves. They didn't know how to just play. They didn't know how to discover the ant hills or the caterpillar or even just running in the grass.

There is danger in such insulation. We are in danger of stunting our own growth, for we were made to live in concert with creation. When we cut ourselves off, we cut off a part of ourselves. But there is a danger to creation as well. We forget that we were called to be stewards and so do not care for that which cannot be replaced.

Today find a way to connect with creation.

May 11
Genesis 2:1-3

Today I read an article in *USA Today* about how business travelers were not universally embracing the chance to use their wireless connections on planes and trains. They complained that travel time was the only time they had to disconnect. It was the only way they could be out of reach of the office. They knew they needed a time to slow down, a time to relax and rest their brains. They needed to read novels or do puzzles or let their minds wander or just plain do nothing.

In today's text, God takes a day of rest, a day of doing nothing. I can hear a modern boss' response now. "Sure, God could rest. But God's work was done. We'll rest when our work gets done – and you know that'll be never."

Physically, emotionally, psychologically and spiritually we need Sabbath times. We need time to rest and to relax. It's part of how we're made. We are not perpetual motion machines. But we also need to rest because it is a statement of faith.

Resting means trusting. We trust that what needs to get done will get done. We trust that our days are held in God's hands, the God who will not let us go. We trust that our worth isn't dependent on our doing so that we can stop a while and yet still be valued and valuable people.

How are you finding your Sabbath?

May 12
Genesis 3:1-7

There's trouble brewing in paradise. The snake starts an innocent sounding conversation with the woman. "What a lovely garden. So you say you can eat anything?"

"God said we could eat anything except the fruit of that tree."

"That tree? Hmmmm... what a pity. It looks so delicious." The snake slithers a little closer. "You know why that's forbidden, don't you... If you eat it, you'll be too much like God. God's been holding out on you and this is your chance to grab that power for yourself." The woman takes the apple and eats and then gives some to Adam, who thinks Eve is doing a swell job handling the cooking.

The snake tempts Eve not with a full scale assault but by creating the tiniest morsel of doubt that God is on the up and up, that God really wants what's best for Adam and Eve. Maybe God is just a tad insecure and doesn't want the competition. Maybe God doesn't want you to pull the curtain back and see what's really going on.

This in spite of all of the gifts and care God has already provided. God has given them the best of everything and all that they need. It's more than enough... until the snake suggests that just maybe it isn't. Maybe there's something better.

Do you trust God? Think about your own life. Has God provided what you needed? Maybe it wasn't everything you wanted or even what you felt entitled to have. But did you get what you needed? Has God given you surprises that were over the top and grace that was certainly unearned?

Sometimes temptation slides up beside us. Maybe God doesn't really care. Maybe God doesn't want you to grow and to live a big life. Maybe God's not really going to come through for you. Maybe God gave all of these instructions and commandments just to keep you down, to keep you in your place.

In such a time remember, God does keep us in our place, and that place is in the heart of God. And it doesn't get any better than that.

May 13
Genesis 3:8-20

Today's text has a little bit of everything.

There's a quite active game of pass the buck. When God asks Adam what happened, Adam says, "The woman you gave me made me do it." (Adam executed the nice double pass, blaming both God and Eve.) And Eve says, "The snake made me do it."

There's the beginning of shame. Adam and Eve realized they are uncovered before God just as they realize they have something to hide. They clumsily try to cover over their sin with flimsy fig leaves.

There's confrontation and accountability. There are consequences for this sin. The garden will never will be the same and neither will be life on this earth.

Finally, there is grace. God doesn't abandon them. Like a parent who hugs their child after the punishment is done, God calls them over. God squints an eye, threads a needle and starts whipping up some decent clothes for them to wear. In spite of everything, God is still taking care of them.

In spite of everything, God is still taking care of us.

Today, in spite of everything, God is taking care of you and me.

May 14
Psalm 147

All the stars in the sky... God sifts through each one, counting, naming, scattering them across the heavens.

The invisible guy on the street corner with the cardboard sign....God looks him in the eyes and wraps him in a healing embrace.

God strolls through creation... scattering the grass seed and putting out the corn for the deer.

God sits by the bedside of the dying old woman.

In some ways, this psalm is a bait and switch. We think we know what it's about. The bait is the example of the awesome power of God. This is a psalm for the big orchestra, the bass drum pounding out the glory and the cymbals clanging the power. The switch comes when the psalm doesn't stay with the picture of God as the powerful creator of all that is.

The psalmist switches to God who is the defender of the weak and helpless. God who binds up the broken and rebuilds the devastated. God who sees the invisible people who live on the margins. It's a lullaby sung in the quiet, lonely, night.

Both things are true. Remembering the power of God keeps us from a too easy familiarity that assumes God thinks like we do. Remembering the tender heart of God keeps us from a faith that is too enamored with power and position.

Holy is God. Wholly with us is God.

May 15
John 9:1-12

The disciples saw an object lesson.
    This blind man
    wasn't so much a man
    as an illustration in their theological textbooks.
"Jesus, whose fault is this?" they ask,
    scratching their beards a bit.
And Jesus taught them a lesson
    about assuming blame
    and being too smug.
But he didn't stop there.
        He spat on the ground
        and he made a bit of mud
        and he smoothed the mess on the man's eyes
        and he healed a man.
        A man.
        Not a lesson.
        Not a cause.
        A man who needed to see.
God, forgive me
    when I am so eager to prove my point
        that I am blind to a suffering person,
    when I am so ready to be right
        that I am blind to the needs of a person.
God, forgive me
    and make a little mud for my own eyes.

May 16
John 9:13-34

Talk about taking your power back…

This man has been a beggar. Being blind in that day and age meant he was useless. All he could do was sit by a street corner and beg for a bit of money.

Jesus changed all of that. He didn't just give him his sight. Through his healing, this man found a voice as well. The religious leaders are suspicious of his healing because it came on the Sabbath which meant that Jesus was breaking one of the ten commandments by working on the Sabbath.

"How are you able to see?" the Pharisees ask him, and the man tells his story simply. "He put clay on my eyes, I washed and now I see." This man obviously was trained in the Dragnet school of reporting – just the facts, ma'am.

But it's not good enough for his questioners so they hunt down his parents who act as if they've been lawyered up. "Yes, this is our son and he used to be blind and now he can see but you'll have to ask him about how that happened." They are afraid.

But their son is not. When the leaders return to question him again, he makes fun of them. He taunts them. "This man is doing God's work and you, God's leaders don't know who he is?"

Maybe we should call this the story of the two miracles. He regained his sight. And he found his voice.

Do you need such a miracle? Sometimes we are scared to tell the truth of our experience. Sometimes we are scared of what people will think if we really tell the story of what God has done in our lives. Sometimes we are just scared.

Today ask God for whatever healing you need.

May 17
Numbers 22:21-35

First of all a disclaimer: Many preachers secretly take great comfort in this text. If God can speak through Balaam's ass, there may be hope for us.

When the Moabite royal family was concerned about the numbers of Israelites heading towards them, they summoned Balaam to lay down a curse on the Israelites. God intervened, telling Balaam, "Don't you dare do such a thing" (my translation). God was blessing Israel and wouldn't cotton to any earthly prophet trying to counteract it with a curse.

But the royal family upped the ante, promising a significant

payoff if Balaam would just meet them at the border and do a curse or two. Caught between a rock and hard place, Balaam heads down the road to the border. Much to his surprise his ass turns off the road and wanders into a field. Balaam whips her and gets her back on track. Then in a narrow spot between two walls the ass pushes his foot into the wall. Balaam whips her again until she simply lies down and refuses to go no more.

Enraged, Balaam whipped the ass yet again and the ass has had enough. Turning her head she asks her master, "Why have you whipped me? Balaam doesn't seem to be at all startled to be having a conversation with this animal. "You've made a fool of me. If I had my sword I'd kill you."

"Have I ever," the ass asks Balaam, "done this before?" Balaam admits she has not.

And then he saw it. The angel. The angel with the big sword who'd been in the way all along. "If the ass had not turned aside," the angel says, "I would have killed you."

Great story. Not much to do with us, though...

Except for the part about deciding I'm going to do what I'm going to do, come hell or high water. Except for the part about me trying to crash through God's every attempt to turn me away from going down the wrong road. Except for the part about missing the point for far too long.

Sometimes the door does not open because hate or fear or injustice or just plain complacency has it closed. In that case, we need to keep banging on that door and raising a ruckus. But sometimes the door is closed because God has a different path for us and is trying to turn us aside.

May we have the wisdom to know the difference and the faith to follow.

May 18
Matthew 6:1-6

We all used to love to hear Fred pray. I have to admit that there were times when we kept a running count of how many times he said "Father," for some days it seemed like it came out with every other word. But we did so with great affection and appreciation.

For to listen to Fred pray was something special. It wasn't that he had so many flowery words and memorable phrases. It was that you felt like you were listening in on an ongoing conversation. When Fred prayed you knew it wasn't the first time these two had talked. It was obvious that Fred spent a lot of time praying alone, out of the spotlight. Fred had a way of gathering up the whole group and taking us with him into those private conversations. We were part of an intimate conversation that somehow included us.

My feeling is that a lot of people are slightly (or mightily) intimidated by prayer. Not that we'd ever want to admit that in church. We have a sneaking suspicion that we're doing it all wrong – if we manage to find the time to do it at all. What if we pray for the things we're not supposed to, or pray the wrong way?

Jesus reminds us that it's not about getting it right or impressing other people. It's about getting off by yourself and talking to God. Just talk to God. That's the only place you have to start. Just talk to God, and maybe even listen a bit.

God wants to have a conversation with you as well.

May 19
Romans 8:26-27

You see, this is what I was talking about.

Yesterday I wrote that we don't have to worry about praying perfectly. Today Paul writes that indeed, God's Spirit will jump in and help us. We don't have to know what to pray for, what is the absolutely best resolution to a terrible situation. We simply have to open our hearts to God.

God, this is the person I care about and worry about. This is what I think would be best but, heck, I don't really know. So just take them and hold them.

We don't even have to know what's best for our own lives. We can know what we want and what we fear, and we can let God sort out the rest.

God, I really, really want that job (or that person to marry me or that house sale to go through) because it seems like the best thing. This is what I want. All I can do is offer my desire to you. You know better than I do what's the right road and what's the wrong turn. More than that, you can work in and through my desire.

And then there are times when there are no words. When our hearts are too deeply broken or our minds are too paralyzed by fear or our spirits are simply too confused and lost. Then God's Spirit steps in and makes a prayer of what we cannot say.

Pray.

Pray as you can.

Pray as you must.

Then trust God for the rest.

May 20
Acts 8:26-40

I hadn't planned to go there. I was leading a retreat and the focus was on gratitude. Somehow in the context of our discussion I found myself talking a lot about community and the power of sharing our stories.

Only later did I realize how perfect it was. Several people came up to me afterwards to comment on how important those words were for them. The person in charge of the retreat told me afterwards that my words were the perfect fit for the things that their church was working on. Only later did I realize that it wasn't a detour at all but exactly the road I needed to be on.

Philip didn't know why he was going to Gaza, only that something in him said that he had to go. That's lesson number one from this text. Too often we dismiss our God-given intuition and nudgings as imagination or last night's bad burrito.

The second lesson is this: When Philip stumbled across the reason for his travel, he was ready. When he came upon a man reading and wondering and questioning, Philip was ready to talk with him about God and God's work through Jesus.

As much as I loved my seminary experience, the point isn't that we all need to go to seminary so that we'll be ready to teach when the opportunity arises. Rather, our preparation comes as we think about God and what it means to be a follower of Jesus. It comes as we reflect upon God's working in our lives. It comes as we read and we grow and we remember to love God with our minds as well as our hearts. It comes as we're willing to listen both to the Spirit's leading and to another person's questions.

God may lead you to unexpected places. You may not even recognize that it was God's leading until much later. God may give you unexpected opportunities to share your own story.

You probably won't run into a eunuch reading scripture in

his chariot. (If you do, you know what to do.) You might run into someone who is talking about how judgmental all Christians are. Or about how nobody really cares anymore. Or how religion is nothing more than snake-oil gussied up with holy language.

Or you might run into someone who is hungry and needing food. Or lonely and needing a presence.

Today ask God to guide you in your detours.

May 21
Isaiah 6:1-8

As I write this, we are getting ready to observe the tenth anniversary of the September 11 attacks. Along with the stories about where we were and what we were doing that day are the stories about how that day changed us. Today I heard a snippet of an interview with a man who carried a woman in a wheelchair down dozens of flights of steps on that day. He's struggled with the memories of that day, but said that his goal was to live like the person he was on that day.

Times of crisis can change us. For Isaiah, it was the death of a king. For you, it may be a national crisis like 9/11. It may better a personal loss, like the loss of a family member, a job... Or your health. Or it may be such a private crisis that no one even knows that you're going through it. All you know is that nothing fits and your life just doesn't work.

In all of these things, we have a choice. We can frantically try to put the pieces back together just like they used to be. (The only problem is that never works.) We can pour a layer of cement over the open places and go on with our lives, a little harder and worse for wear.

Or we can open ourselves to God's spirit even in this time. We don't always have a choice as to the events that happen in our lives. We always have a choice, however of the meaning we make of them. It doesn't mean God will make the time easy. It does mean that God never stops creating and re-creating... Even in our lives.

May 22
Matthew 22:23-40

It was a trick question. What's the greatest commandment? If Jesus is forced to choose one commandment, he will surely slight the others and then his enemies will have him in a corner. But Jesus doesn't blink an eye as he neatly sums up all of God's commandments: Love God, and love your neighbor as yourself.

That's a pretty concise summary, but most of us shorten it even further: Love God. Love your neighbor.

You see, a lot of us don't do particularly well on the part about loving our neighbors as we love ourselves. We treat our neighbors much more nicely. We don't berate them if they make a simple mistake – then bring it up again to them ten years later. We don't read them a daily list of their faults and shortcomings. We don't call them names like 'stupid" and "fat" and "failure." We don't do it to them, but a lot of us do it to ourselves.

Jesus is very clear that we are to love ourselves. For some of us, some healing must take place before we can do that. We have to heal the old, distorted images that we have of ourselves. We have to silence the negative voices in our heads with their steady steam of criticism. Others of us have to give ourselves permission. It really is okay to love ourselves. In fact, Jesus said we should do it.

Loving ourselves means being kind with ourselves, even when we mess up. It means doing good things for ourselves, like taking good care of our bodies and souls. It means treating ourselves like any other beloved child of God deserves to be treated.

What's keeping you from loving yourself?

May 23
Acts 10:9-23

When parents complain to me about their teenagers' challenging of them, I often smile sweetly and say, "How wonderful! If your children do this now, they won't have to do it when they are forty." Believe it or not, this does not endear me to parents.

But part of our growing up process is examining those things we were told to be true as children, and seeing if they still ring true in our lives as adults. We do it with the way we dress and the music we listen to and the kind of food we like. If we are wise, we will also go through the same questioning as we grow in our spiritual life. Growing spiritually sometimes means leaving behind the beliefs that we once would have fought for. It's not always a bad thing. It's what happens as we learn more about God and ourselves and the world.

It happened to Peter. He'd grown up with very strict rules. Some foods were unclean. Some people were unclean. A man of faith would keep him apart from those things in order to keep himself pure. But then came this vision of unclean foods, a vision that wouldn't go away. There came a command that turned his neat world upside down: "What God has made clean, you must not call profane." And then there came an unclean man walking into his life, asking for his help. Peter had to decide if he was going to be faithful to his past beliefs about God – or be faithful to God.

Where is God challenging you? What beliefs have you held onto just because someone told you a long time ago, "That's just the way things are"? Is God calling you to grow into deeper understanding?

May 24
Genesis 9:1-17

It is, in one sense, Eden 2.0. The words of God to Noah are hauntingly similar to God's words to Adam. "Be fruitful and multiply and fill the earth. I give you everything." But Adam's legacy now hangs as a shadow. "The fear of you and the dread of you shall be upon every beast of the earth." It is a fractured Eden in which Noah begins to rebuild.

There is a sadness in the words. Nothing will be as it once was. Even if the animals flourish again and the plants grow with wild abandon and the time comes when you can no longer see the watermarks the debris left behind, the shadow is still there. Nothing will be the same.

But the picture is not all shadow. God realizes that no matter how great our sin, such a punishment should never again be visited upon creation. From this day forth, God will only care for creation, not destroy it.

There may be a time in your life when you feel like God must be ready to be done with you, completely and finally done. That feeling may be very well justified or it may be illusion. In those days, remember this rainbow sign. God will never again be about destroying creation and there will be no punishment that does not come hand in hand with grace.

May 25
Genesis 9:18-29

I've met people who've been in churches for most of their middle-aged lives who've never heard this story of Noah passing out, drunk and naked. We sing about Noah building the arky, arky but not Noah fermenting the grapey, grapey. We sanitize scripture for young children, telling the stories that match up to their emotional, intellectual and spiritual development. And that is as it should be.

The problem is that many of us never get past the Little Tykes version of scripture. We don't keep reading past the heroic deeds to find the falling down. The problem with that is that when we have our falling down moments we think we're the first ones to fail. Maybe you've never fallen down drunk. Or maybe you have. Maybe you've never had to have anyone to cover for you when you were at your worst. Or maybe you have.

The point of today's text isn't to book the vineyard tour and drink ourselves into a coma because hey, if it was good enough for Noah... The point is that our biblical characters are terribly flawed.

As are we.

And God still chooses them and uses them.

As God does with us.

May 26
Ephesians 4:25-32

Anger

God, help me let go of this anger.
    It does not serve me.
    I keep chewing it
    over and over and over again
    but there is no nourishment here.
It keeps me stuck.
It keeps me spinning my wheels.
It takes my energy
    and my focus.
God, help me to let go.

God, help me hold onto this anger.
This anger over the things that should not be
    but are.
This anger over the way
    some people are treated.
This anger over injustice.
    It keeps me focused.
    It gives me energy.
It drives me on
    to speak up or speak out,
    to work for change.

God, may I have eyes to see
    when anger is a distraction
    and when it is gift.

May 27
Acts 18:24-28

Thank you, God, for the teachers.

Thank you for teachers in schools,
   schools that are good, bad or indifferent
      who nonetheless do their job faithfully
      who never stop caring about their students
         no matter how many times their hearts get broken.

Thank you, God, for the teachers
   who teach us about you.
Thank you for the ones
   who challenge our minds
   and open our hearts.
Thank you for every teacher
   who has been content to be behind the scenes,
   rejoicing when their students
      go on to do great things.

Remember the teachers in your life.
Thank God for them.
If you are able, write a note of thanks to them.

May 28
Romans 8:28-30

I made a suggestion to her and she responded, "It's all good."

Through the years these verses have been edited down to say the same thing. "It's all good," we say with what we hope is appropriate faith and piety.

Well excuse me, but I don't think it is. It can't be good for parents to bury their children. It can't be good for a person to throw away a perfectly good life in a haze of addiction. It can't be good for a child to be beaten up, terrorized or raped. It can't be good for a parent to die while children are still too young and too needy. It can't be good for senior adults to lose their life savings and their security because someone else got greedy. I'm sorry, but that's not all good.

And that's not what these verses say. Paul doesn't say that everything that happens is good if you just believe enough. Paul says that no matter what happens, God doesn't stop working to redeem any situation.

Some things are bad and some things are terrible. Some things just ought not to be, and their presence in our lives testifies to the brokenness of this world. But that brokenness isn't the end of the story. God doesn't quit nor does God give up.

If you're dealing with terrible things you don't have to pretend that they're all good. But maybe, just maybe you can hold onto the hope that God's already working to find the way to being good back into your life.

May 29
Luke 16:10-13

You brought a brand new book home from the bookstore (or library, if you so chose.) It's called Profiles in Faith and you cannot wait to read the stirring stories. You know the book will be filled with stories about people who faced persecution, people who stood up for their faith even under the threat of death, people who founded charities with nothing more than a nickel and two dimes and wound up changing the world.

So you open to the first chapter. It's about Jim who refused to cut corners at work even when everyone else said they did it and it would be okay. And Maria who took meals to the shut-ins every month. And Walter, who made it a point of speaking kindly to everyone he met, especially the stressed out retail clerks. And Kim who made it a point to speak to every child at their own eye level and never, ever patted them on their heads. And Mark who spoke up when they gave him too much change. And Louisa who spoke up in the church business meeting to ask if they were being the best stewards of God's gifts. And Steve who gladly served as a sponsor for others trying to be recovering alcoholics. And Carolyn the teacher who made it a point of looking for God's image in every student she taught. And Amy who rescued the animals who had no one else to care for them and stand up for them.

You close the book in disgust. This isn't what you expected at all. Why, these were all such little things. Then a quote on the back cover catches your eye. It's Jesus talking about being faithful in little.

We think about the tests of faith coming in the grand, dramatic moments. In truth, they are at our elbow every day.

In what small things will you be faithful today?

May 30
Isaiah 65:17-25

What in your life needs the touch of a new creation?

You know the places I mean. The places in your life that feel old and cramped, that feel worn out and useless. The ones that seem to be so messed up they are beyond redemption. The same old stuff that you're tired of dealing with again and again but see no way to make it different.

I've moved three times as an adult. Every time, it seems that there's that one box that never quite gets unpacked. You know the one. It's the one that you know is full of important stuff but not quite important enough to be actually needed over the years. Sometimes our lives feel tired and full because of all of those old things we've been lugging around. Sometimes they feel sour and not quite right because they need a fresh wind to blow through them.

Here's the good news. God's Spirit still blows among us and through us and in us. God never retires as Creator and is endlessly waiting, looking, seeking the chance to create anew.

Even in our lives.

Today talk with God about the parts of your life in need of renewal and re-creation.

May 31
1 Corinthians 3:1-9

Our minister of music sighed. "This is why I hate basketball season," she said. Her planned orderliness of choir practice had been disrupted by the trash talking flying back and forth. With four colleges from the same conference very close by, passions run deep. I belong to Wake Forest. I belong to Carolina. I belong to State. I belong to Duke. We claim our allegiances and defend them fiercely.

The people of Corinth were no strangers to such things. But instead of dividing up over basketball teams, they were lining up behind preachers. Some of them were Paul's people. Other's stood with Apollos. They argued over who was best and who had done more. And Paul said it was all nonsense.

Paul has laid the foundation. Now Apollos was building on it. And neither man mattered as much as the God whom they were serving. Once again, the Corinthians were missing the point. It wasn't about who was the best minister. It was about what God through Jesus had done and still wanted to do among them.

It's easy for jealousy to sneak in through the back door. We wonder why she always gets to sing the solos. We wonder why he always gets the choice committees. We wonder why the visiting preacher always eats with that family. Sometimes things are skewed. But sometimes, as Paul would remind us, focusing on such things distracts us from the real questions:

How has God gifted me?

How does God want me to serve in this place?

Seems to me those aren't such bad questions for us to think about today.

June 1
Romans 14:1-12

Used to be doing the Wednesday night dinners was easy. Slap some boiled ham on the plate, add a scoop of peas and a roll, maybe a Jell-O salad, and you were good. Now there's that vegetarian option to worry about. And what do you do about the gluten free crowd? Are you sure no kid has a peanut allergy? So many things to worry about.

No, actually it's so many people to worry about.

And that's Paul's point. We worry about each other. No, that's not quite right - we care about each other. There are a hundred different things that can split a church wide open, from doctrinal disputes to how you sing the doxology to the color of the carpet to who makes the coffee on Sunday mornings. Paul isn't foolish enough to advocate for total agreement. We come from different places and see life from different eyes, even the life of faith.

It's also not the case that whoever is in disagreement should just give up for the sake of everyone else. Throughout the church's history we have needed those gadflies who push us ahead in matters of justice, who push us to expand our vision instead of limiting it.

What we are all called to do is to make a space where all can be heard. We can listen to each other with care, seeking not the next point we need to make but listening in order to understand what is important to the other.

The family of God is messy. Sometimes it is downright difficult. Often it is frustrating. But it is also the body of Christ and in this body we are woven together with threads of love.

Think about a situation in your faith community in which there is disagreement or difficulty? How can you bring a word of grace to the discussion?

June 2
Luke 11:9-13

After I'd left home for school my father built a large storage barn in their backyard. It was well built with a loft on the top. I came home for Christmas and exclaimed, "You built a barn. I'm finally going to get my pony!"

Having an unusually strong case of horse crazy as a girl, I'd begged for a horse of my own. I took riding lessons. When visiting my grandmother's farm I volunteered to clean out the stalls just for the sake of being around horses. (I told you it was a bad case.) But my father, having grown up on and around farms, knew how much time and money a horse required. (Just for the record, the barn housed his lawn mower and yard tools.)

I suppose I could go around with my nose out of joint because I never got the horse I wanted. After all, I asked. But that seems rather silly to me after everything else he'd given to me.

I suppose that we could come to God with a chip on our shoulder because we never got our pony. But when we look at everything else God has given us, can we really hold that grudge?

I know that sometimes we ask for things far more important than ponies, things of life and death. I have no answer as to why those are not always answered in the way we'd like. But I do think that God wants us to keep asking, to keep coming to God with our requests.

June 3
Deuteronomy 10:10-22

"It's for your own good."

I'm just stubborn enough that when I heard those words, I wanted to do the opposite. If it was something I needed to eat for my own good, I'd have none of it. If it was something I needed to do, I'd head in the opposite direction. Maybe it was for my own good, but I needed to discover it for myself.

In today's text, there's a grocery list of all that God requires of us:

Fear the Lord
Walk in all of God's ways
Love God with all of your heart and all of your soul
Keep God's commandments.

And here's the kicker - all of these things are for our own good. God asks these things of us not because God needs a big power trip, but because this is the path in which we find our greatest well-being.

It's hard to understand that sometimes, what with all of the surface distractions... All of the things we think we have to have or have to do or have to be. But when we get right down to it, our joy lies in the things closest to our hearts - and to the heart of God. Love God with every fiber of your being. Seek to follow God in steps large and small. Live the way God has mapped out for you.

It's not good for you in the way the yucky tasting medicine is good for you. It's good for you in the way of finding the place where you belong, where you feel most free and you feel most you.

God, help me live the life you have intended for me.

June 4
Acts 2:1-13

We were college students on foreign study traveling around through Israel and Italy. In the narrow streets of the old city of Jerusalem we happened upon a couple of college students from North Carolina. You would have thought we were greeting long, lost friends. We were excited not only to find other English speaking Americans but people from our part of the world. People who understood us.

I think that's a little of what it was like for those strangers at Pentecost. There they were, stumbling about the narrow streets of Jerusalem, visitors thumbing through their travelers translation guides. Suddenly they closed their books and just listened. Listened to words they understood.

Even in these past Pentecost days, we still need the experience. We need to hear the gospel in words we understand. We need to hear the gospel in words that understand us. This good news isn't a one size fits all kind of message - it's custom tailored. Not to fit what we think we want to hear but what we need to hear.

Sometimes it is the words we long for and sometimes it is the words that we run from. No matter which way we turn, they are the words that being life to us and bring us to the fullest, grandest and best life possible for us.

So today, just listen.

Listen for the whisper of God's Spirit. Look around for a flame or two. Open yourself to all the ways in which God wants to speak to you today. You'll recognize the language not so much by your ears but by your heart.

God is speaking to us in our own language.

How can we not be amazed?

June 5
Matthew 23:1-14

A friend and colleague often reminds me to take the sandwich approach to scripture. That doesn't mean eating a sandwich while doing Bible study. It means considering the text under study as the "meat" or filling of the sandwich while taking into account the "bread," the texts that come before and after. He reminds us that context of scripture isn't accidental.

The context of today's text is that things are heating up. The religious leaders keep coming to Jesus, trying to trick him. Jesus himself has an eye towards the end. He knows where this story is headed and the dark clouds are starting to gather. So what does it mean to look at Jesus' admonitions about servanthood under the shadow of the cross?

It's the so-called great men of the day who put him on the cross... the religious leaders, the Roman governmental officials. It's the humble nearly nameless people, both women and men, who keep watch with Jesus until his last breath, who carry his lifeless body to a tomb not even his own.

They didn't do it to get gold stars or certificates of recognition. They did it because they loved him greatly and loving Jesus greatly, they could do nothing else.

The men who put Jesus on the cross, from Pilate to Caiphas the chief priest to the soldiers hammering in the nails were killing Jesus because they could. They had the power. The women and men who stayed with Jesus were doing it because it was the only thing they could do. They had the love.

What is it that you do today for the sheer love of God?

June 6
2 Timothy 1:3-7

My father's mother died of cancer when I was a young teenager. I'd seen her on our monthly visits to my parents' hometown and one glorious summer got to spend an entire week with her on the farm. Fresh vegetables, biscuits on the table at any given hour, a pony to ride every day - what wasn't to love?

As I've gotten older I've loved learning more about her from other family members. Part of the legacy that she passed down was a love of great books, great music and an insistence on correct grammar.

I have no grandchildren of my own but love spending time with the youngest generation of my family. Occasionally I wonder about the legacy I'm passing on to them. What are they learning from me? What values are they seeing modeled in me?

Whether or not we have young children in our lives who are connected by blood, we are connected to children through the family of faith. What are you teaching them about God and about faith and about how we as Christians live in this world? Sometimes the teaching happens in a Sunday School classroom or during a bedtime ritual. Sometimes it happens in a chance encounter in a hallway. Sometimes it happens as an adult volunteers time out of a busy schedule to be with and to teach a child.

Timothy had a wonderful legacy of faith that he received from two women in his family, his mother and grandmother. What legacy are you sharing?

June 7
Psalm 130

Do you know what it's like to be in the depths?

If you've lived very long at all, you've probably had a moment or two… or more. Maybe for you it was a time of financial difficulty, with more month than money. Maybe you lost your job or hated your job or couldn't find a job. Maybe your marriage had ended and you couldn't see how to go on. Maybe your marriage was dead, and you felt stuck with no good options. Maybe death took the one person in this world that you would have given your life to save. Maybe the news from the doctor wasn't good. Or maybe loneliness, depression or anxiety has been a fog that will not lift.

Have you been there? Maybe you're there now. If so, take heart from the psalmist.

The psalmist cries out from his gut, a soul wrenching cry from the pit. God, please hear me! Then the psalmist reaches for the only bit of light he has – a hope in the hope that God does hear and God does care and God has not forgotten him.

We sometimes talk about hope as if it is something that comes on its own accord, but there are times when hope is a choice. We make a choice that we will hold onto hope. We will hold onto the hope that morning is yet coming, no matter how dark the night seems now.

In working with my clients, hope is a crucial element. When they are not able to claim it for themselves, I tell them that I will hold it for them until they are ready. Hope keeps the door of possibility open, even if only a crack.

Cry out of your depths.

And then hope in the Lord.

June 8
1 Corinthians 16:1-4

Our retreat was going even better than I'd hoped. I was leading the retreat for the women from my church. I'd scored big points by finding a fantastic new retreat center, overflowing with both beauty and hospitality. The discussions had been both lively and heartfelt. Women talked about how much they enjoyed getting to know women they hadn't known very well. Women talked about what a gift this break from their routine was. Everything was perfect.

Until the Sunday morning session.

That's when I asked them to talk about money. Specifically, how money fit into their lives of faith.

I split them up into small groups to make the conversation easier. Still, there was a lot of awkward silence at the beginning. Nobody was looking at anyone else. "It's just not a comfortable topic," one woman said.

I don't know how we got to this point. Paul had no shyness in asking the church at Corinth to set aside a little bit of money at the first of every week to be give in support of mission work when he came. Paul certainly needed the money. But I think he knew something else. They needed to give. They needed to give in order to be a part of this larger work in the world. And they needed to give as a physical sign of a spiritual trust in God.

As do we.

Challenge yourself this week to begin to talk with a trusted friend about money. Choose someone whose confidentiality is without question, who won't broadcast your conversation. Be honest with them about where your faith stretches you... and where your faith has been hands off.

In the end, our Sunday morning discussion became one of the best of the weekend as the women learned that other people shared the same struggles and questions.

June 9
Exodus 18:13-27

As he finished up the job, he gently confronted me. Yes, it was theoretically possible for me to keep up with the mountain of leaves in my yard as well as keep up with my job. (I'd spent several eight-hour days in my yard before calling him to finish the job - a two day endeavor.) If I let him do it all along, it would actually be cheaper for me. Plus I might be able to do something in October and November other than just rake leaves.

It's one of my weaknesses, thinking I have to do everything all by myself. As a solo business owner, sometimes that's the reality. But not all of the time.

Moses faced the same dilemma. He was wearing himself out trying to settle all of the disputes that arose among the children of Israel. (Thinking back to their near constant whining throughout the journey from Egypt, it's not hard to imagine that there were many such disputes.) Moses' father in law asked him what he was doing. Moses replied that he was their leader and this was what he did from morning until night. His father in law put his pipe on the table, folded his newspaper and fiddled with the buttons on his cardigan.

"Can't do it, son," he said with his best fatherly tone. "It's too

many people, too much work. You need to get yourself some help." He told Moses that his job was to be teacher and trainer and facilitator. Others needed to take the day to day load.

Are you in the same boat? Maybe you're not trying to mediate all of the disputes of a people, but you're trying to do too much by yourself. You feel like you're somehow less or you've failed if you have to have someone help you.

And it's a lie. God calls us to do many things. God doesn't call us to do ALL things. Maybe your place is on those front lines, leaving the administration to someone else. Maybe your place is helping others do their jobs better. Maybe you need another mom to help you with your kids every so often. Maybe you need the guidance of someone else to help you figure out what to do next.

It's okay to ask for help.

In fact, it might even be required.

June 10
Matthew 6:19-24

One of the unforeseen consequences of being a minister is that for many years I'd attended or been a part of a lot more funerals than most people my age. Whether or not I have a part in leading the service, it's always an occasion for me to think about legacies. I think about what sort of legacy that person left behind. I wonder what mine will be.

As I talk with a family, I've never heard them mention the size of the deceased's bank accounts or investment portfolio. Instead, they tell stories about what was special about that person – a sense of humor, a devoted faith, how they could make the best coconut cakes. The way they visited folks or sent cards. They way they stood up for doing the right thing. The way they set a quiet example. The way they disciplined their kids so that years later the kids could see through the discipline to the love that was behind it. The way they took in any stray.

They may talk about their loved one's work, but it's in the context of how hard they worked for their family. Or about how passionate they were about the work they did, how it was really their calling. Or how they strove to work with integrity. No one ever mentions how many raises their loved one got.

When the day comes that the people who know you are sitting down to tell stories in your memory, what will they say? What will be your legacy?

What do you want your legacy to be? Do you need to make any changes in your life now in order to start investing in that legacy?

June 11
John 5:1-9

If you look ahead to tomorrow's devotion, you'll see the same scripture text listed. That's not a misprint. When I was working on that devotion, I was intrigued by another aspect of this same story. It's about the angel troubling the waters.

Sometimes the waters are troubled in our lives just because it's a part of the journey, like traveling down a mountain river and having to negotiate the occasional whitewater.

But sometimes it may be an angel – or the spirit of God – troubling those waters.

Time after time I see it in my counseling practice. Someone comes to see me because they've been depressed or they feel anxious. Or restless. Or something just doesn't feel right in their lives. On the surface, everything is fine but beneath that surface, the waters are troubled.

As we work it becomes evident that their symptoms are merely the warning lights telling them to pay attention. Pay attention to the work that no longer works for them. Pay attention to the relationship in disrepair. Listen to the dream that won't go away. Don't listen any more to the critical thoughts that have been pummeling them for as long as you can remember. Take the time to heal that old wound.

It's only human to want to avoid such things. It's no fun to allow ourselves to finally feel the grief or the pain that we've pushed down for so long. We may have to leave our comfort zones for a path that is nowhere near as familiar.

And yet, in the story it is those people who are willing to go into the troubled waters who come out healed.

So are the angels stirring up any water in your life?

June 12
John 5:1-9

The pool at Bethesda was known for its healing waters. After the angel troubled the waters of the pool, it was a case of "First one in the pool gets to be healed." Jesus comes upon a man who was lying by the pool seemingly waiting for his chance to be the one.

"Do you want to be healed?" Jesus asks. The funny thing is, the man never really answers him. He doesn't say, "Yes, with all my heart." He doesn't say, "Yes, but I've given up hope of it happening." He doesn't even say, "What do you think, Einstein? I'm just working on my tan?"

No, he answers with an excuse. "I have no one to help me. Every one else always beats me."

Sometimes I think that it's not so much our big sins that get in the way of our full and faithful lives but our little excuses...

I tried that once, and it didn't work...I've never (fill in the blank) before, so why should I try now?... Yeah, I'd really love to start my day with prayer and reflection, but I always seem to stay up too late and then I can't get up in the morning… I've just always been this way… Yeah, that'd be great, but…

Yes, but… Yes, but… Yes, God, but…

Today, imagine that you're sitting by that pool. What's the question that Jesus has for you?

And what's your answer?

June 13
Luke 13:1-5

Sometimes my clients will ask me why… why they have no confidence, why is their self-esteem chronically low, why are they unable to trust anyone, most of all themselves. Sometimes we can trace the lines of cause and effect, the experiences and events and messages that shaped them and wounded them. At other times, it isn't at all clear. At times I just have to say, "I don't know why. So now the question isn't so much why but what next."

It's a common thing to want to break things down into manageable, easily understood pieces. If we know why something happens, we have a measure of control. We know – or can figure out – what to do to keep it from happening again. It's like the old joke: "Doctor, my arm hurts when I do this." "Well, then don't do that."

People wanted Jesus to connect the dots. Terrible things happened to these people so they must have done something terrible to deserve it. Jesus' answer is clear and to the point. It doesn't work that way, Faith isn't a lucky rabbit's foot that keeps bad things from happening. If you work in a church for very long, you know this is true. Some of the finest saints have to face some of the most terrible things.

We cannot always answer the question as to why bad things happen to good and bad people alike, as much as we need to ask it. But after the asking, after the wrestling and wondering, the time comes to move beyond the why to what next.

What next? Maybe it's to reach out to those who are suffering, to offer what we can when we can. Maybe it's to reach out in our own times of pain, to reach out to God and to God's people. In the end, the one question we are left with is how to live as God's people, in season and out, in times of celebration and in times of mourning.

Today you may be in a season of asking "why." Ask away. But if that season has grown stale for you then open yourself to asking a new question.

What now? What's next?

June 14
1 Corinthians 15:50-58

I stand at the pulpit, look out over the congregation, and take a deep breath. Family members fill the front rows. Some of them stare vacantly at the carpet. Others look up at me with puffy, red-rimmed eyes, begging for some shred of comfort. Behind them are gathered friends, co-workers. Some who were as close as family. Some who come because it is the right thing to do.

Standing over a casket that's holding a body that is now but a shell, I read these words. "Lo, I tell you a mystery…" No matter how many times I say the words, I am always surprised by them. They come rolling and tumbling one after the other and I feel a power in them much greater than my own feeble voice. I cannot explain them. But beyond all doubt, I know in my bones they are true.

I tell you a mystery, that this life we see is not the only life we will know, that there is something grand and glorious and beyond our power to understand fully.

It's a comfort when it is our own loved one whom we mourn. It is a hope when we see our own days growing short. But more than that, it is a gift for any day, for this ordinary day. For the God who makes the trumpets to sound and for death to go slinking away in defeat is the same God who holds our minutes and hours and days, the days when we feel rushed or defeated or just confused. Even on those days, we are held in the light of this same God who has already won the ultimate battle. We are not alone.

Indeed, it is a mystery. Indeed, it is a rejoicing.

June 15
Joshua 2:1-14

If I was pastoring a church, I might be tempted to do a sermon series on "God's Best Hookers." (Perhaps this is a reason I am not pastoring a church...) Today we have yet another prostitute playing a significant role in God's story.

Joshua sends two men to spy out the land of Jericho. In the sparse language of the narrative, we're told they spend the night at the house of Rahab, the prostitute (no explanation of why they chose that spot for spending the night.) Someone rats them out and the king tells Rahab to give them up.

But Rahab has no intention of surrendering them. She tells them that she knows they're on the winning side. She provides an escape plan and then is clever enough to ask for a way for her household to be protected when the Israelites do take over the city.

Rahab has sex with men as a way of supporting herself and her loved ones. (In reality, one of the few options for a woman of that time who was not supported by male family members.) But she's also insightful, courageous and clever. And she is God's servant.

It's easy to come up with all kinds of reasons as to why God can't use us. We're not smart enough. Or good looking enough. Or we don't have enough education. Or we've done terrible things, shameful things.

Rahab looks down on us from her window and says, "So what?"

Indeed... So what?

June 16
Mark 10:17-27

Maybe we shouldn't be so glib about teaching our children to sing, "Jesus loves me." After all, look where it got this fellow.

He came to Jesus asking about eternal life. He told him that he'd kept all of the commandments faithfully since he was a boy. The text tells us that, "looking at him, Jesus loved him." Then Jesus dropped the hammer. "You just have to do one more thing," Jesus said. "Sell everything you have and give it to the poor." Think what Jesus might have said if he didn't like the guy!

I've puzzled over this text for a long time. I've known some people of great resources who were very faithful stewards of those resources. They came by their wealth honestly and shared it generously. Or maybe I'm just trying to water down Jesus' words to make them more palatable and easier to swallow.

For me, the key to this story comes when Jesus says to the young man, "This one thing you lack." For whatever reason, his wealth was getting in the way. His true freedom could only come after he let go.

What's the one thing you lack? Maybe it's your money and property that's taking center stage in your life. Maybe it's a business that's calling you to sacrifice family and friends and even your own good health. Or maybe you need to let go of something different – a destructive habit, a fear that has kept you paralyzed, a resentment that has kept your spirit sour.

If you are very brave, talk with God today. Ask God what you are lacking. Then ask God to give you what you truly need.

June 17
Psalm 91

Wrap me up, God.
    Like a man shivering in the cold, wrap me up
        in the quilted warmth of Your presence.
    Like a woman greeting a long lost love, wrap me up
        in the fierce embrace of Your heart.
    Like a child awakened
        from the screaming nightmare, wrap me up
        in the safety of Your Spirit.

Wrap me, up, God
    for too many days I feel
    like I go into the battle alone.
        Decisions to make.
        Crises to face.
        Everyday challenges that turn into mountains
            just because they never go away.
Wrap me up, God, in Your grace
    that is stronger than anything the day will bring.
Wrap me up, God, in Your grace
    that is brighter than anything the night will conjure.

Wrap me up
    and hold me close
    and all will be well.

June 18
Micah 6:6-8

"Do justice and love kindness"

Only as I started working on this devotion did I think about the perfect joining of these two commands. They are truly made to walk hand in hand.

Doing justice can be a hard task. It can mean stepping outside of our comfort zones, considering the needs of others just as important as our own desires. Sometimes it demands that we take unpopular stands and speak words others don't want to hear.

Those are the external dangers of doing justice. The internal danger is that we begin to see everything in terms of black and white, us versus them, just versus unjust. Injustice makes us angry, and the danger is that we will become angry and bitter people.

Loving kindness can be hard in a different sort of way. As justice calls us to speak out, sometimes kindness compels us to say nothing. While justice asks us to stand up and demand what is right, kindness sometimes asks us to let go of our need for everyone to see that WE are right. Kindness sets the scales aside in favor of holding the heart of things. The danger in loving kindness is that kindness degenerates into conflict avoidance, that we mistake kindness for being nice.

Doing justice without kindness can make our edges too hard. Loving kindness without doing justice can make us too soft and passive. That's why Micah reminds us that we need both. It's not justice or kindness. It's justice and kindness.

Not always an easy balance to keep. But it is the way of those who are walking with God.

June 19
Joshua 4:19-24

When the children of Israel crossed over the Jordan, they brought twelve stones with them. Now they are setting up the stones as a marker. "When your children ask you," Joshua tells them, "what these stones are all about, you tell them. You tell them that we were slaves. You tell them that God gave us freedom and God led us through the sea and through the wilderness. You tell them the story of what God has done."

More than rules and regulations, our faith is at its heart a story. We were slaves. God heard our cry and led us out.

What's your story? Maybe God didn't lead you out of the wilderness of your grief but gave you strength and hope for bearing it. In any given church sit people who have been led out of a hundred different kinds of slavery.

What's your story? This may be heresy, but I don't think people care about Roman roads to salvation or twelve points for believing. They care about our stories. I was here and I reached out to God. I was here and God reached out to me.

If you have children, share with them your own story. And if you do not, there will still be someone to ask what this means in your life. Then it will be your turn to tell your story.

(If you have the time and inclination, take some time to write out your story. Not for an English essay but to help you get the words around it.)

June 20
Amos 8:4-12

God, help me to care...

to care about the woman in worn out bedroom slippers buying the lottery ticket because it's the only hope she can find for herself. Help me to care about the Hispanic kid behind the counter who struggles with my English and is struggling to create a better life. Help me to care about the guy who lives in a slum but drives a nicer car than mine because when he's in his car he can feel like he is somebody who matters.

God, help me to care...

to care about the woman who takes my dry cleaning, the man who waves my car through the road work, the child who comes to school with an empty stomach and no coat in the midst of winter's bite.

God, help me to care, even though caring can be frustrating. Needs are so great and I am so small. Help me do what is indeed in my power to do, whether through a soup kitchen or a voting machine.

Most of all, God, help me live in such a way that I recognize and honor the dignity and worth of each person, no matter their bank account nor neighborhood.

June 21
John 20:11-18

We go looking for Jesus,
    wondering why he isn't here
    just when we need him most.

In our sadness, we do not hear his voice.
In our grief, we do not recognize him among us.
In our great darkness, we cannot take in his light.
    We keep bumping about the tombs,
            looking for him
            longing for him
            missing him.

Until he calls our names.
And we know.
    He was here all along.
    He is here with us.
            We just didn't know.
            Lord, we just didn't know.

Keep your eyes - and heart - open today.
You just might be surprised...

June 22
Colossians 3:12-17

In the preceding verses, Paul has described the old life that the believers buried with Christ. The old ways are buried; the old divisions are no more. Now Paul flips the coin to describe the positive side. These are the new clothes the believer puts on.

Compassion. Kindness. Lowliness. Meekness. Patience. Forgiveness. Love. All wrapped together and held together by love.

I don't know about you, but it seems like a lot to aspire to all at once. I wonder what would happen if we just took them one by one and for a time focused on one aspect. For example, this week I might want to focus on cultivating compassion.

To do that I might have to look at what got in way of my being compassionate. Where is it more difficult for me to cultivate that compassionate spirit? With whom do I find myself being more judgmental? Cultivating compassion would mean consciously choosing it day in and day out. It would mean having to figure out where having compassion means practicing tough love. It would mean asking myself what compassion looks like in various situations, for it doesn't always look the same.

If we so choose, we can find here a nice framework for our own spiritual growth. Not a checklist to be checked off, but a way of expanding our spirit and deepening our practice of faith.

Are you game?

June 23
Luke 13:10-17

They were so intent on their spiritual correctness
    that they didn't see the woman,
    they didn't care about her.
They didn't see her stretch,
    didn't see her looking at the sky
    for the first time in eighteen years.
They didn't see the tears
    of gratitude and joy
    streaming down her face.

They are so vehement in their argument
    over abortion being right or wrong
    that they never notice
    the terrified girl standing on the edge of their debate.

They are so passionate in their argument
    over whether or not gays should be accepted or changed
    that they never notice
    the excluded man standing by himself
        on the edge of the crowd,
        always on the edge of the crowd.
God, as your people sometimes we disagree.
But never let us commit the sin
    of thinking our positions and our arguments
    are more important than your children.
Always…
    may we first and foremost
    be about your work of healing and compassion.

June 24
Exodus 35:20-35

When I cleaned out my childhood home, I found a list of my father's woodworking projects. Along with the furniture that he'd built for family members were the pieces he'd made for churches. When his church refurbished its organ, he made the wooden pieces that held the pipes in place. When they started a new church, he made the furniture for the children's Sunday School class. When his church celebrated a significant anniversary, he painted three large oil paintings of the three historic church buildings.

He was an ad man by trade, and I found in his files records of many church campaigns he'd helped with. Renovation campaigns... beginnings of new ministries and worship services... Over and over again I saw his creative skills and advertising experience put to good use.

I thought about him as I read today's text. The people are bringing items to be used for the creation of the furnishings of God's house. But they did more than bring stuff.

God gave some women the ability to weave fine cloth or do beautiful embroidery... and they did just that. God gave some people the ability to work with gold and silver and precious stones, and they did just that. God gave some people the ability to be fine woodworkers, and they put their gifts to work.

God has given you gifts as well. It may be a creative sort of gift, like the ability to paint a picture or sew clothes. One of our deacons was a gifted interior designer, and he shared his gifts with us in helping to make our building space not only more functional but more beautiful. Or your gift may be in rocking babies, cooking dinner or hammering a nail. You may be gifted with numbers or organization.

Whatever your gifts, God can use them.

June 25
Isaiah 53

This is one of those texts that feels far too rich and deep and full for my mere words on the page. We should have a great work of art to stand before, so big and so engaging that we gaze at it for hours. We should listen to Bach's St. Matthew Passion as we look. This is a text that really needs all of our senses to take in, and even then it is not enough.

Despised. Rejected. Wounded. Oppressed. Grieving. Humiliated. Shamed. Unjustly accused. Unjustly killed. Suffering every depth of suffering we could imagine or that we could know.

Not because suffering is wonderful and we should all aspire to it but because suffering is inevitable if we live for more than a minute. Sooner or later suffering becomes our companion. Sometimes for a brief moment and sometimes for a lifetime. And sometimes for a moment that feels a lifetime long.

But suffering isn't our only companion. For there is One who also sits down with us, who will wait with us no matter how long our dark nights, who will walk with us no matter how hard the road and how badly we limp, who can bear to hear any cry we may need to scream. The One who holds the whole world in his hands can hold our battered and bruised hearts.

Because he knows. He was real flesh and blood and he know what it is to have bones ache and pain pound. Because he was a real man he knows the sting of being misunderstood, of being excluded. He knows what it is to wish you could give your life for one simple sip of water even as your life is winding down.

My God, he knows.

June 26
Luke 14:25-33

Being as I'm the one picking out the texts for this book, and being as there's no one looking over my shoulder, it's a great temptation just to skip over today's text. I can substitute some teaching of Jesus that's not quite so harsh, something a little more warm and fuzzy feeling. Maybe that story about the children coming to see him? Yes, that would be easier to write on.

But this is the text that's staring me in the face today and the one I must consider. I notice we never use this text on Mother's Day or Father's Day. The price of following me, Jesus says, is hating your family. I can see it if you have a terrible, abusive family. But what if you have a pretty nice family?

The only way I can understand this text is by looking at its context. Jesus goes on to talk about figuring out the cost before you begin any endeavor. You can't get started and then stop when it gets too hard. The cost of following me, Jesus says, is everything.

What are you willing to give up in order to follow Jesus? What price are you willing to pay in order to be faithful? Think about it before you sign up because you don't know beforehand what will be asked of you.

Jesus may show up at your work, asking pesky questions about what you do and how you do it. Jesus may show up in your relationships, making pretty pointed observations about how you treat people –or how other people are treating you. Jesus may be there at the soccer game or when you're balancing your checkbook. There's no part of your life that he's not going to stick his nose into and there's no telling what parts of your life he might change.

Are you willing to take that kind of risk?

June 27
Hebrews 11:1-3

When our church contemplated capital campaign renovations a new pipe organ was at the top of the list. Our old electronic organ was on its last legs, adding an element of unpredictability to our Sunday worship. Besides that, many of us yearned for the sound and feel and beauty of a pipe organ.

There's just one hurdle in replacing an electronic organ with a pipe organ.... the pipes. More specifically, room for the pipes. Turns out, that was no hurdle for us at all.

Back when they built the sanctuary the church didn't have the money to put in a pipe organ but they trusted and believed that this would not always be the case. When they built sanctuary they included space for organ pipes. That's faith.

Many of the people who were involved in making those

decisions and giving that money didn't live long enough to see their music dream realized. But they were willing to make it possible for another generation to carry it forward. That's faith

It's no news flash that we are an instant results oriented culture. No book promising that you can lose twenty-five pounds in two years in going to be a best seller. And while it's important in the church continually to assess whether our work is working, as people of faith we also hold the long view.

We believe in faith that the seeds we plant may bear fruit, even if we will not see it for ourselves.

We believe that investing in people who cannot repay us is worthwhile for we have faith that somehow, someway what we do may make some small difference in those lives. And who knows — some of those lives may go on to make a huge difference. We have faith that what we do matters even on the days when all of the evidence available seems to scream otherwise.

We have faith that all we see is not all there is. We have faith that we do not work and dream and hope alone but in concert with God's own Spirit. We have faith that grace is meant for even us, even and especially on our worst days.

Today, have faith.

June 28
Genesis 12:1-3

It was the beginning of so much. It would be the beginning of years of wandering and wondering and waiting. It was the beginning of holding onto hopes so long that they became threadbare and worn, hopes so faded they hardly seemed worth holding onto. It was the start of leaving all that was familiar for nothing more than a promise, and an outlandish one at that. It would be the beginning of growing old with dreams seemingly unfulfilled. What would Abram had done if the Lord had come to him and said, "Go... and this is what you will have to face."

It's Abram's story, but it's also ours. Maybe we're not promised a child... but we are promised a new life, different than any we could have imagined. Maybe we're not promised a literal home, but we're promised the gift of feeling at home in our own skin, of being at peace and at home wherever we find ourselves. But God's promises always involve movement. We have to leave what is comfortable and familiar in order to venture to a new land. Sometimes our journey moves by fits and starts. Sometimes our hopes grow faded and tattered and like Sarai, we can only laugh hollow laughter when we think of them...

Then we see Abram (now named Abraham) over in the corner. He's got a brand new name and a brand new son. The boy is the light of his cataract-clouded eyes. You ask him if it was all worth it, the waiting and the wondering and the wandering. Abraham can only laugh in answer, cradling close the child whose name itself is Laughter.

June 29
Psalm 131

The baby is restless. Okay, let's be blunt - the baby is screaming her little head off. Her face turns purple as howls of outrage fill the air.

Her mom doesn't shame her for expressing her need in the only way she knows how to do. A hungry baby cannot pick up the phone and call for take-out. Her mom picks up and holds her close. Finding her mom's breast, the child relaxes her tense and angry body. With tear stains still on her cheeks, she relaxes into nursing, taking in exactly what she needed.

This is the image the psalmist uses in today's text. I am calmed and quieted, the psalmist says, just like a nursing child.

What's your day like today? How has it been or how do you think it will be? Are you stressed? Are you upset about something? Does anxiety buzz around the edges of your hours or depression lie heavy on your soul?

Imagine.

Imagine for just this moment that you can be a child again,

a toddler still small enough for laps. Imagine crawling into the lap of a parent who does not shame you or belittle you. A lap

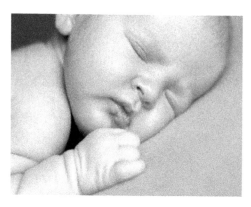 that's safe, encircled by arms that love. A dad or a mom who rests a chin on the top of your head and wills their steady breath into your own soul until you breathe more freely. Until your tight muscles relax.

You can't stay there forever. But the love of it does go with you forever.

Calmed and quieted.

May you be so this day.

June 30
Acts 20:7-12

There was a man in our church who is known for falling asleep in worship. He was a man of deep faith and generous spirit who has given selflessly through the years. He just tended to nod off during the sermons.

When it came time to call a new pastor, this man wound up on the search committee. The joke was that if he could stay awake during a candidate's sermon, that minister was a keeper!

He would have found a kindred spirit in Eutychus. Paul is filled with all he wants to share before he has to leave town, and talks for hours on end, long into the night. Eutychus found a cozy spot in a window to listen to Paul, but as the hour grew late his eyes grew heavy. Falling asleep, he lost his balance and fell out of the window. The three story fall was enough to kill him.

Paul went downstairs, picked the boy up and reassured everyone that there was life still in him. Then he went back upstairs, broke bread, and continued the discussion.

I don't know about you, but if I'd just raised someone from the dead, I'd want to savor the moment a little bit. I'd want to receive the gratitude and congratulations and adulations. I'd want at least a little bit of fanfare.

But not Paul. Paul just goes back to what he was doing before they were so dramatically interrupted. Paul was clear about his priorities. It wasn't about him putting on a show. He raised the boy up because it just needed to be done. For Paul, his focus was on sharing as much as he knew to share about this Jesus who had both saved his life and changed his life.

What's your priority today? What's most important to you?

July 1
1 Corinthians 10:23-33

We're getting close to July 4, the day in which our country celebrates the birthday of its independence. One of the foundations of that struggle was the belief that we, the people, had certain rights. Over two hundred years later, we still struggle to know what it means to have such rights.

The apostle Paul was concerned about community, not a country. The church in Corinth had its problems, not the least of which was knowing how to get along with each other. It may be technically okay to do some things, Paul tells them, but it's not helpful. The question isn't so much do I have a right to do or say this but rather, how does this serve the greater good?

How would life in your community of faith be different if everyone asked that question? I may have a right to say anything, but does what I say serve the greater good? The new ministry/ alternative service/budget line item may not be my cup of tea, but does it serve the greater good? How am I helping to build up the body of Christ?

What's hard is that there is no cookie-cutter, decision tree driven way to sort this out. Sometimes we have to risk offending others in the body in order to follow faithfully the way we believe God is leading us. At times in relationships we have to risk offending another person in order to speak truth to them.

But at the very least, if we heed Paul's admonition we can avoid being like a bull in a china shop, heedlessly breaking things. At the very least, we will not beat people over the head with our rights. With humility, we seek the discernment of God's leading to know when we must hold back in order to build up and when we must act and speak (no matter the consequences) in order to move forward as God's people.

July 2
Galatians 5:22-26

Love. Joy. Peace. Patience. Kindness. Goodness.
Faithfulness. Gentleness. Self-control.

What a to-do list!

Thankfully Paul's point is that it isn't a to do list. These are the things that naturally happen when we live in partnership with the Spirit of God.

Like that's so much easier.

Actually, it is easier in one sense. It's not all up to us. It's not something we have to do by strength of will. But we do have to be willing to open ourselves to seeking.

My parents were wonderful examples of what we used to call churchmanship. They knew how to be good church members. They tithed faithfully. They supported programs and services if they thought it was for the greater good of the church even if it wasn't something they were personally interested in. They remembered that their ministers were people and allowed them to be so. They refused to engage in gossip. They shared their many gifts, whether it was building furniture or baking a much in demand cake for the bake sale. In short, they loved God and loved their church.

As I think about how to go about being a member of my own church I think of them often. I make the decisions I do not because I'm checking something off a list but because I want to honor the example they gave to me. It's not a burdensome thing but part of the gift of being Joe and Gerry's daughter.

Today think about what you've learned from God about living in love. Think of the grace you've seen modeled. Think of the people who have blessed your life by their modeling of such graces. Then ask the Spirit to lead you in living in a way that honors all you have received.

July 3
Matthew 5:13-16

At the midpoint of our pastoral care residencies, we had a major evaluation. It was the cause of much anxiety among the residents as we prepared all of our materials, reflecting back on the work we'd done and the things we'd learned over these first six months.

When my turn came, I sat down at the conference room table facing the supervisors gathered there. I talked about how I was taking small steps and starting to learn some things. One supervisor finally interrupted me, saying something to the effect that this was all poppycock. I was more capable than I was giving myself credit for. Why was I selling myself short?

"You are the light of the world," Jesus said, and while I don't think it means that we go around like we're God's gift to humankind…

Wait…. What if we ARE God's gift to humankind?

Not in a "Look how great I am" kind of a way, but in the sense that we have been blessed to have met up with this Jesus person in our lives and to have experienced his grace. We do have a gift to share. As we live as followers of this Jesus, his light shines through us.

It is a boldly preposterous thing to think. And yet, it is exactly what Jesus said. "Let your light shine," he told the disciples and he says the same to us.

So as you go about your day today and tomorrow and the next, let your light shine. Whatever gifts God has given you, delight in them and let them shine. Whatever joy God has delighted you with, let it shine. Whatever hope God has encouraged you with, let it shine. Whatever promise God has graced you with, let it shine.

You are the light of the world.

July 4
Galatians 5:1-2

I knew David McCullough's book 1776 was well-written when I found myself thinking halfway through, "It's not looking good for these colonists. I'm not sure they're going to pull it off." Of course, they did win in the end and today all over the United States we celebrate the gift they gave to us. Freedom. One of the consequences of reading a book like 1776 is a new appreciation for what intoxicating, heady and — dare I say it? — revolutionary stuff this was.

And yet, what Paul is writing to the Galatians is even more revolutionary. Freedom. Absolute spiritual freedom to live, not according to a set of rules and regulations but to live out of relationship. To live not out of fear of punishment but to live out of love for God.

As we've found in this experiment called the United States of America, freedom can be messy. And hard. One of the things that makes it hard is that there are other people here who expect to be free as well. Where does my freedom end and yours begin?

In dealing with the Galatians, Paul knew full well that spiritual freedom was hard as well. When you live by rules and regulations, it's easy to know who is in and who is out. It's easy to see if you measure up. But that's not the life Jesus calls us to live. "This is how people will know you belong to me," Jesus said, "that you love one another." What does that mean, to love one another? That's what we have to keep working out, day in and day out.

Freedom is messy and freedom is hard. Hard for a country. Hard for a church. Hard for a Christian. Hard for us, for you and me.

On this revolutionary day, let us give thanks for freedom… all of it. May we be wise and faithful stewards of the gift.

July 5
Galatians 5:22-26

A prayer for today…

Spirit of God,
    let me walk in your way.
There is too much hate and division in this world.
    Let me walk in the way of love.
There is too much despair in this world.
    Let me walk in the way of joy.
There is too much conflict in this world.
    Let me walk in the way of peace.
There is too much demand for immediate gratification in this world.
    Let me walk in the way of patience.
There is too much mean-spiritedness in this world.
    Let me walk in the way of kindness.
There is too much manipulation in this world.
    Let me walk in the way of goodness.
There is too much fear in this world.
    Let me walk in the way of faithfulness.
There is too much violence in this world.
    Let me walk in the way of gentleness.
There is too much unthinking action in this world.
    Let me walk in the way of self-control.
Spirit of God, let me walk in your way.

July 6
Amos 5:18-27

This is not my first pass at today's devotion. Early on I'd written something, a sly and smug bashing of mega-churches that can double as shopping malls. But here's the thing that happens when listening to folks like Amos. You can't go too far pointing out how other people are falling short in the justice department before the prophet turns to you and brings it home. Amos doesn't say, "Take away from me your fundamentalist noise, but you moderates and liberals are fine."

We all have times when we miss the point, when we pedal rather earnestly and fervently completely in the wrong direction.

As much as I hate to admit it, there are times when I find myself judging someone simply on the basis of how they look. There are times when I change the channel or turn down the volume so that I don't have to be confronted with injustice I'm called to address.

There are times for holding hands around the campfire and singing *Kum Ba Yah*. And there are time for linking arms along the street and singing *We Shall Overcome*.

What if Amos was sitting down with you, pulling up a chair in your Bible Study class, sitting on the front pew of your sanctuary. (Yes, I know it's uncomfortable even to imagine such a thing.) What would he say to you? What would he say to your family of faith?

May we have the courage to listen.

July 7
Acts 11:1-18

He didn't have to do it, you know.

After all, Peter not only had been among the select twelve chosen by Jesus, he'd been one of the inner circle. Whenever Jesus is calling a few of them out to go with him, it seems that Peter is there. Sometimes (often?) he stuck his big old foot in his big old mouth but he was always right there with Jesus. Sure, he'd flunked the biggest test of all when he denied ever knowing Jesus. But Jesus forgave him and put him right back, front and center.

Peter had position and Peter had clout. Peter could call on actual, intimate conversations with Jesus to support his position. So Peter didn't have to change. Peter didn't have to challenge himself. And yet he did.

Actually, God did the challenging and Peter was awake and aware enough to recognize it and allow it and allow himself to undergo a profound change. No longer was the world divided into clean and unclean but all was blessed by God.

Too often too many of us tend to be fearful of change, even and especially theological change. We don't know where we'll end up. What if it's just the proverbial slippery slope? Are we saying that we were all wrong?

It takes a lot of faith to allow change. We acknowledge that we know in part, and that as we continue to grow and to seek and to ask some of God's answering may surprise us. We are called to let go of the good for the better, of the safe answer for the grace answer.

I know that I am often as goofy as Peter. I wonder if I can be as courageous as him. What about you?

July 8
Romans 8:31-39

Every time I read this text, I get the picture of Paul writing furiously, his hand going faster and faster until he almost cannot keep up with the words that are tumbling out. It's a tough life at times, this business of following Jesus. But there is nothing that this life brings that can tear them away from his all-encompassing love.

Just as there is nothing that can tear you away.

Jesus loves you, you know. No, I mean he really loves you. The kind of love that makes a person's face light up when their loved one walks into the room. The kind of love that cannot wait to see you, to sit down with you. The kind of love that hurts when you hurt and wraps you up in a great big embrace. The kind of love that celebrates with you when the good things come. The kind of love that will speak truth to you when you are hurting yourself or someone else – or just plain living as less than you are meant to be.

He loves you when you're climbing the ladder and he loves you when you're in the pit. He loves you when you are filled with faith and he loves you when you're so depressed you can hardly get out of bed. He loves you when you triumph and he loves you when you fail.

There is nothing you can do that will make this Jesus love you any less. There is nowhere you can go where his love will not go with you. There is nothing that can happen to you that will take you away from his love. You can get sick or go bankrupt or get fired or make a mess of your marriage… and he will still love you.

There is nothing in heaven or on earth that will keep God from loving us, love made flesh in Jesus.

If you remember nothing else today, remember this… you are deeply, intimately and magnificently loved.

July 9
Proverbs 3:5-7

Proverbs 3:5 is one of those verses that's so easy to memorize... and so hard to do. "Trust in the Lord with your whole heart..." I'm pretty good with trusting in God with most of my heart. I just try to keep a few pockets tucked away under my control.

Like, the "what if" section where I anticipate and worry about every terrible possibility, no matter how unlikely. Or the "Man, I really screwed up" section where I beat myself up for failings large, small and imagined. Or the "I don't need no help from nobody" section where I try to figure out how I will face all of my challenges all by myself. Then there is the shadowy section. I find it hard to trust God with that because I don't even like to go there myself.

Funny thing is, the psalmist doesn't say, "Trust in God with the vast majority of your heart." Or "Trust in God with most of your heart." We're invited to trust God with our whole hearts.

What about you? What part of your heart do you have a hard time trusting God with? Are you afraid of letting go of the control (real or imagined and probably mostly imagined)? Are you afraid of revealing your whole heart to God? (Somehow I think God knows anyway.)

Today, just for today, allow yourself to risk trusting in God with your whole heart. You'll be in good hands.

July 10
John 3:1-15

Born again.

It's like the man rescued after many days at sea. The woman getting the news that all the cancer is gone.

They walk out, blinking in the light of the days they didn't expect to see. All of the things that used to fill their hearts and their minds with pointless clutter don't seem so urgent any more. They see the world with new eyes, and lo, it is a wonder.

Born again.

Babies come into the world, not holding on to the space that's been home, the only world they've known. In fact, for anything to happen at all the last, nourishing connection with that old life has to be cut. It was safe but it was too limiting.

Be born again, Jesus says. Walk out into days you'd never thought you'd get. Blink in the brilliant light of grace. Refocus. Adjust. See life with new eyes and a new heart.

Be born again, Jesus says. Cut the cord with everything you thought you knew, what you thought you had to have to live. Your old life may have felt safe but it was too limiting. It kept you too small.

Are you willing?

Are you willing to let go?

Are you willing to cut the cord?

Are you willing to step into the days you'd never dreamed you could have?

It's birthing time....

July 11
Genesis 16:1-6

Who could blame Abram for wanting to move the process along? After all, God helps those who helps themselves, right? God had promised Abram that he was going to be the father of nations. God had also promised Sarai, his wife, that she would become a mother in her old age, but that didn't seem to be happening. It wasn't an unheard of thing for a master to sleep with his slave. Surely it was the right thing to do for Hagar got pregnant.

Very quickly, everything turned out all wrong. Sarai was so jealous she couldn't see straight. And Hagar did nothing to help her cause around Sarai when she casually mentioned feeling the baby kick. Caught between a pregnant woman and an angry wife, Abram threw up his hands and told Sarai to deal with it. Sarai took out her anger on Hagar, who ran away. What a perfectly fine mess Abram had gotten himself into.

How many times have we done it? How many times have we given up on God, figured that God couldn't possibly deliver on a promise that was seeming more remote by the day? How many times have we messed things up by thinking we needed to take over for God?

That's not to say that we should just sit and fold our hands and wait for God to come through. Receiving God's promise often requires action. After all, God told Abram to go and leave his father's country to journey to a new land. But it does require that we be patient as it unfolds in ways we could not have imagined and on a time line we did not create.

Today, ask for patience to allow God to work in your life.

July 12
Genesis 16:7-15

In some ways, Hagar only did what was asked of her – had sex with her master in order to provide him with a child. Her trouble began when she "forgot her place" and lorded her pregnant state over her master's (to this point) childless wife. Sarai complained to Abram that the maid was not being respectful and Abram told Sarai he didn't want to get involved in a spat between two women he'd slept with. Okay, those aren't the exact words we're given, but they well could have been. What we are told is that Abram told Sarai to deal with it, and we're told she dealt with Hagar harshly.

So harshly, in fact, that the pregnant woman fled into the wilderness. An angel finds her there and promises that God will not cast her out. Go back to Abram's household, the angel instructs her, and God will look after her. (Funny how many times people come across angels when they're in the wilderness.) Hagar returns and gives birth to Ishmael. Just as the Jewish people trace their spiritual lineage back to Abraham, so Muslims trace their spiritual lineage back to Ishmael.

It's an interesting action on God's part. Hagar and Ishmael weren't a part of the plan. They were what happened when Abram took things into his own hands and tried to force God's hand. As a servant woman, she had no rights and Ishmael's place was even lower. But God reached out even to them. God took care of even them.

Who are the outcasts in your world?

July 13
Hebrews 12:1-2

I was on the final leg of my first triathlon. I'd managed to get through the swim, had endured a flat tire on the bike route and now was on the last leg of my run. I was tired and frustrated. All of a sudden a friend emerged from the crowd, one of my running buddies. "You're doing great," she said, running alongside me until it was time to turn toward the finish line.

The following December it happened again at the end of my first half marathon. It was cold and rainy and I couldn't imagine anyone being out there if they weren't running. But as I got closer to the finish line another friend stepped out from the crowd and ran alongside me, encouraging me. "You can do it, Peggy. You're almost there."

There was something about those friends running alongside to support me that gave me energy and strength. As tired as I was or as frustrated as I was, I suddenly knew that I could do it. I wasn't running alone.

The writer of Hebrews reminds us that we're not running this race of faith alone. We are joined and supported and encouraged by those who have gone before us, some of whom we knew and loved and some whom we knew only by their stories. When we feel like our journey is nothing but detours, they are there reminding us of roads we cannot yet see. When we feel weighed down by loss or struggle or doubt or a hundred other challenges, they are there reminding us that there is One on whom we may lean. When we feel like the task is too big or the hurdles too high, they are there to remind us that in Christ, miracles still happen and grace still flows.

Remember the saints. Remember the saints whose stories have inspired you. And remember the saints whom you've had the privilege to know and to love.

Because right now they're stepping out from the crowd to run alongside you. "You're doing great… you can do this," they say. And you breathe deeper and easier because you are not running alone.

Ever.

July 14
Jeremiah 31:1-4

Israel lost everything. Trusting too much in their own resources and paying too little attention to God, they had been defeated by the enemy and now faced captivity and exile. Jeremiah had tried to warn the people that this was coming if they did not change their ways, but they didn't listen to him. Now, instead of gloating or thundering judgment, Jeremiah brings an amazing word from God that is nothing if not love.

God speaks of surviving the sword to find grace in the  wilderness. Then God all but sings tender words of love, a love that is there even though everything else is lost.

Where is your wilderness? Maybe it was a time in your past or maybe you're feeling lost right now. Maybe you found yourself there seemingly out of no fault of your own. Maybe you know full well all of the bad choices and selfish actions that landed you there. Maybe you're not sure because you're just not sure of anything anymore. Maybe no one knows or even suspects that beneath the looking good outside there's a lot of desert.

Grace is there. Grace is there as we remember and see with new eyes the ways in which God was working when and where we least expected it. Grace is there even now, even if we don't see it quite yet. If you can see it, give thanks. If not, ask to be open to it.

And then listen. For God is whispering in your ear and in your heart such tender words of love: I will never stop loving you. I will rebuild your life. I will bring you joy. I hold you in my hands, and I will never let you go.

July 15
Luke 23:44-56

It was the only thing left that he could do for this man. He hadn't agreed with this plan of having Jesus arrested, but his voice didn't carry any weight. With a lump in his throat, Joseph asked for the body and gave him his own tomb. It was too little. Way too late.

The women stood helplessly by while Jesus died. They couldn't bear to look but they couldn't bear to leave. They couldn't take his pain away, but they could make sure he didn't face it alone. Now there was only one thing left to give him, only one act of caring left to do. They could bathe his body and embalm it. Much too little. Much too late.

Of course, it would be a few days before they would learn that is wasn't too late at all. It would be a few days before Joseph got his slightly used tomb back.

It's easy to feel helpless in the face of great suffering, whether it's a village of AIDs orphans in Africa or your suffering neighbor next door. We can't make it all better. We don't have the resources. We don't have the time. We don't have the knowledge. We don't have the power.

And yet, too often we let what we cannot do keep us from what we can do. We can't solve global poverty. But maybe on one night a month we can help make sure that the homeless people in our town get a good and decent meal. We can't take away the grief of a friend, but we can listen when they need to talk and sit with them when they just need to be.

Today, ask God what you can do. Even if it seems too little, too late.

With God, you just never know.

July 16
Amos 5:6-15

God, I know that you call me to care about the poor. And I do.

But God, it's not such an easy thing. In these days. In this world.

I don't know if you've noticed it, but the world has gotten big. And complicated. So much bigger than that scrap of Middle Eastern land that Amos called home.

At any given moment I can find pictures and video that will take me into the slums of Calcutta, the poor of Johannesburg, the cold and starving Syrian refugees. So close. So remote.

Am I unwittingly selling the poor for the shoes I put on my feet or clothes I wear on my back? Do I casually put on the sweat and tears and life of a young child when I get dressed?

It's hard to know, hard to keep up, hard to do anything different. Does my fair trade coffee make a difference? Is the beggar on the corner truly homeless and hungry or just slick at running a scam? If I advocate for laws that will help the poor, will there be a law of unintended consequences? Can I trust this relief agency with my funds?

God, I pray that I never grow so weary of the questions that I quit asking them. Let me not be so overwhelmed that I stop trusting what I do know and doing what I know I can do.

God, let me never get so overwhelmed that I stop caring.

July 17
Mark 7:14-23

I went to college in Greenville, SC, home of fundamentalist school Bob Jones University. (In case you were wondering, I went to the other school in town.) In my Sociology class we took a field trip to Bob Jones, in part to visit their well-regarded museum of sacred art and in part to observe another culture. Somewhere along the way I picked up one of the demerit slips. Infractions were listed, including categories of both major and minor horseplay. Reading it, I felt fairly certain that most of my freshman hall wouldn't have made it through the first semester there.

I also remember thinking about how fear-based it all seemed. A hand holding here, walking too close there, stepping out of the box just a little bit meant danger.

The Pharisees had their own checklists. Every aspect of life was monitored and not following all of their rules meant not following God.

Jesus would have none of it. It's not about what we eat, Jesus said. It's about what we cultivate in our souls. You can skate through life demerit free and still be far from the life God intends.

The important things cannot be measured and checked off, things like kindness and grace and charity. Serving one another. Loving one another.

What are you cultivating in your life?

July 18
Romans 16:1-24

For some reason, in reading today's text I was reminded of an utterly random line from *The Andy Griffith Show.*

"Goober says 'hey.'"

Here Paul is doing the greeting, not Goober, but it's something of the same sentiment. "Tell Dorcas Paul says 'hey.'" Paul gives us a long list of people to whom he sends special greetings. It's a little like picking up a church directory. There's Dorcas, the deacon and Prisca and Aquilla who hosted a church in their home. Mary, a hard worker. Rufus and his mom who adopted Paul like a son. Paul gets so cranked up that Timothy has to throw his greetings in as well. And Paul's secretary, Tertius, says hey, too.

So what would your list look like? Maybe it's Mrs. Smith, who was your Sunday School teacher in kindergarten and always made you feel special as she passed out the juice and the butter cookies. Maybe it's Devon in the choir whose music never fails to touch your spirit. Maybe it's Susan who so faithfully visits the homebound. Maybe it's Harry who has steered the finance committee with both faithfulness and financial wisdom. Maybe it's Maria who gives you the best hugs and somehow seems to know when you need one the most.

The community of faith has many faces. Some of them are well-known, like Paul. Some of them are leaders, like Dorcas. And some of them are like this long list of names, known only to history by a name in a directory.

Today, give thanks for some of the ones who bless your life. If you get a chance, you might even drop them a note to say hey… and thank you.

July 19
2 Corinthians 3:1-6

I'd been looking forward to leading the women's retreat. They'd had me lead the group before, so I was going back to familiar faces and, in some cases, old friends. The retreat began on Friday evening with dinner and continued on Saturday morning.

That Thursday I got a call from my dad's retirement home. He wasn't looking well, and as we talked we decided the best course of action would be to take him to the Emergency Room to get him checked out. Between one thing and another, I didn't get to bed until three o'clock the next morning. I slept far too few hours then spent a few hours at the hospital. Mid-afternoon I went home to get ready for the retreat.

I stood in the shower feeling my exhaustion. I wondered how in the world I was going to have the energy to lead a retreat as tired as I was. Suddenly the words came to me as clearly as if they'd been spoken out loud. "It's not all up to you."

It's not all up to you. I took a deep breath and let go. "You take it, God," I said, "and do what I cannot." Relieved, I gathered up my materials and headed to the church.

I suppose it will be no surprise to you to hear that the retreat went well. I had all of the energy I needed to lead the group. More than that, I felt led as well. The casual conversation that meant more than I could have known. The random comment that became the most important insight for someone. It was fun and energizing and challenging and exhausting – as all good retreats are. And it wasn't all up to me.

Sometimes we find ourselves in situations that seem too hard for us. We don't have the energy. We don't have the wisdom. We don't know what to do or we don't have the stomach to do what we must. The demands are too big or too constant.

In those times, in all times it's a good thing to remember.

It's not all up to us. Let go and trust. It's not all up to us. Let go and breathe. It's not all up to us.

July 20
Luke 10:29-37

In the very fine movie, Lincoln, one of the things that comes through is Lincoln's love of story-telling. Waiting for news of a critical battle, one of his cabinet members flees the room. "You're going to tell a story, aren't you?" he says to the president. "I cannot take another one of your stories."

I wonder if the disciples or the religious leaders or even the crowds that followed Jesus felt the same way. "Oh Lord, there he goes with another story."

Today's story is pretty familiar. Most of us know it: the man beaten by robbers, ignored by the religious leader and the chief layperson. It's the Samaritan, the one who was an outcast, who stopped and tended to the victim's needs.

Just before this story, of course, a lawyer pressed Jesus on what he should do for eternal life. (I suppose the Roman Road to salvation had not yet been written.) When Jesus turned the question around the lawyer answered that it was to love God and love neighbor. "Very good," Jesus replied, but before he could get away the lawyer tugged at his sleeve. "And who is my neighbor?" he asked.

Maybe he wanted to draw the lines tight, to make the boundaries clear. Jesus would have none of it. "Who was being neighbor?" he asks at the end of the story, and the lawyer replied that it was the one who showed mercy to the man in distress.

What does it mean for you to show mercy in your life? Don't get it confused with trying to rescue people in ways that actually do not help them. And it's not about giving people whatever they want regardless of consequences.

Sometimes mercy is as small as a smile, acknowledging the personhood of the service person in front of you. Sometimes mercy is as bold as speaking up when others have no voice. Sometimes mercy is as courageous as giving a kidney. Sometimes mercy is a pragmatic as wielding a hammer. Sometimes mercy is as soft as a hug.

Are you showing mercy?

July 21
Psalm 139:1-12

She cannot look me in the eye. "If you only knew," she said. Or sometimes she says, "If everybody only knew… they wouldn't think so well of me… they wouldn't like me... they'd know who I really was." How many times have I heard women and men tell me such things? Their secrets weigh heavily upon them, hidden deep beneath layers of shame and guilt. Occasionally the guilt is justified but usually it's more about what was done to them.

We all have our secrets. Sometimes they are silly. And sometimes they are heartbreaking. Hand in hand with the secret comes the fear, "if you only knew…" If I'm found out, no one will respect me. No one will love me. Everyone will know who I really am.

Perhaps today's text should be read with more fear and trembling than joy. "You have searched me and known me." You God, know everything about me. You know my secrets. And yet, there is no threat here.

God know us deep in our bones. There is nothing that you

have done or said or thought that God does not already know. There is no hell we find ourselves in that we do not find God there with us.

We are known right well. And we are loved right deep. And we are held, right now and forever.

July 22
Psalm 139:13-24

Knit together.

Were God's hands gnarled as they held the needles?
Did God smile to see the beauty of the yarn
    and then sigh a satisfied sigh
    as the stitches came together?
    Fearfully and wonderfully made.
God, you made us to be a wonder,
    sinew and bone and blood and spirit
    all woven into one.
God,
You knit for us a life
    and we have stretched it out of shape
    and dirtied it
    and found it wanting.
Fearfully and wonderfully made indeed.
God, if we could just believe it.
If we could just believe it was true.
For us.

Knit together by God.
What a wonder...

July 23
2 Samuel 11:2-5

It's a story worthy of a soap opera — or perhaps even MTV.

A king sits on his rooftop deck one fine day and discovers even finer scenery. A beautiful woman on another rooftop is bathing. After appreciating the sight, the king sends for the woman and they hook up. A couple of months later the married woman sends back word to the king that she's pregnant.

Even in today's times, adultery has been known to wreck a career or two (at least in this country.) Even more so when that leader is supposed to be God's own chosen leader. What's a king to do?

Whatever the right thing is to do is precisely what King David does not do. As the story unfolds, his choices go from bad to worse. And yet this is THE King David, one of the most celebrated kings in the history of Israel. More than that, the gospel writers don't blush at pointing out that this King David is part of the family tree of none other than Jesus, the Messiah.

I don't think that the moral of the story is that our sins don't matter. David and Bathsheba will face their own terrible consequences. But I think that it does remind us that our sins are not the end of the story. They do not have to have the last word in our lives. God the creator is endlessly creating new opportunities for us to reclaim and redeem our lives, no matter how badly we have messed up.

What sin are you holding onto today? Talk with God about it and let the Creator create a new heart in you.

July 24
Luke 12:13-21

Stephen Covey has a wonderful line about people being so focused on climbing the ladder of success that they never notice that it's up against the wrong building. Today as I read this text I'm struck by the image of mindlessness. The rich man doesn't give a lot of thought to his plans. He has a lot of stuff, more than he has room to store. The thing to do is obviously to tear down the old storerooms and build bigger ones. Let's be honest, who among us wouldn't want to have THAT problem!

While he may have had bigger storehouses, he never stopped to ask the bigger questions. His wealth brought just ease, not responsibility. He was focused on keeping his money, not investing his life.

No matter the state of our bank accounts, it's easy to fall into the same boat. Asking the bigger questions means that we have to stop and to think about our lives. It means we have to be willing to ask questions whose answers may not come easily. We have to ask questions whose answers we may not even like. Like a good sailor, we have to stop every so often, chart our progress and make course corrections.

We live in a reactive culture, and that kind of intentionality takes reflection. It takes time and effort to ask, "Where is God in all of this and what would God have me do?" And yet, that's exactly what we're called to do.

Where's your ladder leaning?

July 25
Galatians 6:1-5

She'd supported me through some tough times, always there to encourage or to be a listening ear. I much appreciated the gift of her friendship. However, it was a different story when the tables were turned. When she hit a rough patch, it became clear to me that the burden bearing could only go one way. She could help me but I couldn't help her.

Paul writes that we are to bear one another's burdens. I let you lean on me when you need it but I also lean on you in turn. Such mutuality is at the heart of Christian community. There will be times when you are strong and I am stumbling. There will be times when I am strong and you need help. In helping each other along the way, there is grace for both the giver and the receiver.

I see a lot of people who are very good at helping others. They are there with a card, a call or a casserole. But they somehow think themselves as less than strong or less than faithful if they allow themselves to lean on someone else for a while.

Life can be wonderful but sometimes life can be very hard. Part of the gift that God gives us is the gift of each other. Sometimes that gift means that we reach out to someone else who's struggling. For all of my formal ministry, I think sometimes that my best ministry takes place in the church parking lot after choir practice as we take a moment to talk about our lives.

At other times it means having the humility to know that you cannot do everything on your own and the wisdom to know that you need not even try. You are surrounded by brothers and sisters who may not be able to take your burdens from you, but they can make them a little lighter.

Is there someone you need to help with a little burden bearing today? Or do you need to allow someone else to help you?

July 26
Galatians 6:6-10

We want results. And if we had our druthers we'd have those results sooner rather than later. We want the thirty-minute oil change and the three day cure. At the very least, we want to know when we can expect those results.

Which is why this whole business of well-doing is hard. We may be faithful day after day, week after week and not really know if we have made one thimbleful of difference. You work with teenagers and there are times that you swear that all you are doing is providing them a chance to work on their bored stares and eye rolls. You volunteer and you visit. You work for change in your community. You reach out to the person who seems to be on the fringes only to get little response. Sometimes it's hard to keep going.

But here's the thing with sowing. You never really know when that harvest will come. You might not even be there to see it. It may be years later or a lifetime later. You may never see the difference you made.

Except for the difference it made in you. We do not grow weary in the doing of it because it's not about reaping the biggest harvest. It's about what we learn and how we grow in the doing of it.

There are times to ask if something is the best use of time and resources. When I served on a church staff I was labeled by some as the one who "killed" the visitation program. In truth, I'd done an analysis of our records and found that I could find no evidence that years of making visits to newcomers had yielded even a single visitor. There were better ways to do outreach.

There are other times, however, when we cannot measure the response but we must remain faithful in the doing nonetheless. Today ask God where you are called to give, and then ask God for the strength and patience to be faithful in the doing of it.

July 27
Psalm 121

When I got out of the hospital I was pretty helpless. Actually, I was pretty much completely helpless. The collision between my backside and a Buick left me with a pelvis fractured in three places and unable to do much of anything for myself. Since I lived alone, I went from the hospital to my parents' house where I could be cared for. Each night I settled in for the night, knowing that if I needed anything all I had to do was call. If I needed to go to the bathroom or if I needed more pain medicine. Even in the middle of the night, all I had to do was call and my mom would be there.

So it is with our God, only more so. We don't have to yell loudly in order to wake God up, for God is by our bedside, not napping, not sleeping… just waiting. While we sleep, God is beside us. While we struggle, God is waiting for us to ask for help. When we fear what we face or what we might face, God is waiting to walk with us even through the valley of shadows, even the shadow of death. God doesn't take a day off or walk away for an afternoon. God is waiting for our call. The God who made the heavens and the earth is waiting, just waiting to reach out to our need.

You may be rolling along and doing just fine today. If so tuck this truth away for the day when you'll need it. And if this is one of those days, lift up your eyes. You're not alone. God is by your side and God will not leave you in distress.

Just ask.

July 28
Luke 15:1-10

When workers were fixing the air conditioning unit in my dad's house his cat took advantage of the open door opportunity and took off in the big, wild world. She's a particularly special cat, for I'd given her to my mom for Mother's Day several years before my mom's death and I was crushed when I learned she was missing. After a week or two, I discovered that some students had seen it in the condo complex across the street.

I went by there after work. I went back at 11 p.m., for someone saw her late at night. I went back at 6:00 in the morning, a prime hunting time. After a couple of weeks, I finally stopped cruising slowly and walking through the condo complex out of fear that someone would turn me in for suspicious activity. It looked like I was casing the joint.

As I looked for that cat, I actually thought about this text. Whatever lengths I was going to for Little Bit, God would go that much farther for one of us. In fact, God would never give up on us.

Jesus tells these parables in response to the people who are grumbling at his choice of company, turning up their nose in a huff because he was hanging out with people who were known to be sinners. (Truthfully, he'd be pretty lonely if he wasn't!) Not only does God tolerate sinners, Jesus says, but God goes to great lengths for them.

That addict who's begging on the street corner? God's looking for them in order to embrace them. That hooker who's publishing her ads on the internet? God's looking for her as well to show her what true love looks like. That kid whom everyone else has written off? God is waiting, just waiting for him to look up long enough to notice that a welcome hug is waiting on him.

When we really get this, it makes a difference in how we see the world. It's a lot harder to divide the world into us and them. It's also a lot harder to keep our hearts closed. It also makes a difference in how we see ourselves. Even at our worst, God is still cruising through the neighborhood, looking for us, wanting to tell us to just come on back home.

By the way, more than two months after she disappeared, Little Bit showed up at a neighbor's house, four houses down from my dad. As I write, she's home and fattened up again and perfectly content.

July 29
Luke 15:11-24

He got what he deserved.

Parents work to teach their children the importance of making good choices and reinforcing that bad choices bring negative consequences. Here we have a younger son with a whole string of bad choices. First of all, he asks for his inheritance up front, not content to wait until his father actually dies.

Like a trust fund baby who gets the money too soon, he takes off on a perpetual spring break. He's the life of the party... until his money runs out. He's made a whole bundle of bad choices. Faced with not a lot of options, he goes to work on a pig farm and hits the proverbial bottom when he finds himself envying the slop he's dishing out to the pigs. For a nice Jewish boy, you couldn't get much lower. He thinks about how well his dad's servants were treated. He gladly kicked himself out of his family but maybe his father will hire him back.

Here's where the story breaks down. If he'd gotten what he deserved, he'd be bunking in the servant's quarters – and even that would be grace after what he'd done. If he was ever to regain his father's trust, he'd have to earn it.

 Instead, his father meets him halfway down the road and nearly knocks him down with a hug. He throws a party for him and spares no expense. God knows it's not what the kid deserved. "It doesn't matter," the dad says. "All that matters is that you're home."

God knows that we make some terrible choices. We make bad choices that everyone sees and bad choices that we hide like guilty secrets. And when we think about showing up before God we don't have much of a leg to stand on. We've squandered our inheritance as God's children either by throwing it away or by just not believing that it's true… or that it's true for us.

We think we don't deserve much and maybe we don't. But God races down the road to meet us, nearly knocking us over with a hug. In-between kisses, God beams at us and says, "You're here. That's all I wanted. You're here." And God strikes up the band and gets the barbecue going and sets the table. The party is for you.

No matter where you've been, no matter how willful or negligent you've been, all you have to do is come back home. God is waiting with such a welcome.

July 30
Luke 15:25-32

There's nothing like having an older or younger sibling to bring the issue of fairness front and center. Younger kids complain because older siblings get to do more things and do them sooner. Older kids complain because their parents aren't nearly as strict on their younger siblings. (I tell my brothers that it's not my fault that by the time I came along our parents were too worn out to put up much resistance.)

Let's face it; what happened to the older brother wasn't fair. We try to explain our way around it by assuming all kinds of things about his character – he was jealous, he was a rule follower who worked without any sense of joy, he was a stick in the mud who never had any fun anyway. But give the guy a break – wouldn't you be at least a little upset if the same thing happened to you? You were the one hanging around when your brother (or sister) broke your dad's heart. You had to watch him look hopefully down the road every time he saw someone coming and the disappointment when it wasn't his child. You had to witness his heart breaking again and again. You had to shoulder the burdens that didn't go away when he left. Now he comes waltzing back home and gets treated like the little prince?

We can spend a lot of time and energy grousing over what is and isn't fair. Jesus says that's not the point. The point isn't if someone else gets what they deserve. The point is that none of us gets what we deserve. Sooner or later, it comes back to grace. It always comes back to grace. Grace may take different forms at different points in our lives but it's always there. God embraces you not because of what you have or haven't done, but because you are.

Today, whether you're feeling like a prodigal or like an elder brother, let yourself receive the embrace of God's love, the great big old bear hug of grace.

July 31
Psalm 73

As a child I met up with and came to know a very terrible man. For a very long time he abused me in many horrible ways, things unimaginable to most good folk.

At the very least he deserved to be imprisoned for the rest of his life, kept far away from any children. At the very least he deserved to have the things he did in the shadows brought to the light. Really, at the very, very least he should have reimbursed me for the large sums of money I spent healing from his cruelty.

I don't know if he is living still, although I strongly suspect that he long ago died. As far as I know, he lived his days with his secrets intact and his crimes hidden. Seemingly successful, probably with a wife and (God forbid) kids, he lived his life as the poster child for the prosperity of the wicked.

From time to time I've had a few conversations with God about this. Like the psalmist, there seems to me to be something terribly wrong in a system in which such things happen and such people go unpunished.

Not all questions that we must ask can be answered. The psalmist never really resolves the issue of prosperous evildoers but comes around to something more substantial.

Even so, the psalmist declares, even among these very wrong things God has not abandoned us.

Sometimes we wish God had been with us in ways a bit more active (would zapping this creep with a few thunderbolts been too much to ask?) But in the end, through it all and in the midst of it all and in the hope that lies beyond it all, God does not abandon us. Sometimes God's presence means rescue and protection. And sometimes it means binding up our wounds.

You may have had to wrestle with some of these same questions. Maybe it was an accident or an illness that took the life of the young woman who was born to be mother to her young children. Maybe it is a friend or family member who has to endure an inexorable, progressive and cruel illness. Or maybe you faced things in your life as a child or teenager or adult that no one should have to face.

Ask your questions. Know that God is present even now to hear them.

And even when the darkness threatens, the light cannot help but win out. For the light shines in the darkness and the darkness has not overcome it.

Amen and amen.

August 1
2 Corinthians 12:7-10

We're still getting to know each other, this new church and I. So the other week when I limped my way into choir practice several people observed that I was limping and wanted to know what had happened. I explained that as a parting gift from the Buick that hit me, every so often I get a bit gimpy. I've learned to live with it and it's not such a big deal, especially considering what could have been. It's like a tiny thorn in the flesh.

We're not told what Paul's thorn in the flesh was. Scholars have speculated on everything from epilepsy to stuttering. Whatever it was, it was something he didn't want to live with but in the end had no choice. God wasn't going to take it away. In the end, Paul realized that grace would come not with healing but with acceptance. The healing came in the realization that he didn't have to be perfect and without flaw for God to use him.

What's your thorn in the flesh? Maybe you have a limp, a physical or emotional or spiritual one. What limitation do you keep bumping up against and banging your head against? What would you beg God to change if you had the faith to ask?

Beg God for change if you must but be willing to accept acceptance. And then ask God to use your own flawed self.

August 2
Acts 24:22-27

One of the famous quotes from baseball legend Yogi Berra is, "When you come to the fork in the road, take it." It seems that Governor Felix could have learned from Yogi.

The governor was well-versed in matters regarding this new religious group that were known as followers of the Way. He kept their preacher Paul imprisoned but sought to make his stay as humane as possible. He also took advantage of the opportunity to learn more.

As much as he hated to admit it, what he learned was more than a little off-putting. This fellow Paul kept talking about things like discipline and accountability. Who wants to hear that?

Still, he was intrigued. Maybe he could find out more if he kept this fellow around. Better yet, maybe Paul would wise up and slip him a bribe.

Felix never got his bribe. And he seemingly never got the point. He leaves the stage a curious but uncommitted man.

The gospel of our Lord is grace but it is also demand. Jesus asks of us things and sometimes those things are hard. Sometimes they take us out of our comfort zone. Sometimes they turn our lives upside down.

In short, when you come to the cross in the road, take it.

August 3
Psalm 20

When I was growing up, it was still the tradition at some schools to have a minister offer a prayer before a football game. For the minister in question, it could be a bit of a ticklish proposition. After all, did God really care who won the game? What if both sides prayed for victory? Did God merely flip a coin? Was the dropped touchdown pass God's will or an exercise of man's free will to sin and fall short?

Today's psalm is a prayer for victory; however, this time it's victory in battle, not a football game. So, what do we make of such a psalm in our world?

I don't have a quick and ready answer for that. I do not want our men and women killed. I helped officiate at the funeral of a young man who'd grown up in our church and was killed in Iraq. Following the service, the participating ministers waited on the front steps while the casket was brought out of the church. With tears in our eyes, we hugged each other tightly and prayed fervently that we would never again have to lead such a service.

I don't want our men and women killed. But more than that, I want to live in a world where no one's son or daughter has to be killed in battle. I know, you're probably rolling your eyes at such pie in the sky. And yet, are we not called to be peacemakers?

The psalmist speaks of God granting the desires of our hearts. May we sing this psalm along with the prayer that our heart's desires be for living lives that bring peace – peace among our neighbors, peace among our countries.

Maybe it is just a pipe dream. But then again, God has been known to do an impossible thing or two.

August 4
Exodus 16:1-10

My next door neighbor used to have a "no whining" sticker on her car. I'm sure Moses wished he could have borrowed it. It wasn't enough that he stood up to Pharaoh. It wasn't enough that he had called down the plagues upon Egypt. It wasn't enough that he'd led them out from slavery and through the parted waters. No, in a first class pity party the children of Israel accuse Moses of doing all of this just so he could lead them out there to die.

It's not Israel's finest moment.

But for God, that doesn't matter.

God feeds them anyway. God doesn't magically transport them out of the wilderness or give them tickets on the express train. However, God does give them what they need, feeding them day after day. Just what they need. Just enough of what they need.

Like Israel, sometimes we just have to throw a pity party. Sometimes I prescribe them for clients. If we had more faith or were peaceful and trusting and big of heart, maybe we wouldn't need them. I don't know about you, but I'm still prone to an outbreak every now and then.

God hears all of our whining. And then the most amazing thing happens. God doesn't magically transform all of the hard places in our lives, but God does give us what we need. Just what we need. Just enough of what we need for this day.

And for today, that is enough.

What do you need for today?

August 5
Exodus 16:13-30

Talk about your slow learners…

God provides the miracle of food in the wilderness. The only stipulation is that they only take what they need for that day. Of course, some of them have to gather up as much as they can, and the extra promptly becomes rancid. On the sixth day Moses tells them to gather up enough for the next two days since God's take-out is going to be closed on the Sabbath. But some of the stubborn people insisted on going out for food on the Sabbath (of course, finding none.)

I'm thinking that they weren't real good at following directions.

Sometimes, neither am I.

It takes a lot of trust to follow such directions. Sure, God has provided what I needed today… but what about tomorrow? Sure, God has led me this far and not abandoned me in the wilderness… but what about the next step? It takes a lot of trust not to stuff our pockets full of manna. We want faith to be a once and for all decision, but in reality it can only be lived out today… and then the next day's today… and then the next day's today.

I don't know what sort of manna you need today. Maybe it's actual food or the mortgage payment. Maybe it's the strength for sitting beside a hospital bed. Maybe it's the courage to live one more day sober. Ask God for the faith to ask for today's manna. And faith enough to trust that tomorrow will be provided for as well.

August 6
1 Corinthians 11:17-33

I was a last minute fill-in to assist with Christmas Eve communion. People were invited to gather at the kneeling rail where the pastor served the bread and I followed with the cup. We were taking by intinction, which means that people dip their piece of bread in the cup.

Well, with it being Christmas Eve and what all, some people didn't know. Others who knew perfectly well forgot. As a result, a number of people had already eaten their bread by the time I came along with the cup.

Some looked at me in puzzlement. Some sheepishly whispered, "Oops." Some reached for the cup to drink directly while I, being mindful of cold and flu season, pulled it away from them. I felt like the grace nazi (after Seinfeld's famous soup nazi.) "No grace for you!"

It was just one of those things, one of those crazy, confused things that will happen if you hang around churches long enough. But Paul was talking about a different kind of confusion. He wasn't talking about forgetting the order of things. He was talking about forgetting about each other. He was talking about forgetting about the whole purpose of it all.

When you gather at the Lord's table, however you gather... remember. Remember that this is a table set by love. This is a table where all of our footing is equal. This is a table where the taking of our meal goes hand in hand with the giving of our lives. This is a table of death. This is a table of life.

No matter how familiar it may be, remember. And tremble for the shock of it. And catch your breath for the grace of it. God in flesh invites you here. God who suffers so that we do not suffer alone invites you here. God who dies so that we will not pass through those waters without a friend makes a place for you here. God who lives so that we will yet live as well bids you take and eat.

Remember.

August 7
Matthew 4:12-22

How did Jesus know it was time to begin his ministry?

In Matthew's gospel Jesus is baptized and spends a season in the wilderness, wrestling with temptation. And yet, neither one of these two events are the precipitating event, the nudge that pushes Jesus forward into action.

Jesus learns that his cousin, John, has been imprisoned. For whatever reason, this is the event. He leaves home, and begins to gather his disciples.

So how do you know when it's time? How do you know that it's time to go back to school or start a family or take a risk? How do you find the balance between gathering the information that you need to make wise decisions while avoiding "paralysis by analysis"? How do you know when it's time to begin moving beyond your grief and back into life? How do you know it's time to let go of the "what if's" and move to the "what nows"?

The Christian scriptures speak of two kinds of time. The first, chronos, is time measured by the clock and calendar. The second, kairos, is usually translated, "in the fullness of time" or "at the right time." There's no way to count the days or measure the minutes until kairos time.

Sometimes something happens, and it seems clear. John was being moved off the stage, leaving an empty space with Jesus' name on it. It was time.

Something happens. You get laid off and now there's no reason not to follow your dream. A good friend dies, and you realize that it's time to stop putting your own life on hold. A need sneaks its way through your defenses and into your heart. Now is the time.

And sometimes the only clue you have is the feeling in your gut, the nudge that your spirit can't ignore.

Jesus had done all that he needed to do in order to be ready when the time came. And then, when it was time, he set off on his new beginning.

May we be as wise.

August 8
Matthew 5:1-3

When I originally did the planning for this book, I chose Matthew 5:1-11 for this day, the text that we know as the beatitudes. But when I sat down to write, I decided that each one of them was rich enough to stand on its own. So you'll find them sprinkled through the next few months.

Today Jesus blesses the poor in spirit. I started wondering just what that meant. Being as I was at my counseling office and away from my theological library, I had to turn to my friend Dr. Google. The problem was, a lot of what I read didn't read true to me. I cannot read this text without thinking of the many people with whom I've worked. Their issue isn't an excess of pride. It's being beaten down too many times and in too many ways. If being poor in spirit means thinking you're next to a worm, then I know some mighty blessed people who seem decidedly unblessed.

What if that's not what Jesus meant? What if he meant knowing that all our heart deeply desires, all for which our spirits truly long, all that we need to become fully human and fully ourselves, all that is key to a truly abundant life... all this lies with God.

"Give me Jesus," the old spiritual sings, and the poor in spirit sing it as well.

August 9
Ephesians 4:1-6

I was talking with the social worker about her work in helping children get adopted. The children she worked with were grade-schoolers, children old enough to have had a history – and plenty of disappointment. She said that one of the issues that can arise after adoption is that the children will push themselves to be perfect. They are terrified of being sent back and of losing their home so they try to avoid giving their new parents any reason to do just that.

It was hard for me to imagine. I always knew I had a home, a place where I belonged. I always knew that my family would claim me. Okay, there was the one time I went to camp and returned home to find a note from my brother on the back door: "Don't come in. We've rented your room out." But I knew that he really did love me, and the note was just a sign of that love.

But these adoptive children have never known such security. For some of them it takes a very long time before they can trust that this home is truly their home.

We are the daughters and sons of God. We are truly and firmly and forever in this family. We don't have to be perfect to earn our right to stay. We don't have to be smart enough or good-looking enough or accomplished enough to earn our place. We're not going to be kicked out.

So live big and be bold. If you fall on your face, you've got a brother who's there to help pick you up and dust you off. Be your own bad self, knowing God delights in your uniqueness. You're in the family, and nothing is going to change that.

August 10
Genesis 18:1-8

The visitors came,
 and Abraham made a place in his home,
  a place at his table for them.
He stopped what he was doing
 to welcome them
 to care for them.
  He didn't know.
  God, how he didn't know.

How many times have angels stopped
 by my way, God?
How many times have they stopped
 and I was too busy
 and my life was too full
 and I just couldn't be bothered...
What dreams have I missed?
How many times have you wanted
 to come to me
 and to sit with me
 and to grace my heart with promise,
But that heart was too full
 of old hurts and mistakes
 and worry and fear
  and there was no room.

God, teach me the grace of hospitality
 in my home and in my heart.

I can't keep turning the angels away.

August 11
Genesis 18:9-15

Sometimes, God, I have to laugh
    with the kind of laugh
    that never quite gets to my eyes,
    springing from bitterness and not joy,
    disappointment and not delight.

Sometimes, God, I have to laugh
    because it seems impossible
    that your promise should come true,
    that it should come true for me.
I have to laugh
    because I know in my bones
    that I cannot get there from here.

You know that I'm laughing at you.
And you know that you'll have the last laugh with me.

God,
    even when I cannot see any way
    for your promises to come true
    and my heart dreams to take flesh,
        help me to trust
        that you know the way.
God,
    help me to believe
    that my heart may yet truly laugh again…

August 12
Genesis 21:1-7

If yesterday's reading was filled with laughter born of bitterness, today's is filled with laughter born of... well, birth. Abraham and Sarah keep pinching themselves and sharing "Can you believe this?" looks as they take turns holding their baby boy. Their faces grow tired from grinning. When someone asks the name of the boy, they look at each other, chuckle and say in unison, "Isaac... Laughter." What else to call such a boy?

You know about those kinds of moments, don't you? Okay, maybe not in the same way as Abraham and Sarah, but you've had your own impossible moments – those times when the pieces fall into place or doors open in unforeseen ways or you discover that detour was the road you were meant to be on all along. And you cannot help but smile, maybe even laugh.

I had one of those moments when I received the phone call telling me that the Personnel Committee was recommending me for their staff position. I was a year past my seminary graduation and job prospects were few. In those days even having a woman on staff was a novel idea for many churches and one that many churches would not consider. I'd toiled away working retail, wondering if I was ever going to have a chance to follow God's calling in my life.

I hung up the phone after talking with the pastor and grinned from ear to ear. Maybe I even chuckled a little. I remember telling myself to remember this feeling, this moment. Anything was possible.

What about you? When have you had your moments? I know that sure there have been at least one or two. Look for them if you have to, but remember the feeling of being in sync, of things falling into place, of being smack dab in the middle of where God most wants you to be. Remember and give thanks.

And laugh.

August 13
Psalm 3

I feel so beaten down.
> They have twisted my words
>> into shapes I do not recognize.
>
> They have made judgments about me
>> when they do not know me.
>
> They have misrepresented
>> what I did when I was only trying
>> to do the right thing.
>
> They have been quick to decide
>> that I do not measure up
>> and quick to let me know
>>> where I have fallen short.

So beaten down,
> I can only look at the ground.

But God, you come
> and lift my weary head.

In your eyes there is no condemnation.
In your look there is only love.
Your gentle hands lift me up
> and remind me that I am not alone.
> In the end, only this matters.
> Only you matter.

August 14
Matthew 5:4

Today's beatitude is a blessing for those who mourn. Maybe it's no accident that Jesus begins with this – it's hard to get through life without mourning some kind of loss.

Loss of loved ones. Loss of jobs. Loss of marriages. Loss of dreams. Loss of homes. Loss of physical abilities. We mourn the

loss of what used to be and the loss of what never will be and what we never got to have. Life, by its very nature, carries with it loss.

Jesus didn't say that his followers would be spared mourning, although I've heard Christians try to argue that point. ("I shouldn't be sad if I know he's in heaven.") Grief is a part of honoring those whom we have loved and that which has mattered to us

What Jesus does say is that those who walk through the valley of grief shall find comfort. Contrary to what a lot of people believe (or hope), comfort doesn't take the pain away. Comfort slides in beside the pain, pulling up a chair so that we have something more than sorrow in our hearts. Comfort gently expands our spirits so that we can breathe again. Comfort opens our eyes so that we can see possibility again. And on those days, whether it is the next day or five years removed, on that day when grief rears its dark head again, comfort helps us remember that pain is not all there is

Blessed are you who are courageous enough to walk through the tough journey of mourning. Comfort shall be, indeed comfort is at hand and comfort is yours.

August 15
Psalm 51

They look down at the floor or out the window or at nothing at all. Their words come slowly, stumbling and hesitant. "I've never told anyone this before," they say and I know that it's my cue to wait. However hard it is to say and however long it takes to get the words out, they are about to share with me one of their secrets. Most of the time it's a secret about what was done to them. Sometimes it is a secret about what they have done.

Today's text is one of our most well-known psalms of confession. Reading it today, I wondered what the whole point of confession is. When a client shares with me their secrets, they are telling me something that I usually don't know. It's not as if God doesn't know everything I've done and everything you've done. Maybe we need to confess not because God needs to hear but because we need to say it.

Saying it makes it real. We can't pretend that it didn't happen. Saying it to God means taking responsibility – this is what I chose to do or not do. And through our confession we hand over our sins to God, letting go of the burden of them. It is a first step in living more freely and more faithfully and more as the people God created us to be.

My clients are often terrified of telling their secrets. They fear that I will judge them, that I will now be able to see their secret shame. They fear that I will agree with every terrible thing they've been telling themselves. They fear that once the truth is spoken out loud, something in their worlds will split open and they will never be the same.

They're right about that last one. They are surprised that once the words come out, they breathe easier and sit up straighter and feel a lot lighter than when they began.

What sin are you trying to keep from God – and yourself? Gather up your courage and talk with God about it. Your world may break open but grace flows through the cracks.

August 16
Luke 17:5-6

What does it mean to have even a smidgen of faith? I've been thinking about that question as I've been thinking about this devotion. I know what it doesn't mean.

I know it doesn't mean ignoring our brains and their capacity to plan, analyze and evaluate. I know it doesn't mean ignoring the very real bumps and bruises of our heart. We weep when we grieve out of love, not lack of faith.

Jesus talked about the power that comes with even a smidgen of faith, the power to accomplish things that seem impossible at first blush. I don't think that the point of his story was that landscaping would become easy if we had enough faith. Maybe it was that the old boundaries that seem so set and solid are really quite flexible when one approaches them from the position of faith. Things are not always as they seem.

When I was in college I had the honor of hearing Dr. Benjamin Mays, one of the pioneers of the civil rights movement. The large, bare stage dwarfed his small frame but the power of his life filled the auditorium. "I've seen changes," he said over and over again. He was not so many generations removed from slavery. He'd grown up with segregation. And now he was addressing this mostly white audience.

He'd seen changes because people had enough faith to dream a dream of a different world and a different way. People had the faith to speak out against injustice. People had the faith to take action, sometimes (oftentimes) even courageous and dangerous action. People had the faith to believe that the God who led slaves out of Egypt could lead them to freedom as well.

Like the disciples, we can ask Jesus for more faith.

If we dare.

August 17
Ecclesiastes 3:1-8

Decisions

Should I stay or should I go?
Should I speak or just keep silent?
Do I keep working in faith
     or do I shake the dust from my feet?

God, I'm trying to be faithful
     and to follow you
     but discernment is hard.
               There are no easy answers
               when every path is a gift
               and every path is a loss.

Help me, God, to get clearer,
     to be clear about the path
     with your name on it.
And if I cannot be clear
     help me to live in the uncertainty.
And when I must act
     give me the grace
     to step out in trust,
               knowing that even if
               I take the wrong turn
                    you will not quit
                    trying to make it right.

August 18
James 1:5-8

My first thought in reading this text is, "Man, that's a little harsh." James instructs us to ask for what we need from God (like wisdom) and God will give it to us. But we have to ask without any doubts, for the doubter is like a sea wave that's pushed about by the wind.

If receiving from God is dependent on me asking without any doubts, I'm in trouble. I suppose I have a least a garden variety faith, but not without a few weeds popping up here and there. To be honest, I've always believed that a little doubt can be invigorating for faith, keeping it from being stale and too small.

My only hope is that James is describing a consequence, not a condition. When doubt gets in the way it keeps me off balance. It keeps me from receiving what I have asked for, not because God isn't giving but because I am all over the place. I'm not open to the possibility of receiving. My doubt crowds out the possibilities of my faith.

Perhaps there is doubt that keeps my faith lively, ready to ask questions and to grow. And then there is the doubt that closes doors... doubt that God could reach out to me, doubt that changes are possible, doubt that God can do anything with my life and in my life.

So maybe on our way to faith we can live with healthy doubt.

August 19
1 Kings 19:1-8

Worn out, burned out,
    the weary prophet sleeps until awakened by a touch,
    an angel by his shoulder,
    bread and water by his head.
"Take and eat," said the angel, "lest the journey be too much
for you."

Worn out, burned out,
    half-asleep we stumble through the motions
    until we see him there,
        as unexpected as a rainbow,
        as familiar as our breath,
In his hands, Jesus holds the bread, the cup.
"Take and eat," he says.
"Take and drink," he says.
Lest this journey of your life be too much for you.
Take and eat of my strength.
Take and drink of my grace.
Lest this journey be too much for you....
    take me into yourselves.

August 20
1 Kings 19:9-18

What are you doing here?

My clients are often surprised when I prescribe for them a pity party. I then explain to them that sometimes we just need to wallow. But pity parties also have rules, chief among them being that they aren't allowed to last longer than two hours.

Elijah was having a very fine pity party, and maybe he'd earned it. In trying to be a faithful prophet of God he'd earned the wrath of the queen and now he was on the lam, hiding out in the wilderness. Strangely enough, God offers no words of comfort for his broken spirit or praise for his faithfulness. Instead, God asks, "What in the world are you doing here?"

When Elijah starts in on his litany of woe, God waves a hand and says, "Oh please... you are SO not the only faithful person left. Get over yourself and get moving." (That's a rather free translation of the text.)

You may need to have a pity party... today, next week, next month. At that point you will be convinced that you are the only one doing anything (laundry, housework, church work, washing the dishes in the office sink) or the only one who cares about anything (the unbridled power of the neighborhood association, people driving slowly in the left hand lane, world hunger). You may be flooded by the great unfairness of life.

You may need to find your own cave and do your own pouting. But don't be surprised if at some point God shows up – not in the great signs of a fire or earthquake or wind but in that still small voice that somehow feels like a loving and gentle but firm slap on the back of the head.

What are you doing here? You are SO not the only one. Get moving because I have work for you to do and I have work to do through you.

What are you doing here?

August 21
Mark 16:1-8

They couldn't do it. Mary Magdalene and Salome and Jesus' momma were given a very specific task. Go and tell the others that Jesus was no longer dead. He was alive and would meet them in Galilee. As Mark tells us, they said nothing because they were scared.

It's understandable. They'd gathered up the spices needed for a proper burial. They dreaded having to take care of his body but they were glad to be able to do something, this one thing, out of their love and their grief. Approaching the tomb they realize that there's no way they can move the stone – how are they going to get in? Their relief at seeing the tomb opened soon turns to confusion when there's not a dead Jesus inside but a very alive young man. A young man who gives them extraordinary news.

I don't know that I could have switched gears that fast. How about you? Eventually, of course, they find their voice and spread the news to the disciples who can't quite wrap their minds around it either.

The women said nothing because they were afraid. Fear has a way of paralyzing us. It constricts our voices and saps our energy.

Is fear keeping you from something? Maybe it's keeping you from following that nudge that your spirit keeps feeling. Or maybe it keeps you from even paying attention, too afraid of what you might hear and what God may ask of you. Maybe it's a fear that keeps you from saying something or doing something or being something.

Today take note of your fears. Then ask for God's help in healing them.

August 22
Genesis 28:10-17

"I will give this land to your descendants, and your descendants will be like the ants covering the earth…" Land and children. That's the promise that God gives to Abraham. Except today's story is about Jacob.

When Jacob shuts his eyes for a good night's sleep, his eyes are opened to the holiness that surrounds him. God comes to him with a promise that is no longer just a promise for Abraham but a promise for him as well. God will give him children and God will give him land.

Elsewhere in this book I've written about the importance of story, of the need to pass down from one generation to the next the stories of God's working… "We were slaves in Egypt and the Lord rescued us with a strong arm and mighty hand." But at some point their story needs to become our story.

The promise that God gave to Abraham and Jacob, God also gives to us, the promise of a family and a home. The family may or may not manifest in physical children as it did for Abraham and Sarah. But in Christian community we find family as well, a place and a people to whom we belong. We find grandparents from whom we can learn and we find children… from whom we can learn as well. We find brothers and sisters who laugh with us and care about us.

We may not receive a physical plot of land, but God gives to each of us a place. A place that is centered in God's grace. A place of belonging, of acceptance, of freedom. We can be at home in God's creation… and at home in our own skin.

Today consider how God's promise to Jacob is taking shape in your own life.

August 23
Philippians 1:1-3

I'd asked my college chaplain to autograph a book he'd written. I expected him to write the usual "best wishes" and so I was surprised when he asked to keep the book for a day or two. One afternoon he gave the book back to me, and I waited until I was out of the office to open the front cover. As I walked along the path tears came to my eyes as I read what he'd written. To my surprise, I found words of encouragement and affirmation, along with this scripture reference: "I thank my God every time I remember you." I was stunned. I admired this man tremendously. Receiving this affirmation and appreciation from him was a gift that left me speechless.

He became my mentor, unfortunately dying of cancer within a year of writing those words. As I write this, I find it hard to believe that it's been nearly twenty-five years since his death. But I would be less than truthful if I didn't tell you than even now those words sometimes inspire me, stun me, uplift me. On days when I feel as if I can't do anything right, I remember his words.

Have you had people in your life like that, people who have been such blessing to you that you cannot help but be thankful when you think of them? If you have (and I hope you have), give thanks to God for them. And if they are still on this planet, take a moment to express your appreciation directly to them. You may never know what it will mean to them to know what they have meant to you.

Who are the people you are grateful to have in your life? Tell them today.

August 24
Psalm 137

A hurricane washes away a city or a tornado flattens a house. And on the front pages of our newspapers or the covers of our magazines or on our computer screen we see the pictures. Vacant eyes staring out from haggard, haunted faces. The look of a people who are now living in a world that is more nightmare than home.

If we could have taken a picture of Israel during the time of this psalm, we would have had such an image. The nation was destroyed. The best and the brightest were carted off to Babylon, where they had to live out their lives in a place far away from home and the home of their faith. The opening verses of this psalm are a gut-wrenching cry.

But it's the ending that takes our breath away, startling in its raw anger and bitterness. "Happy shall be the ones who kill your children by beating their brains out on the rocks." We cannot read it without flinching. Seldom do ministers choose it as their sermon text. Why should such sentiments be in our scripture, especially in this book that we think of as such a lovely collection?

Perhaps it is here because this, too, is the truth of our existence. Not the highest and noblest truth, but true nonetheless. When you have lost everything, when someone or something has taken away everything that was familiar in your life and everything that was treasured in your life, you want to lash out. Our anger is a part of our grieving.

Perhaps it is here as reminder that we do not need to censor ourselves with God. We don't have to worry about making our prayers nice. We can trust God to hear our anger as well as to heal our grief.

Today let yourself be completely honest with God.

August 25
Mark 10:46-52

Jesus enters the town of Jericho, and above the noise of the crowd, he hears a man calling out for mercy. He asks that the man be brought to him, and the people lead blind Bartimaeus, the beggar, to Jesus. And then Jesus does the most extraordinary thing. He doesn't reach out and lay his hands on his eyes. To me, that would be the obvious thing – after all, he is a healer and Bartimaeus is a blind man. But Jesus first asks him a simple and direct question: What do you want me to do for you? Bartimaeus' answer is equally direct: Let me see again.

So what would you say if one day they came to you and said, "Take heart, get up, Jesus is calling for you." What would you say if Jesus was suddenly standing before you, asking, "What do you want me to do for you?"

It's not a rhetorical question. He really is right here, you know. Sitting beside you, standing before you. He can see where you're blind, but he'll ask you anyway. What is it you want me to do for you?

Let yourself be as bold as Bartimaeus. Tell him the secret hope, the deepest yearning of your heart. In some ways, I think we all want to see again. We want to see the true wonder of this world... we want to see the grace that weaves itself through all of our days... we want to see the love that holds us and does not let us go... we want to see ourselves as we truly are – God's dear and beloved children, called to live full and free lives.

What is it you want me to do for you?

Jesus is here, asking you. Let your heart answer him.

August 26
Ecclesiastes 3:9-22

Talk about a change in mood!

The opening verses of this chapter are sheer poetry, and those of us of a certain age cannot hear them without also hearing the soundtrack of the Byrds singing, "to everything, turn, turn, turn, there is a season, turn, turn, turn; And a time for every purpose under heaven."

But now the song's over and the Preacher takes a hard look around. When you come right down to it, he says, there's no proof that we're any different than the cows who are here one day and food for the worms the next. So we might as well enjoy ourselves.

Well, I feel terribly spiritually uplifted; how about you?

Of course, as Christians living on this side of Easter, we have a different perspective. We have no proof but we do have faith that this life is not the only life there is. So what should we do with such a text today?

For me, the text is a reminder to live the gift, all of the gifts, of this life. Part of the gift is the work that lies before me... the work of making a living, the work of making a life. The challenge for me is to be present in the midst of it, and to be present to God who is in the midst of it as well.

For today, just for today live the work of your life (work-work or life-work) as if it's the gift God has given you. Depending on your day, you may have to look a little harder. But I bet that if you asked, God would help you find the eyes for seeing.

August 27
Matthew 5:5

I struggled with this text. Lots of the images I had for being meek weren't things I was aspiring to be - letting someone else make all the decisions, never speaking up. I finally turned to Clarence Jordan's book on The Sermon on the Mount and he helped me understand it better.

Both Jesus (Matthew 11:29) and Moses (Numbers 12:3) are called meek and neither man was a shrinking violet. In the biblical sense, the meek are the people who have given themselves wholly to God. Their lives are completely interwoven with what God desires. Their passion is for what God has called them to do, even when it is more challenging, more uncomfortable or even more dangerous than what they'd chosen if left to their own devices.

How can such people not inherit the earth when they are already living as citizens of God's kingdom?

So the question is (and one I never thought I'd be asking): How are we to be meek today? You may feel that stirring in your bones of a specific task or ministry you're called to do. Or a call you feel the urge to make.

Or you may not have anything specific stirring in your soul right now. It's enough just trying to love God and love neighbor. It's enough to love mercy and do justice and walk with God for this day.

Shall we be meek?

August 28
Luke 10:1-12

I jokingly referred to our church as the French Foreign Legion of churches. It's the last outpost, the refuge for all the people who weren't welcome anywhere else. We laughed about it but then we listened of the stories of some of the people who came to us.... People who were just about to give up on church altogether for one reason or another, people who'd been made unwelcome in places where they'd grown up, people who'd been told it wasn't okay to ask the kinds of questions they wanted and needed to ask.

We listened and remembered that what we do as a community of faith matters.

Before when I've read this text I've tended to focus on the part about shaking the dust off of your feet and moving on. That's what I started to write about for today. But then I read the text again and I'm struck by Jesus' sense of urgency. Don't take anything that will weigh you down. Don't stop to chat in the road. If they don't want to listen, don't try to argue them into it, just keep moving.

If there ever was a time for an urgent faith, this is it. Perhaps that could be said of any age, but this is the age that you and I are living in. People have been fed a Lean Cuisine® in the name of Jesus and told that it was a feast and they've decided there must not be much to this faith stuff after all. People see folks who bear the name of Christ who are acting loudly out of fear and have decided that peace must be found elsewhere. People are hungry to be a part of something that matters and to know that they matter.

What does it mean for you to live an urgent faith? Don't confuse it with frantic or hurriedness for the sake of hurry. But let yourself ask the question: How would this day be different if you lived it knowing that passionately living out your faith is what the world needs you to do?

August 29
John 21:1-14

If nothing else, Peter led with his heart. When Jesus spoke of being betrayed, Peter spoke up first, declaring he would never desert Jesus. When Jesus asked who they thought he was, Peter again was the first to reply: "You are the Christ, the son of the Living God!"

He does it again here. Jesus is risen, but the disciples are still a bit at loose ends, caught in-between the miracle and the mission. Peter does what comes naturally. He goes fishing. With nothing better to do, the others follow him.

What follows is a familiar script – long night, no fish, stranger on the shore. After they've pulled up the nets filled to overflowing, one of the disciples recognizes this stranger. It's Jesus.

Peter doesn't wait on formalities. He grabs his clothes and jumps into the lake, swimming to shore to meet Jesus. When the boat comes ashore, it's Peter who jumps up to pull in the nets.

Sometimes Peter's quick reactions get him into trouble. But surely they made Jesus smile. Even when he was shaking his head and sighing, somewhere he had to be smiling. Peter wasn't afraid to lead with his heart.

There are certainly times for careful planning. There are times for using the best of our minds to weigh the options and consider the facts. But if that's all we do in faith, then we're only halfway in. We need our heart as well.

When was the last time you let yourself love Jesus without hesitation? When was the last time you plunged into the waters of grace, unwilling and unable to wait even one more minute to be in his presence?

I wonder what it was like on the beach that morning. Did Peter envelope Jesus in a wet bear hug, nearly knocking him down? Was Peter grinning from ear to ear or was he stumbling over himself or his words? What a picture it had to be.

Sometime, sometime soon, let yourself lead with your heart. It's Jesus standing over there on the beach, and he's made breakfast just for you.

August 30
Job 2:11-13

He was the college chaplain, teaching a class on the wisdom literature of the Old Testament to a bunch of college students who mostly didn't like having an eight o'clock class. While L.D. was a brilliant man and a faithful student of scripture, he also came at these texts with his heart. He'd had his own dances with suffering, first with a son who'd been born too sick and lived too briefly, and then the shattering death of a daughter who was killed in a wreck just as she was becoming a young woman. Later he had his own battle with cancer.

I'll never forget Dr. Johnson reading this text in class one day, commenting about the friends who sat with Job in silence because his suffering was so great that they just didn't know what to say. "That was the last kind thing they did," he said.

Over and over again people confess their awkwardness to me. They want to reach out to friends who are facing grief or illness or some other form of suffering. "I just don't know what to say," they tell me. The truth is, you don't have to say anything.

If you and they are so inclined, wrap them up in a hug. Tell them that you are so sorry that they are facing this terrible thing. Tell them that you care very much. Tell them that you have no words but that you love them. If need be, just sit with them in silence. If they need to talk, they will and you don't have to do anything but listen. And if the two of you just need to sit together without any words, then that will be blessed as well.

August 31
Psalm 63

It was late last night when I left the office, which isn't such an unusual thing. I often have clients who can only come after they get off of work.

Sometimes when I know I'm working late I'll bring my dinner with me to the office. I didn't do that yesterday. So as I prepared to leave I considered my options for getting fed.

I could throw something together at home but I didn't want to have to clean up the kitchen. I could order take out from any one of several restaurants in the area but I didn't want to deal with getting in and out of the car in a cold, dark rain. (Just so you know, I'm not usually this much of a prima dona.) I was hungry but not allowing myself to be fed.

Today's psalm presents us with an interesting contrast: Hungry for God. Full as if at a feast. Thirsty for God. Satisfied.

The fullness comes as the psalmist turns his attention to God. When he meditates upon the working of God in his life or the works of God in creation. When he seeks out God in the sanctuary and through worship. In other words, the psalmist is willing to get out of the car or dirty up a few dishes.

Sometimes we complain about how spiritually hungry we are but never put ourselves in a position to receive. What about you? Are you willing to "dirty a few dishes" today?

September 1
Job 42:7-9

One of the most valuable lessons I learned in my clinical training is that sometimes there are just no words. There are no words to make things okay for the couple who are cradling their stillborn baby. There are no words that will provide adequate explanation for the father of young children who has just found out that he has a nasty and terminal form of cancer. There are no words that will be enough for the patient who has just learned that she has a chronic, disabling and ultimately fatal disease.

Job's friends thought otherwise. When confronted with his suffering they insisted that Job must be to blame. It's what they believed. It made things easier when God acted in such a linear fashion. If I do x God will afflict me with y. They were only repeating what all the faithful believed.

Job had once believed it as well, but it didn't wash with his life anymore. While they are giving their pious pronouncements Job is shaking his fist at the heavens, demanding that God come down here and explain. The world wasn't working like it was supposed to and God had some 'splaining to do.

In the end when God does speak, it is not the pious friends who are commended. God tells then they have been guilty of misrepresenting God. Only Job – only angry, defiant, doubting Job has been faithful.

The story of Job reminds us that God is not offended when we question. Indeed, if anything God is offended when we speak too glibly.

Make room in your heart for the angry, defiant and doubting questions. You may find God there as well.

September 2
Luke 24:1-12

They couldn't believe it.

Not even when the women connected the dots for them and told them what the strangely bright young men said to them about how it all made perfect sense. Even when they reminded them of everything Jesus had said and how it all pointed to this point, the disciples couldn't believe them. It was too good to be true. Such things just didn't happen in this world. Such things didn't happen in their world.

God, I understand. Sometimes it's hard to let Easter in. Big Easter and little ones. It's hard to let it in when death seems too much present and much too much the final word. But it's also hard when those little deaths come – the defeats, the hopes that wither before they really even bud, the closed doors and fruitless detours.

God, forgive me but in such times it's easy to think that anything else is just wishful thinking. Thinking that something could be different. Thinking that something could be different for me. Thinking that there could be new life for my life.

God, forgive me when, in being your disciple, I act too much like your disciples. Help me to believe and to trust that you are still in the business of making all things new. Help me believe and to trust that you won out over death not just for that one time but for all time, not just for end of life deaths but for all of the death that comes before.

Help me remember all that you have said and all that you have done.

Remember.

September 3
Matthew 5:6

When author Geneen Roth leads workshops for people who want to address a lifetime of compulsive eating, one of the first orders of business is teaching them what it feels like to be hungry. For a hundred different reasons they have disconnected from their bodies. They have also disconnected eating from hunger; one has nothing to do with the other. They have to learn how to listen to their own physical signals, to know how it feels to be hungry and to know how it feels to be full.

It's easy for us to do the same thing with our souls. There's a lot of spiritual junk food out there. We can keep devouring it and never have to go beneath the surface of our lives. Better than that, we can fill ourselves with distractions. With going and doing and worrying and planning and ceaseless motion.

So stop. Right now. Take a deep breath and see what you feel. You may be physically hungry. What are you feeling in your soul?

Are you restless? Bored? Anxious? Scared? Longing? Satisfied? Peaceful?

Longing for righteousness flows in two directions. We long for God, for our spirits to be in the flow of God's spirit, to be fired with the fire of God. But we also long for that righteousness to be done here on earth. We long to live in ways that are pleasing to God, that are lives of integrity and compassion. We long to help dig the channels through which God's righteousness can flow. We keep wishing for that world which we do not yet see and yet somehow still hope is possible.

Stop. Right now. In your soul, what do you feel?

If there is longing, then congratulations. Jesus has a blessing for you... and with the blessing comes a deeper, richer fullness than that you could have dreamed for yourself.

God, make us all a little hungry.

September 4
John 16:16-24

It's completely understandable if the disciples were a little off balance. On the one hand Jesus has been talking about persecution and about leaving. He talks about being gone and then being present. And when he guesses the questions they are whispering among themselves, his answer only deepens the confusion. "You will be very sad," he says, "and then you will have great joy."

It's the joy that makes up the refrain. They'll have joy when he comes back. The day will come when they can ask anything of God and God will grant it, not so that they'll have their own magic genie but so that their joy will be full.

Where is your joy? We who live on this side of Easter have a perspective the disciples lacked in those crazy, chaotic days. We can have the joy they couldn't yet glimpse, standing on the other side of Easter.

Where is your joy? Is something lacking in your life that would help make your joy full? I know, you want to break into a chorus of "O God, won't you give me a Mercedes Benz." If that's what you really need to ask for, then ask away. But be willing to talk with God about where the joy lies. (You might be surprised when God's joy-full gift comes in a completely different package.) Is there something you need to let go of that will enable you to receive God's gifts – and God's joy – for you? You might need to ask for help in letting go. Is there something you've always wanted to ask of God but you felt like you just didn't deserve? Ask away, but be willing to talk with God about where the joy lies.

You might be surprised.

Ask and receive, that your joy may be full.

September 5
Genesis 45:1-15

All of those years. All of those years of wondering how they were and where they were. All of those years wondering about his father, wondering if he'd ever see him again. In an instant, all of those years crowded upon Joseph's heart and he knew he couldn't keep his composure. He sent all of the Egyptians out of the room while he broke the news to the waiting Israelites that he was their long lost brother. The brother they'd sold into slavery.

Needless to say, this was not completely joyful news to his brothers. Joseph was the one with the power now and if he wanted to make them pay he could make them pay handsomely. Instead, Joseph embraces them and tells them to move their families close by so he can provide for them in this time of famine.

While we hear a lot of stories about Joseph in the interim between his brothers selling him off and Joseph reuniting with them, we're not told what Joseph was thinking. Late at night what did he think? He had a few close calls as well as some great opportunities. What seems certain, however, is that Joseph didn't spend his time plotting how to get even with his brothers. He hadn't been turning over in his mind all of the ways he could make them pay.

He manipulates the situation a bit when they arrive, making them sweat. But he does so in the service of getting his youngest brother and father there as well. Several times he has to turn away because he cannot keep his tears from coming. When his identity is revealed, he embraces them with love, affection and grace.

Joseph didn't waste his time in Egypt chewing over his resentments, although who could have blamed him if he did?

Instead, he kept moving forward.

What are you chewing on? Is it taking too much of your energy? Is it holding you back? Maybe Joseph can help a bit with letting go.

September 6
Genesis 50:15-21

In the sixties, the comedy team of brothers Dick and Tommy Smothers had a routine based around, "Mom always did like you best." In Joseph's family, it was more of a call to battle than a family joke. He was the youngest, doted on and spoiled and not above flaunting the fact a bit. His older brothers, being older brothers, didn't appreciate this.

They took their sibling rivalry a step further. They debated leaving Joseph for dead by the side of the road, but finally settled on selling him into slavery, telling their heart-broken father that he had been killed by a wild beast.

But now the tables are turned. Their father is dead, and Joseph is in power. There is no reason for Joseph to hold back from exacting his revenge. Joseph's response, however, is to embrace his brothers. "You meant it for evil," he said, "but God meant it for good."

Pay attention to what the text doesn't say. It doesn't say, "God made this terrible thing happen so that the good could come." No, God took the actions of his brothers – born of blind jealousy – and by grace transformed them into something that was life-giving.

Sometimes very terrible things happen to us. I don't believe that God sends those to us. What I do believe is that there is nothing in our lives that is beyond the power of God to redeem and transform.

Nothing.

September 7
Psalm 142

I've just been reading the opening verses of this psalm over and over for several minutes. Here's what I found it doesn't say.

I told God what was going on but then, to be honest, maybe I shouldn't really be so upset. I mean, if I was more faithful I could probably love my enemies and I guess what they've done isn't so bad after all. After all, what right do I have to complain? This shouldn't bother me. You know what, God? Just forget I said anything.

The psalmist is much more direct.

"I pour out my complaint before (the Lord), I tell my trouble before him."

God doesn't want the edited, make nice version of our prayers. At times we may feel petty, self-serving and short-sighted. If that's the prayer we have to pray, then that's the prayer we should offer up to God.

We can offer up such a prayer in trust, knowing that it doesn't have to stop there. God hears our cries for help. God also hears the deeper heart cries that long for more than fear or anger or bitterness.

We offer up such a prayer in trust, knowing that God will not shame us or abandon us. God will heal us and help us to come out of the cave.

Today, offer your very real prayer to God.

September 8
Mark 12:28-34

Love God with all your heart.
> Love with the fearful places.
> Love with the joyful places.
> Love with the grieving places.
> Love with the dreaming places.
> Love with the grateful places.

Love God with all your mind.
> Love with your wise mind.
> Love with your anxious, obsessive mind.
> Love with your curious mind.
> Love with your seeking, questioning mind.

Love God with all your strength.
> Love with your ready to face the world strength.
> Love with your almost gone strength.
> Love with your tired strength.
> Love with your unexpected strength.

Love God with all your soul.
> All of it.
> Everything.
> Forever.

> > Loving God.
> > Amen.

September 9
Genesis 27:41-46

Perhaps Rebekah didn't think things through. Jacob had always been her favorite boy but he'd had the misfortune to be the second son, even if by only a few minutes. That meant Esau was the one in line to receive the best of his father's blessing.

But as old Isaac lay dying, Esau was nowhere to be found, and Rebekah devised her plan. She'd disguise Jacob as his brother. Isaac, with eyes failing, would be none the wiser. The blessing that could only be given once and only to one child would fall to Jacob.

And that's exactly what happened.

I wonder if Rebekah thought about Esau's fierce disappointment and anguished rage? Surely she didn't foresee having to plan again and to act again and to scheme again to keep one son from killing the other.

It's a tempting thing to think just in terms of what's good for us. It all seems so easy, so doable, so very simple. But all of our actions have consequences, and not just for ourselves. As we strive to become better stewards of creation, we're learning that our actions have consequences not only for ourselves but also for our children and our children's children.

As you anticipate the consequences of your actions, consider not only what will happen today, but also what will happen next week…next month… next year… as a result. Then ask God to help you choose wisely and compassionately.

September 10
Matthew 5:7

When I looked up "mercy" in the dictionary, I found two different shades of meaning. One was to have mercy towards someone, who was under your power; for example, not giving out the full measure of punishment. The other was to have compassion for someone who had no power; that is, to do an act of mercy.

In both cases, the giver has no need to hold on. No need to hold onto a demonstration of power. No need to hold onto resources. No need to remind people that we are better than they are or more powerful than they are or more prosperous than they are, that we are healthier than they are.

To be merciful is to step into a wider perspective. It is to open our hearts to the mercy of God's heart. It is not to count how much we have or what we're owed but what we may give... because we have already received, by God's grace.

Here's my challenge to you: Spend one day looking for occasions to be merciful. Ask God to open your eyes to the opportunities before you. If you are very brave, ask God to bring such opportunities into your day.

Open your heart.

Let go of needing to be right or better or on top.

Let yourself meet human being to human being.

Let the mercy you have already received be the mercy you give.

And then let yourself delight in the surprises that come.

September 11
Matthew 7:1-5

My sisters-in-law and I were skiing the wonderful mountains of Colorado together. Riding up on the chairlift together we watched the skiers down below us. We admired those who were smooth and skillful. And (I'm ashamed to admit it) we made fun of those who were clearly a fall about to happen. After all, we were long past the beginner stages ourselves.

Once at the top of the slope, we decided to explore a new trail. It was marked as a blue route, which meant medium difficulty. Once we started (and could not turn back) we realized the error of our ways. The trail was narrow and steep and filled with moguls (bumps.) The only way we could get down was to crisscross the slope, slowly and awkwardly. As we stopped halfway down to catch our breath I commented, "We have become the people we were laughing at."

"Don't judge other people," Jesus said, "because you will become the people you were judging." It can be easy to fall into a habit of judging other people. Did she actually think she looked good in that dress? He's put on quite a few pounds – he should be more disciplined. It's especially easy to judge people we do not know and who, in some manner or fashion, are strange to us. A good clue is when we start talking about "those people."

Jesus reminds us that none of us is perfect and so we have no right to judge others. Just as we judge them, others could judge us. When we sit in judgment over others, it distances us from them. It builds a wall between us, a wall called "you're not quite good enough" or "You're not like me." Jesus calls us to break down the barriers and build connections. That comes when we reach beyond our judgments to get to know the real person.

Who are you most tempted to judge?

September 12
Psalm 61

I adopted my dog Ralphie from a rescue group. A stray, he'd had the good sense to wander into the yard of a woman who worked with this rescue group.

Our first attempts at walking were quite an adventure. Eager to ride in the car, he stubbornly sat down on the driveway when I attempted to walk. He tried to tell me that he was perfectly fine waiting there until I came back. Not only was he not leash trained, he was terrified of cars. Whenever one passed, he became anxious and agitated and wanted to run home. In his fear, he did the only thing he could do – he scrambled up into the yard and stood behind me. I was his protection from those fearful machines.

It's something of the picture I get from today's psalm. Like Ralphie hiding behind me for protection, the psalmist wants to hide behind God. The psalmist wants a safe resting place, a place where he can catch his breath. You know the feeling, don't you?

I don't know about you, but sometimes I get tired. Like the psalmist, my heart is faint. Sometimes I just want a resting place where I don't have to worry or wonder, where I don't have to fear anything that's on my current top ten list of fears.

The good news is that we don't have to go to a tower or scramble up the rocks. That place is right here, as close as our breath and as near as our heartbeat. God is that close, and in God is both our peace and our safety. In God is our rest and in God is our renewal.

And in God's house we may dwell forever.

September 13
James 2:14-26

I've never been very good at what's called a "forced-choice question."

Would you rather vacation at the mountains or at the beach? Well, I love them both.

Would you rather go to a football game or a symphony concert? Actually, either one. I get frustrated with some of the security questions that pop up on web sites now, the bits of information they can use later to make sure you are who you say you are. Name of your favorite teacher. I couldn't pick just one. Name of your first pet. Well, there was the family cat, George, but he wasn't really mine. My first pet was Kitty, unless you count the turtle named Greenie or the goldfish who never lived long enough to have a name… You see why I don't do well on these things?

I don't think the writer of James would do very well with such questions either, at least not when it comes to faith. He remind us that we cannot choose between faith and works, they are inevitably woven together. It does no good to talk about your faith if it never gets past the point of just talking. You may have the most inspiring testimony in the world but it will fall short if you don't get your hands dirty.

The things that we do don't get us into the express lane for heaven. They don't prove our worth or make us more lovable to God. But the faith that we do must always go hand in hand with the faith that we profess.

Where does your faith manifest in works? What are you doing because you are a child of God? The call to service may take different forms at different points in our lives, and yours will probably not look like the person next to you. For two nurses in our congregation, the call manifested as an opportunity to go to Haiti after that country's devastating earthquake to provide medical relief. Another man uses his carpentry skills  to build houses through Habitat for Humanity. Other people stuff backpacks with food each Wednesday night that children will take home on Friday, giving their families food for the weekend. One person serves as a point person for refuges, helping them navigate the maze of legal systems and customs. Another person visits the folks who can no longer get up and go to church, reminding them that they are not forgotten.

How does your faith manifest in works? Your call won't look like mine. But as God's child, the call isn't optional.

September 14
John 13:12-20

Sitting around with my friends in one of our rooms after we'd finished running a race, I offered to massage their feet. Runners' feet are generally gnarly, and these were no different. There were the obligatory black toenails that strike most runners sooner or later. There were the callouses that manicurists had to be warned not to remove in a pedicure because they were hard won. Training for a race means putting a certain number of miles under our feet, week in and week out, and when I massaged those feet I felt the weary muscles and tendons in my hands. It was a surprisingly intimate experience.

As is serving one another. You can't wash feet from a distance. You can't serve remotely. You have to get close up, in the middle of things.

. In the middle isn't always pretty. Sometimes people stink, either because they haven't had a chance for a bath or they've lost the parts of their brains that tell them to take one or the disease that's eating away at their body leeches out the smell of decay.

Close up isn't always pretty. People disappoint you. People sometimes act out of their woundedness and fear instead of their highest selves. Sometimes you can't find that perfect answer. Sometimes you find it and even that isn't going to be enough to take the pain away or magically transform the situation. Some days you wonder why you're washing feet that are just going to get dirty all over again.

And yet, for all of that Jesus pulls up a stool and a basin of water and towel and bids us take, serve.

Wash the feet that you can.

Trust God for the rest.

September 15
Luke 18:15-17

Standing in the pool I was enjoying the relief of the cool water on a hot summer day. Suddenly I heard a familiar voice. "Aunt Peggy, catch me!" I turned as the two year old launched himself from the side of the pool into my arms. He didn't have a moment's doubt that I'd catch him and that we'd do it all over again (and again… and again… and again.)

The disciples thought Jesus was too important to be bothered with children, what with their runny noses and sticky hands and everlasting questions. Jesus told the disciples (and not for the first time) that they had it all wrong. Jesus had a habit of welcoming those whom society excluded… prostitutes, tax collectors. Why should children be any different? But Jesus took it one step further. He turned things around. The children should be welcomed as our teachers. "You have to be like them," Jesus said.

He makes me think of a kid's utter trust, flying through the air to my arms. I think of a group of grade schoolers hunkered down, patiently waiting and utterly fascinated as a butterfly emerges from a cocoon before their very eyes, noisy children now quiet with wonder. I think of a child's innocent question about how it feels to have a different color skin, innocent because for the child different does not yet mean inferior.

I've done too much babysitting and led too many children's groups to completely romanticize children. I've suffered through the temper tantrums. I was even locked out of a house once by the children I was supposed to be watching. (The kids, now responsible adults, swear they don't remember this incident.)

But Jesus said we needed to be like them. In order to make our way into God's kingdom, we needed to have that kind of trust, that kind of wonder.

How will you be like a child today? (A temper tantrum doesn't count. Neither does locking someone out of the house.)

How will you trust?

How will you wonder?

September 16
1 Samuel 20:30-24

Once David had been Saul's balm. David's music was the only thing that could bring the king relief from whatever was tormenting him. But that was before David took on Goliath and emerged with the adulation of the people. That was before David had become a clear rival to the king. Now David was the enemy and had to be snuffed out.

All of which posed a dilemma for Jonathan. David was his best friend. Yet, as Saul reminded him, as long as he lived Jonathan had no chance to secure the throne. Jonathan made a choice to help David escape, not out of his own self-interest but out of love for his friend. Jonathan did what was right even though it meant considerable loss on his part. He risked losing his father. He risked losing his future. In the end, he risked losing his life.

One of the hardest things as a community or a church is to look beyond our own self-interests. Not in my backyard. What's in it for me? There's nothing for me here. I've got to protect my own.

Yet God calls us to have the courage of Jonathan, to be willing to do what is right, to be willing to make the choice that comes from love. In the midst of a contentious political campaign a man wrote a letter to the editor saying, "Why do you tell me not to worry, that it won't affect me? Do you not think that I care about my children and grandchildren and the world in which they live?"

Today, if you are brave, ask God for both the courage and wisdom of Jonathan. May we choose what is right. May we choose out of love.

September 17
Matthew 5:8

There's a lot of talk about purity these days, what with purity rings and purity pledges. Without exception, it's referring to choosing to refrain from sexual activity until marriage. That's not what Jesus is talking about here. In this context, purity of heart means single-mindedness. "Purity of heart," wrote the Danish theologian Soren Kierkegaard, "is to will one thing." The focus is on willing the thing that is also God's will.

I call Ralphie my little ADHD dog – except when it comes to tennis balls. When there's a ball to be chased, he's the model of focus. One night in obedience class the leader of the group on the other side of the ring was tossing a ball. Ralphie stood statue still, his complete focus on that ball. His head literally vibrated from the power of his focus. A herd of cats could have been line dancing in front of him and he would not have noticed. I could have waved a steak under his nose and he would not have wavered.

While I hardly hold Ralphie up as the example of good mental health, he does help me understand what it means to focus completely on one thing. For the pure in heart, nothing gets in the way of that one thing. They don't allow anything to distract them from their desire to follow God.

What does it mean for you to be pure in heart? For me, it means refining and reordering my focus each day, day after day. What does it mean for me to seek God today? With what am I in danger of distracting myself?

What does it mean for you to be pure in heart?

September 18
Mark 14:66-72

He failed.

There's no way to sugarcoat it. In the biggest test of his life, he failed. He didn't fight for Jesus and save him. He didn't stand up for him. Peter didn't even admit knowing this man whom he'd given up everything to follow, this man with whom he'd eaten and traveled and talked. He blew it.

I've heard tell that there are people who've never failed in this life, people older than two or three. Personally, I'm not sure I know any. If you happen to be one of those lucky souls, just move right along to tomorrow's devotion. Because the rest of us mortals need to talk.

We've failed at some point, in some way. Maybe you cheated on your spouse and betrayed the vows you took.

Or you didn't stand up for your friend when everyone else in the office was trashing her. Or you took that drink after you'd promised your friends and your family and your sponsor that you'd never drink again.

Maybe you screwed up on the job and it cost you your job. Or you cheated on the test. Or you knew so clearly what God was calling you to do or who God was calling you to be and you deliberately, with forethought, took another route. Or you had a chance to give, a chance to reach out in love and compassion and you just kept walking.

We've all failed God at some point. We've all betrayed the best in ourselves.

Today's text is gut wrenching and heart breaking. With every oath and categorical denial, we feel the fear that's choking Peter. Maybe we've not been in that kind of danger, but we know about bad choices made out of moments of fear.

Today's text ends with a broken hearted Peter weeping, perhaps weeping with shame and regret. But this isn't the end of the story. There are yet chapters to be written for Peter.

As there are for us. If you have failed, then welcome to the club of humanity. Depending on how you failed, you may have to face some very stiff consequences.

But that's not the end of the story.

It's not for Peter.

It's not for us.

September 19
1 Samuel 1:1-8

Don't be thrown off by the strange customs and funny sounding names. For all of the ways that the characters in these stories are different from us, in at least that many ways they are the same. Take today's text, for example.

There is a man named Samuel whose wife, Hannah, has been unable to get pregnant. She is inconsolable and weeps in the night. Samuel tried to make her feel better but his attempts fall on deaf ears – or a broken heart. (Not so different from us.)

God gets involved in Hannah's story – just as God gets involved in ours. To be sure, we may feel God's closeness in a moving worship service. But God is also there in the everyday stuff of our lives, the disappointments and challenges. The trick of it all is to be willing to allow ourselves to reach out to God in the midst of it.

Maybe like Hannah you've longed for a child who through whatever circumstance has not come. I cannot promise you a nursery in your future, but I can promise that God will not stop bringing new life into your life. Maybe there's some other dream that to this point seems empty and hopeless and remote. Let God show you the next step toward that dream – or the way to let go of one dream in order to receive an even better one.

Wherever you are and whatever stuff you stumble over in your life, God is there and God wants to help. I know it's an utterly audacious and preposterous thing to say and I wouldn't dream of being so bold. But I'm surrounded by too many stories of too many people who testify to exactly that truth. People like Hannah and Samuel.

And you and me.

Today let God be a part of your ordinary life.

September 20
1 Samuel 1:9-20

Talk about pouring salt on a wound. Hannah is at the temple, praying her heart out. Her prayer is raw and honest and filled with emotion. Eli the priest, seeing her lips move but hearing no sound, accuses her of being drunk and tells her to shape up. Personally, I think Hannah's response shows remarkable restraint.

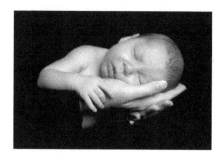

Hannah wants a child with everything she has. Paradoxically, she wants him enough that she is willing to give him up, to surrender him to God's service.

It's a gift to be able to hold things lightly, to desire something with all of our hearts and then not to have to hold onto them. Maybe you started a Bible study or support group. It was your great passion and you spent countless hours and untold energy in getting things going. As passionate as you are, as a leader you realize that there's a time in which you have to let go. You have to let the group become what it wants and needs to become, which may be quite different from your vision.

It's a gift to be able to hold our own lives lightly. We dream what we dream for our lives, holding our desire fiercely and fondly. But there is grace is being able to let go of the expectation of how and when that dream becomes real in our lives. We offer it to God, trusting that God can work things out in ways beyond even our greatest expectations. Sometimes God transforms our dreams into something quite different than what we thought we wanted or needed... but something that turns out to be even more perfect.

What do you need to offer up to God today?

September 21
1 Samuel 3:1-9

There was no frequent vision…

God…
    I know about those dry times.
You know I'd gladly walk in your way
    only I don't know what that way is.
You know I'd gladly follow your lead
    but no lead comes.
You know we'd gather up our courage and our faith
    and work to make your vision real
    but there is no vision.

God,
    in the dry time, give me patience.
Give me faith enough
    to keep seeking
    and to keep listening
    and to keep looking.

And God,
    help me not be too surprised
    when you wind up speaking
    through the person I'd least expected.

September 22
1 Samuel 3:10-21

He was between a rock and a hard place. He was the junior guy, the intern. It was bad enough that God was choosing now to speak to him and not to his priest, Eli. What was worse was the message he was being asked to convey. Eli had been too soft as a parent and a priest and had not punished his sons for their arrogant disregard of God. Eli and his family would reap the terrible consequences of their actions – or inaction.

When morning came Samuel didn't want to tell Eli the news, but Eli insisted. A word from the Lord had come, and he had to hear it, no matter how hard the words. That took a lot of courage.

Our actions have consequences, and like a good parent God does not rescue us from those consequences. If you smoke for forty years, you'll probably have to deal with some kind of lung problems. If you treat your friends poorly and take advantage of them, you will probably lose them. If you only yell at your children and tell them how they've screwed up, they probably will not want to visit you in your old age. If you spend your day at the job surfing the internet and doing slipshod work, you'll probably lose it. Our actions have consequences.

It takes courage to face those consequences. One of the twelve steps of AA is to take a fearless personal inventory of all the people whom you have hurt through your drinking. It is an incredibly hard thing to do. But also, in the end, also incredibly freeing.

For once we name our sins (and that's what we're talking about) and face the consequences we've been trying to avoid, we can quit hiding. As a matter of fact, didn't Jesus say something about knowing the truth and the truth setting you free?

What is the truth that you need to face today?

September 23
Psalm 145

When I was a child, my bedroom was across the hall from my parents' room. If I woke up in the night and was sick or scared, all I had to do was call out and my mom would be there to do what needed to be done. Take care of me. Comfort me. Soothe me.

That's the picture that the psalmist gives us of God. Really. Not the junior grade minions of God but the God who called forth creation and all that is in it. The God who is beyond our ability to comprehend fully. The God to whom we sing and pray and the God whom we worship. When we call out, the psalmist says, God is there.

Are the words too familiar to you? Do you really understand how incredible they are, how earth-shaking they are? If you, you who are one of tens of millions of people on this planet, call out to God, God is there to listen. And not just to listen but to care.

As I type the words, the smile spreads across my face. God is really listening to your cries and to mine. We are never, ever left to face this world and this life alone.

Call out to God today. Maybe you just need to express your appreciation for many good gifts in your life. Go ahead and thank God for all those things. Or maybe you're facing a decision that you don't know how to make, a situation you don't know how to resolve. You can talk about that as well. Maybe you're hurting or heartsick. You don't have to carry it alone. Or maybe it feels like night to you, a night that never seems to end. God cares about that as well.

Like a good parent, the God of the universe comes close by your bedside (or chair or kitchen table), leans over and lends an ear. "What is it, my child? What is it?"

What is it?

September 24
James 3:13-4:6

What do you want?

James gives us a picture of a community grown toxic, in part because people want all of the wrong things for all of the wrong reasons. What do you want for yourself? What do you want for your community of faith? What do you want for yourself as a member of that community?

What are you holding onto? Does it give you strength or does it burn your insides like acid? Is it a grudge or a hurt or a gratitude?

What do you see in your community of faith or in yourself that seems not quite right? Is it because it is an injustice? Or is it because your feelings are hurt? Is it because it is something in your life that you truly need to work on or is it because it's something someone told you about yourself that was never true to begin with?

What's your deepest desire, the one you'd beg God for if you were brave enough to be that honest? What would be different in your life, your family, your church and your world if you received it?

Lots of questions today. But James reminds us that being in community (and indeed, following the way of Jesus) demands of us such questions, such reflection.

Today, allow yourself to sit with some questions.

September 25
Luke 7:1-10

One of the themes of the gospel of Luke is the breaking down of old barriers. In Luke, the outcasts keep finding themselves on center stage, spotlight squarely on them. And Jesus is always there with them, usually giving them some form of praise for their faith.

On the one hand this is a very easy text for me to read and it makes me feel all warm and cozy inside. There's a Roman soldier who not only does not abuse his power but rather seems genuinely to look out for the welfare of the people he rules. There's his care for his slave who could have been no more than property to him. And there is his faith in Jesus. "All you have to do is say the word," he says, "and I know it will be done."

On the other hand, this text can make me uncomfortable. A Roman centurion was the enemy. Their role was to be cruel and godless. The Jews of this town were willing to see him as a person. Jesus was willing to see him as a person of faith. Luke sees him as one more exhibit as to why the "religious people" don't have a corner on faith.

This makes me uncomfortable because I am one of those "religious people" I was on the cradle roll, for heaven's sake, I don't think I can avoid the label. This text forces me to look at who the outcasts are in my world.

Who am I tempted to write off? Who am I tempted to ignore? Who am I tempted to treat as nothing more than a label? Who do I put in the "them" category when it's us versus them?

This story makes me uncomfortable because it reminds me that that's precisely where Jesus might be... standing with them.

Who are the outcasts in your world?

September 26
2 Kings 5:8-14

Naaman the king was in a bad way. He had leprosy, which was just about as bad as it could get. Not only would the disease eat away at his flesh, it would take all of his relationships as well. Even though he was the king, as a leper he was unclean. He was an outcast, best to be avoided by all the healthy folk.

So when Naaman heard that Elisha, known as a holy man, was in town, he was ready for the big miracle. He was the king and Elisha was the prophet, so surely he would have to do something grand and heroic in order to be healed. What a story it would be years later. He'd astonish his friends and associates with his determination, his faith, his willingness to do anything in order to be healthy again.

Except for this. Elisha told Naaman to go down to the river and wash himself three times. Naaman was outraged. "This is nothing at all," he sputtered. It was a command that was so beneath him. He wouldn't do it. He just wouldn't do something that was so common, that was so beneath his dignity as a king.

It finally took the nudge of a servant. "Uh… sir, you DID say you wanted to be healed, didn't you?" Naaman swallowed his outrage and went down to the river, only to find healing in its common waters.

So what's God calling you to do today? Maybe you're all revved up and ready to serve. End world hunger? Save the environment? You are so there. But God says, "Hey, why don't you call your friend and ask them how they're doing?"

"But God," you sputter, "that's nothing. It's not big enough or grand enough or important enough." And God gently says, "Uh… you DID say you wanted to be a part of the healing of the world, didn't you?"

God, may I be willing to follow your lead, no matter how small the step may seem to be.

September 27
Luke 5:17-26

For the two months that I was in a wheelchair, I was unable to drive. On several different Sundays, a friend from church came and got me and took me to our worship services.

This was no small thing. My church is about a forty-five minute drive from my house. She drove forty-five minutes to pick me up, another forty-five minutes back to church, another forty-five minutes to take me home plus another forty or so minutes back to her house. Plus wrangling my wheelchair in and out of her car. Although she passed it off as nothing, I knew it was a huge inconvenience endured simply for the sake of allowing me to be a part of the community I was missing.

I can't read today's text without seeing the miracle that comes before the miracle. It's the miracle of four friends who are willing to carry the dead weight of their friend to Jesus if it means he might be able to walk again. It couldn't have been easy to haul around a grown man who could not walk. Not only that, but when they hit a roadblock, they don't give up. If they can't get to Jesus through the door, they'll come through the roof.

You may be the person in need of receiving such help today. If so, allow someone to be inconvenienced for you. You may even need to ask for the help that you need. But maybe today you need to be the one willing to be inconvenienced. It may be as simple (or as complicated!) as giving someone a ride to and from church so that they can connect with their community. Or it may be more demanding. Shortly before I was born my parents took in two neighborhood children while their parents were in rehab.

You may never know when the chance will come. When it comes, be honest with yourself. Is it a time when you truly have nothing to give and so need to say no. Or is it just an inconvenience?

September 28
Psalm 63

When was the last time you were thirsty? I mean, lips cracking, tongue like cotton in your mouth thirsty? Most of us live in places where water is easily accessible, not to mention soft drinks, sport drinks and the mocha frappe. People who know such things tell us that often we misread the signals from our bodies, eating when in fact we are thirsty.

The psalmist wrote of being thirsty for God, but just like our physical selves, we often misread the signals. We think we're hungry for excitement or another person. We think we need the newest movie or newest book or newest video game. We need a buzz. We need... Something.

But stop and listen. Pay attention.

Beyond the distraction.

Beyond the easy and quick and glib.

Beyond the pull of Hollywood or Madison Ave or the bar around the corner. Beyond your to do list for today and long term goals for tomorrow.

Stop. Listen. Pay attention. Let your thirst rise up from your soul. Our hearts are restless, O God, wrote St. Augustine, until they find their rest in thee.

Stop. Listen. Pay attention. Are you thirsty? Do you long for something more or better or deeper?

Stop. Listen.

Then cry to God. Yell out to God. Whisper to God.

I'm thirsty. I'm thirsty. I'm thirsty.

And the God who became himself a thirsty man crying out for relief, such a God will hear.

September 29
Philippians 3:1-11

I confess that in reading today's text in preparation for writing I could get no farther than the first verse. "Rejoice in the Lord."

That's hardly an earth-shattering revelation, I know. We have Advent just around the corner, and one of the Advent Sundays focuses on joy. We'll sing "Joy to the World."

Rejoice. Be joyful. I could be wrong but it seems to me that a lot of Christians and a lot of churches are not hindered by an overabundance of joy.

Sometimes life is like that. Grief can mute our rejoicing, for example. But when you look at your life, when you look at your days outside of such difficult times, is there much joy? Joy is happiness that has gone soul deep, to be anchored in our bones. Sometimes we laugh with it and sometimes we smile for the grace of it. And sometimes joy is a sweet gift that we savor deep into our being.

If joy seems in short supply for you begin asking yourself why. Are you holding on to old hurts and fears that are getting in the way? Sometimes it is enough for us to decide that we are done with it and sometimes we need the help of a counselor. Are you focusing so much on what you think other people should be doing in their lives that you are neglecting to ask what God might be doing in your life? Are you do focused on the things that are wrong - or even simply the things that have to be done - that you miss all the moments for rejoicing?

Rejoice in the Lord.

Rejoice.

In the Lord.

September 30
Philippians 3:12-16

From time to time I talk with people who are struggling with all that lies behind them. Sometimes they carry burdens that were never rightfully theirs to begin with; for example, feeling guilt for not keeping a parent sober. Sometimes part of the struggle is facing the responsibility of having made choices and done things and said things that deeply hurt some of the people they love most in the world.

Sometimes they have betrayed the trust of others. Sometimes they have betrayed the best of themselves.

Sometimes that past does have to be remembered, whether it is to understand what a child could not about the responsibilities of parent and child. Or because amends must be made as a part of healing and restoring relationships.

Paul had his own past, hunting down the people whom he now called brother and sister. Watching the gruesome death of a man being stoned and approving of it all.

Whatever is in our past, whatever we need to do with our past Paul reminds us that it is indeed past. God does not chain us to what has been. God always calls us forward to what may be.

Do with your past whatever you must. But also remember this: no matter what has gone before, God is always calling you forward to a future, to God's future.

October 1
Matthew 5:9

Blessed are those who avoid conflict, for they shall be safe.

Wait, you mean that's not how this verse goes? We tend to get it confused, this business of avoiding conflict and peacemaking. We think that lack of conflict and peace are the same thing while actually they are very different.

A lot of church folks are very good at avoiding conflict. When my church went through an Intentional Interim process, they had to look at all of the conflict they'd avoided for many years. So many things had been swept under the rug that it was beginning to get hard to walk in there. All of the conflict that had been avoided didn't go away; it just piled up and festered.

We avoid conflict because conflict is messy. Somebody's feelings might get hurt. People might get angry. Worse yet, somebody might leave the church.

Avoiding conflict isn't peacemaking. Avoiding conflict means running away from the mess while peacemaking means running into the middle of it.

Peacemaking means addressing those issues that caused conflict in the first place. Peacemaking can never be separated from doing justice. They go hand in hand. Peacemaking means having to stir the waters on the way to peace. Peacemaking means speaking the truth in love, but speaking the truth nonetheless.

Will you have the courage to be a peacemaker?

October 2
Luke 8:1-3

Jesus and the Twelve. It's the bunch of guys gathered around the table in Da Vinci's Last Supper. It's the list of names learned in a third grade Sunday School song, the heavy hitters like Peter and James and John and even Judas as well as the more obscure guys like James the lesser (how'd you like to have that nickname?)

The way we talk about them and the way we think about them, it's almost as if they're a self-contained, self-sufficient group moving through the countryside. Just Jesus and the guys. Today's text presents a different picture.

Along with the twelve chosen disciples, there were also a number of women who followed along, unable to leave this holy man who had healed them. More than that, there were those who helped support their ministry out of their own resources. If the disciples were the stars, these folks were the supporting cast. No headlines, but necessary just as well.

"I can't teach a Sunday School class," she said to me one time. "But I love to do the shopping for our Wednesday night dinners and for our monthly dinner at the shelter." It can be tempting to devalue our contributions when they don't seem to be big enough or important enough. But like the women who followed Jesus and those who supported his ministry, our supporting cast contributions are valuable as well.

Today, celebrate the opportunities that you have for ministry, even if they don't seem very big or very glamorous.

October 3
Philippians 4:10-13

He'd seen me in the hospital a day or two after my accident. "You must have had some mighty fine drugs," he later kidded me, "because you were quite happy."

Well yes, to have full and true disclosure. I did have some fine pain medicine, for which I was terribly grateful. But there was more to my good spirits than that. The fact of the matter is that I made up my mind to be happy, to be content in even this situation.

I couldn't change the fact that my pelvis was fractured in three places but I was being well cared for. I couldn't change the fact that I couldn't walk and that the road to walking would be long and hard and painful. But I was going to get that chance. I was surrounded by people who loved me and cared for me. I could be content.

Look, I know that there is a very real thing as depression that comes as a red flag to focus our attention on changes that need to be made or that comes part and parcel with grief. But for many of us for most of our lives we make a choice. I can be content. I can be unhappy. Whichever road I choose, I can find plenty of evidence to support my choice.

Paul knew this and knew that it goes deeper than just cognitive therapy. I can choose to be content because I am not alone. I am held in God, the same God who will go to the ends of the earth for me.

What are you choosing today?

October 4
Acts 9:26-31

After his baptism, Paul begins preaching. He so stirred things up in Damascus that he had to escape by night, lowered over the wall in a basket, in order to escape a plot to kill him.

So he shows up at the next logical place - in Jerusalem, with the disciples. The only problem was that they thought it was a trap. And why wouldn't they? This man had made a name for himself hunting down Christians. Now he shows up with a story about having seen the light? It sounded too much like a trick to get inside the door.

Had it not been for Barnabas, Paul would have been left out in the cold. It was Barnabas who vouched for him, who opened the door for Paul to be accepted among the followers of Jesus in Jerusalem. It was Barnabas who would later become Paul's travel partner on his missionary journeys. Barnabas never gets first billing but he plays a crucial role.

Who's been a Barnabas in your life? Has there been someone who opened a door for you, made an introduction for you or generally supported you? Have there been people who made something possible in your life?

If so, give thanks to God for them. Even better, if they are still on this earth write them a note and let them know what they've meant to you.

And by the way, perhaps consider how you might be a Barnabas as well.

October 5
Numbers 13:17-33

So here they are. After all of the wandering and wondering and waiting, they are on the brink of the Promised Land. Moses sends a group of spies to scout out the territory – what's the land like and are there people there who might be miffed if we take it?

The spies come back with their report. "We've got good news and bad news. The good news is that you have never seen such a fertile and fruitful land. The bad news is that the people living there are big. Really big. We have no hope against them."

Caleb speaks up to give the dissenting report. "We can take them – God is leading us." But the rest of the spies shout him down. "Us? We're like grasshoppers next to those guys. They'll crush us."

Have you ever been there? Have you ever been on the brink of a dream? Have you ever had something you really, really wanted in your sights? If it isn't yet close, it is at least on the horizon. For days or months or even years the thoughts of this dream have energized you and kept you moving forward. Yes – you're going to do it.

Until that day comes and you take another look at it and you start feeling like a grasshopper. There are too many obstacles – you'll never get over them. It's going to be demanding. On second thought you don't have the strength or the ability or the energy to do this. What were you thinking? Every time that little voice in the back rooms of your soul starts making a ruckus again, wanting you to move forward, you push it away. "Grasshoppers," you say. "Nothing but a grasshopper going against giants."

But Caleb knew the truth. It wasn't all up to them and it's not all up to us. We may feel like grasshoppers, but we're not alone.

October 6
Numbers 14:1-10

I'm sure Moses must have wanted to roll his eyes. There they go again. When the people of Israel hear the report of the spies, they start up engaging in their favorite pastime: whining.

"It would have been better if we had died in Egypt. We need to go back to Egypt. Let's elect a new leader who will take us there." Joshua has to step up and argue for keeping the faith. Later, Moses will have to make the same argument with God, who is just about done with the whole lot of them and wants to start over with a new chosen people who will be a tad more appreciative.

It all sounds ridiculous, doesn't it? Who would want to go back to slavery? But maybe it's not so strange. When you're in an in-between place, it's tempting to go back to the old and familiar. At least it is familiar and there's a certain comfort in that.

It's the resistance we meet when we try to change old, destructive habits. Familiar is easier. It's the temptation that arises as we try to take new steps along our spiritual journeys. So what if maybe we had half a life – at least we knew what to expect.

When you are tempted to go back to Egypt, call forth your "inner Joshua" and remember the reassurance that the gifts of that which is to come are worth the uncertainty of the present.

October 7
Numbers 14:20-5

Most of the spies thought it was impossible to enter into the Promised Land. The hurdles were too great. And they were right. They didn't make it.

Joshua and Caleb thought it was entirely possible given that it had been God leading them there all along. And they were exactly right. They made it into the land of promise that became their new home.

If you think something's too hard, it will be. If you think it's just not possible or not possible for you, then you'll probably be right. If you think it can't be done then you're not the person to do it. Because you'll fail.

The family therapist Virginia Satir helped us understand the importance of our inner beliefs and the ways in which they shape our lives. If deep down you think you're a screw-up, you're going to find a way to sabotage every success. If you think you don't deserve something it's going to be pretty hard for you to get it. Sometimes part of the healing process is examining those old beliefs and changing the ones that are too limiting, the ones that really aren't true in the first place.

Jesus can heal us in many ways. One of those ways might just be opening your heart and mind to what is truly possible for you. For your life.

Are your beliefs limiting your life?

October 8
Matthew 7:24-28

Without a doubt, it was a challenging four-year "curriculum." Beginning with being hit by a Buick while biking (which meant many months of physical therapy after five months of healing), it included the unexpected death of my mother, cleaning out and saying good-bye to our family home of nearly fifty years, watching as our house was literally moved away, the deaths of several friends, the death of my two cats, becoming caregiver for my elderly father (whom I moved five times in three and a half years as his need for care increased) while trying to run a business and being with my father as he died. For both parents I had the difficult conversations about "do not resuscitate" orders and stopping any care beyond making comfortable.

There were no two ways about it. I needed a rock-anchored faith to get through such a time. My foundations were getting rocked on a regular basis. I needed something substantial and real to hold onto.

The things about it is that if I hadn't already anchored myself on this rock it would have been too hard to do it once the storms came and the winds blew. From time to time I wondered how I would have possibly navigated it all without faith, without that rock on which to lean when my soul grew too weary and that rock to hold onto when everything else seemed to slip away.

On what is your foundation anchored?

October 9
John 14:1-4

You give each other a quick hug before she picks up her bags and disappears through the airport doors. "Don't worry," she says. "It won't be so long before we see each other again. I'm just going to get things ready."

Through the days that follow, you miss her. Although there's the phone and e-mail, you miss her presence. You miss the casual conversations that come as you grill fish or bake some bread. You miss the long after dinner walks. You miss the way she makes you laugh and makes you think. She is, in short, the very best friend you've ever had.

But then the day comes when it's time to be reunited. She greets you at the door and welcomes you into the house. Although it's a place that's new to you, you cannot imagine feeling more welcome or feeling a deeper sense of belonging anywhere in the world. It's woven into the walls. It's shining in her eyes. You sit down together on the sofa. You arrange the pillows just right and prop your feet up and know that you've got all the time in the world now.

Jesus told his disciples, his friends, that they would only miss him for a little while. The day would come when they would be together, forever. It is one of the loveliest pictures and one of the loveliest hopes that we share. Jesus has gone on ahead to get things ready for us. And when the day comes that we take our own journey, the ending of it will be that we are there with our best Friend, forever at home.

October 10
James 5:13-18

Pray. Reach out for help. Ask for and extend forgiveness.

That's today's text in a nutshell. The author of James is giving instructions to the church for living together as a Christian community. Most of the time when I've heard someone speak on this text, they've focused on the snippet about praying for the sick. That's important, but as they say in the late night infomercial, "wait… there's more!"

We pray for each other. More than that, we let people know that we need prayers. And that can be the hard part. For some of us, it's a lot easier to be the prayer than the prayee.

I know, sometimes we don't want to let the whole church know that we need prayers because, like the old game of gossip, our broken leg will turn into life threatening illness in a few short days. Sometimes we're dealing with private things that, for whatever reason, need to remain private. But sometimes we just don't want anyone to know that we're weak, that we're hurting… well, to be honest, that we're human.

And yet, our clenched teeth self-sufficiency is actually doing a disservice to our brothers and sisters. We're depriving them of an opportunity to use their own gifts of caring and support. There comes a point when our self-sufficiency becomes selfish, depriving others of the challenge of caring and community.

Are you able to allow someone to give to you?

October 11
Daniel 3:8-18

There's always somebody. There's always some tattletale who wants to tell the teacher that Frankie isn't using a number two pencil or that Clara took three cookies at break instead of just two. Monitoring the world would be exhausting except for the pleasure they get from it. It's a way of being in power.

Because of their service Shadrach, Meshach and Abednego were placed in positions of authority. Evidently that didn't sit well with some of the people. When the king made his decree ordering people to bow down to his image, they saw their chance. "You didn't hear it from me, but there are certain Jews... okay, those three, who are not following your decree." The punishment for such disobedience was being burned alive.

I'm sure those three could have rationalized things. They could do so much more good if they stayed in those positions of influence. Maybe they could even witness to the king and bring him around. But they didn't do that.

"We worship the one true God and no other," they said. "Burn us if you will."

I hope that none of us are every faced with such a choice. We are, however, faced with a hundred smaller choices all of which point back to the fundamental question. Who is God in our lives? Who, or what, are we worshiping?

If someone looked at you, the actions you take and the decisions that you make and the choices that are your choices, how would they answer that question?

October 12
Daniel 3:19-30

I struggle with this text. On the one hand, it's a great story. The three men are bound up and thrown into a furnace. The king looks in, expecting to see their charred bodies. Instead, they are unbound, walking around... and they have been joined by a fourth. The king suddenly realizes Who he's up against and not only brings them out of the furnace, he converts on the spot. (And orders the rest of the nation to convert under threat of some pretty grisly penalties.)

It's a great story but I struggle with it because I cannot help but hear the echoes of all of those Christians who were just as faithful but weren't rescued. Christians in places like China or North Korea. Christians who rot away in jails whose doors stay stubbornly closed. Christians who lose jobs or families as a consequence of claiming their faith. I wonder where the angel is for them?

And yet if we could talk, perhaps they would tell such a story. Not necessarily the angel who delivers but the angel who helps sustain long past what any reasonable person should be expected to survive. Perhaps they would speak of losing everything but knowing God was with them anyway.

I cannot answer all of the questions. But I can keep trusting the God who calls us family... and be willing to claim that family as my own.

October 13
Romans 12:9-21

Around a dinner table
    or in the midst of a choir rehearsal
    or as you transition from hubub to Bible study
    or as you sit together in a coffee shop...

you share things that make you laugh
    for the humor of our lives
you share things that fill you with joy
    for all the good of our lives
you share things that make your heart heavy
    for all of the pain of our lives
you share things that stir your spirit to be inconvenienced
    for all of the need in our lives.

In such honest moments
    we call the connections between us community
    spirit calls such connections family
    love calls such connections real.

Grant us the grace
    and the courage
    to live in community.
    to be family
    to let our love be real.

October 14
Mark 7:1-8

After telling us that some of Jesus' disciples had not washed their hands before eating, the writer of Mark tells us why it's such a big deal. Part of the Jewish tradition was a ritual washing, not only of hands but also of all of the eating utensils. Such washing was a sign of faithfulness.

When confronted about his disciples' laxity, Jesus responded by calling the Pharisees all a bunch of hypocrites, more concerned about looking good than being good.

Traditions are good and meaningful. Traditions link us to a world wider than our world and a time more than just our time. Do we not observe a tradition every time we hold up the bread and say, "Take, eat" and the cup, saying, "Take, drink of it..."?

Traditions provide structure. It is their gift and their problem. The temptation is to hold onto the tradition for the sake of tradition itself, like holding onto a house long after the last resident has moved out and the rooms have become empty, cold and bare.

Take some time to reflect upon the traditions, habits and structures of your life. Are they serving a purpose beyond themselves? Why are you holding onto them? Do they need to be reinvigorated? Or is it time to let go? Wise churches ask themselves the same questions from time to time.

What does the structure of your spiritual practice look like?

Where's the meaning in it?

Where's the life in it?

October 15
Matthew 5:10-11

Let's be honest. I don't know how many of us can relate to this verse. I personally don't know a lot of people who've been persecuted for their faith. In fact I live in a part of the country where a common question is still, "Where do you go to church?" It's the folks who profess no faith who face the persecution.

Oh, I've had folks who disagreed with me. I've had discussions with people who would have gladly denied me the right to be ordained. My former church was kicked out of our association for our beliefs. Having an ordained woman on staff was the beginning of our becoming a part of the prayer lists of other churches. Still, no one was flogging me.

So I'll read this verse today and lift up my prayer for those who are persecuted. For those for whom gathering together for worship must be covert and guarded. For those who cannot talk freely about their faith. For those who cannot walk into any bookstore and buy any Bible.

For all who risk life and limb, work and home and family in order to follow you, God, I pray. May I never take for granted the gift that I have. May we all work for the day when all are truly free.

October 16
Matthew 20:1-16

The council was meeting in Atlanta towards the end of the summer. The head of the group decided that going to an Atlanta Braves game would be a fun outing for the group. The Braves were flat out terrible, so there was no problem getting tickets.

By the time we met, the Braves were no longer terrible. In fact, they were in the midst of an exciting climb from worst to first. Our "fun outing" turned out to be prime seats for a crucial game in a pennant race. One leader never looked so good.

We wouldn't have been nearly so excited if we'd been going to see a last place team. That's just how things are.

Except in the kingdom of God. With God, first or last doesn't really matter. God doesn't use the same ordering system that we do. God has a way of turning our worlds upside down.

Now if I'm one of those last hired folks, I'm thinking this is pretty good news. But if I've been out working all day, sweating through the hours I'm not so sure. If I'm hearing it as a believer who has come along long after the fact, long after the disciples then it may be pretty good news. If I hear it as a person of privilege whose circumstances of birth ensured I am among the first place of the people of the world... is it such good news?

God, let me focus on your grace and leave the ordering to you.

October 17
Proverbs 27:1-6

My friend was visiting from another part of the country. As we walked through the park, people smiled and waved and said "hey," and I smiled and waved and said hey back. After a while my friend asked, "How in the world do you know all of these people?" I told her that they were all strangers. But in my part of the country we wave and smile and say hey to strangers whom we meet.

You see, it's all about being nice. We put a large premium on being nice where I live. If you're rude, people assume that you aren't from around here. Truthfully, it's not such a bad way to live.

Until it is. Sometimes being nice comes at too high of a cost. We don't confront that friend because we don't want to hurt their feelings. We don't speak up because we don't want to make someone angry. Many times the people with whom I work learned long ago that it was dangerous to risk making someone angry. Too often we keep repeating obsolete childhood lessons even though we're in our adults bodies now.

Groups (including churches) can talk about how much they all love each other as a cover for never having real conversation and real disagreement. The problem is that the issues just don't go away if we ignore them. They fester. One day a new member speaks up or a new minister takes a stand or proposes a new ministry. And everything blows up in their faces.

I don't think that the writer of Proverbs was advocating for totally random, all the time willy-nilly confrontation. But there is a time and a place for speaking up. Sometimes it's telling a friend that they are killing themselves with their drinking or their lifestyle and you can't pretend it's not happening. Sometimes it's telling someone that they need to get professional help for their depression or anxiety or that problem they keep bending your ear about.

And sometimes the most loving thing you can do is to speak truth to that person looking back at you in the mirror. No, Disney animals will not come in and magically change your life overnight for you. No, you aren't living the life that God dreams for you. Yes, it's time to say yes.

Sometimes the hard words are the most loving words in the end.

October 18
Jeremiah 32:6-15

And you thought you were trying to sell your house in a depressed market...

Jerusalem was under siege. The Babylonian armies were camped outside the gate. It wasn't looking good for the home folks.

In the midst of this God gives Jeremiah very explicit instructions to buy some land from his cousin (who, I'm sure, was very eager to sell.) For Jeremiah, it was to be more than a real estate transaction. It was to be a sign of the promise of God, the God who would not forget Israel even in exile. In the midst of destruction, God painted a picture of building again. In the midst of everything going to pieces, God invested in hope.

In the midst of everything going to pieces, God invested in hope.

I think God is still in the investment business.

Sometimes everything goes to pieces just because it's a difficult time. You find yourself living some kind of life that you never dreamed you'd be caught dead living. There are a hundred different reasons for hitting the detour. But sometimes, even though you don't know it at the time, everything is going to pieces because that's the only way there can be room for your new life to emerge. The new job. The new opportunity. The new way of living and being alive. Things you wouldn't have dreamed of doing and moves you wouldn't have dreamed of making had not things fallen apart.

Whatever the case, look around. Even if you feel like your own property values are falling faster than a stone, look around. There's somebody walking around the lot next door, putting an offer in on it. When you ask him why in the world he'd bother, he just looks at you and winks. "People are going to be building houses here," he says, and as ludicrous as it seems, the way he says it you can't help but believe it.

Even if things are falling apart, God is there. God is here – ready to invest in the future we can't yet imagine.

October 19
Philippians 4:8-9

Perhaps you've done the same exercise.

I stood beside a classmate, holding my arm straight out while she tried to pull it down. I was pretty strong and she had to work pretty hard. Then we repeated the exercise while I focused on positive thoughts. She could have been a monkey swinging on my arm and it would not have budged. Then we repeated it one more time, only this time I was focusing on negative thoughts, tuning in to a self-critical voice. Although I was just as determined to keep my arm straight, much to my surprise it folded up like an overdone noodle.

Our thoughts are powerful. They affect us in more ways than we realize. Like the Force in Star Wars, we may use them for good or for evil, to help build us up or to bring us down.

Paul gives us a good prescription here. Think about the things that are true and lovely and excellent and worthy of our praise. Those thoughts act as positive reinforcements for our spirits. They lift us up, they give us energy and they give us hope and focus. The more that I am focused on that which is excellent, the more I want to make excellence a part of my own life.

Where have your thoughts been the past few days? What do you want to focus on?

October 20
Luke 6:12-16

It was one of the first and most important decisions of Jesus' ministry. He was about to pick out his disciples, the ones who would become his inner circle, the ones to whom he'd entrust his teaching and who'd walk with him on this journey. So to prepare he contacted an executive search committee and began to comb through the submitted resumes.

Of course he did no such thing. That's silly. He set up a schedule of interviews and asked each candidate to tell something about themselves while his administrative assistant looked for embarrassing pictures on the internet.

No, Jesus didn't do that either. He prayed. It was the first and most important thing he did. He prayed long hours.

I confess that I start getting a little antsy when I hear people praying about a decision. What they often mean by that is that they decided what they wanted to do and then asked God to give a divine blessing to the plan. Their praying comes with a certain selective hearing so that it seems to them that God invariably agrees with them. People have been known to build huge towers and threaten God's wrath if donations are not made... all after a season of prayer.

I get a little antsy when I think about praying about decisions in my own life. First of all, I may be just as tone deaf when it comes to what God really wants me to do. Secondly, I may hear very well... but not hear what I want to hear.

I don't know exactly how prayer works. I do believe that it's wise to allow for the chance that at any given point we could be wrong about things. I do know that as we pray about the choices that are ours to make we are sometimes led in surprising and unsettling ways, led to decisions we would not have made if left up to our own devices.

And yet, we pray.

For what guidance do you pray today?

October 21
Psalm 86

Teach me your way, God....

My soul stays stuffed
   with all it does not need.
      Old hurts that weigh me down.
      Old pictures of my self that hold me back.
      Old resentments that fester but do not heal.

Teach me your way, God.
      I'm scared of where it will lead,
         of what you will ask
         and what you will demand.
God, I'm scared of where
   I will end up
   walking with You.

But I'm tired of stumbling and struggling.
Tired of feeling like
      there has to be something else
      there has to be something more
      there has to be a point
         or what's the point of it all?

Teach me your ways, God.
Give me the wisdom to ask,
            the courage to learn
            and the love to live them out.

October 22
John 2:1-11

President Dwight Eisenhower warned us about the "military industrial complex." What he could not foresee was the increasingly powerful "Wedding industrial complex." It isn't enough to have a nice wedding; one must have a theme. Even people of modest means expect limos or horse drawn carriages and venues festooned with every sort of bling. Numerous shows follow brides choosing a dress, competing to see who has the "best" wedding and, of course, brides behaving badly.

I'm sure the wedding in Cana had no expensive wedding planner. For one thing, they seriously underestimated the amount of wine needed and had the very embarrassing situation of running out. What's a host to do when there's no wine shop down the street?

Mary's solution is to tell Jesus, "They've run out of wine."

"Mom, what does that have to do with me?"

Mary, in essence, calls him out, telling the servants, "Do whatever he tells you to do."

What's a messiah to do? Tell the servants not to listen to his mother? Sigh like an angry adolescent and ignore her?

Like a good boy, he takes care of the situation like she tells him to do. He turns the water into wine and the party keeps on going.

Have you ever stopped to think what a weird way this is for a Messiah to begin? The Gospel of John uses a series of signs, miracles that weren't ends unto themselves but were pointers, pointing to Jesus' true identity.

So the first such sign comes when he's at a party. And they've run out of wine. And his mother tells him to do something about it, even though he doesn't really want to go public yet. Do we really think God doesn't have a sense of humor? Who else would write a messianic script that started this way?

Maybe this was the first sign, not only that Jesus was the Son of God but also that Jesus wasn't going to fit into predetermined molds.

Today, as you go about your day, be open to the places where God's unexpected humor might just be breaking through.

October 23
Mark 1:9-13

Sitting in Sunday School, en route to looking up another text, these verses caught my eye. Following Jesus' baptism we're told that "the Spirit drove him into the wilderness." The wilderness was the place of temptation. It was the place where wild beasts threatened. And finally, it was a place of angels.

Jesus doesn't get off track and wander into the wilderness. It's not punishment for his lack of faith, like the Jews fleeing from Egypt the long way around. Jesus has just stepped forward into the public beginning of his ministry... and the Spirit drives him into the wilderness.

First of all, if we harbored any thoughts about living a faithful life sparing us from such places, this text should take care of it. Sometimes we wind up in the wilderness because of our faithlessness. Sometimes it's because of our stubbornness. But what if some of the time we are exactly where God has led us?

Looking back at my life, I cannot truly say that any of my own wilderness wanderings have been fun. Looking back, I can see where some of them have been necessary. Looking back I can see where many of them have turned into places of growth, grace and blessing.

If (or should I say when) you find yourself in the wilderness and you need to pout and complain for a while you will be one in a long list of God's people who have done just that. But then, if you are very brave or very foolish or both, open yourself up to the possibility that being there isn't a detour but is a necessary part of the journey.

And then start looking for signs of grace.

October 24
Judges 2:16-23

Israel lost their focus. Against all odds, God brought them out of Egypt. Against all odds, God led them through the wilderness. God raised up wise people to give counsel and direction.

But eventually, Israel stopped listening. They stopped paying attention. They stopped caring whether or not they were following in God's way. They worshipped the god *du jour*. They'd remember God whenever they were oppressed and forget God as soon as the coast was clear.

Finally, God had enough. God wasn't going to wipe them off the face of the earth. But God wasn't going to make things easy for them either. God used to clear the way for them, but no more. The people who stood in Israel's way would continue to stay in Israel's way.

We have our own Egypts, places of being held down and held back - even if that place is our own mind. We have our own wilderness journeys, the times in which we wander, feeling like we're putting in a lot of steps but not getting anywhere. There are times when we can do nothing but cry out to God from our very bones. Help me.... help me.

In our dark nights of the soul and in our days of struggle, we find our way back to God. Yes, we will seek to follow God and to be faithful. Yes, we'll work on that relationship. And we do very well... Until. Until things get easy again. Until we get distracted. Until we get careless and sloppy and convince ourselves that it's really not that important.

We don't make a commitment of faith just once or twice in our lives. We make it over and over again, day after day after day.

The person in recovery says, "Today I am choosing not to drink" or "Today I am choosing not to use." We are called to make our own kind of choice:

"Today I will follow God."

Each day, every day the choice is still there. Today I will follow God.

What's your choice today?

October 25
1 John 1:5-10

You're a sinner.

Oh don't get so huffy. So am I. We could go anywhere in the world and start a 12 step group. "Hi, my name is Peggy. And I'm a sinner." But is it really possible to be a recovering sinner?

Today's text reminds us that it's not our sins that create a wall between ourselves and God. It is our unwillingness to own up to them. Like we could really hide them from God. "Oh no, God, I didn't eat that cake" we say earnestly while chocolate is smeared from ear to ear.

So you sinned. I have, too. We've had sins of commission, where we did something wrong. And we've had sins of omission where we didn't do the good thing. Guess what? God already knows.

Even better? God still loves you. God wants to help you do better so that you can be freer.

So let's just quit this charade of acting like we're prefect – or even that we're supposed to be. Admit to God where you've screwed up and missed the mark and fallen short. I'll do the same.

Then we can look Jesus in the eyes as he tells us, "Does no one condemn you? Neither do I."

October 26
Acts 4:13-22

Maybe you've heard the argument, too. "The reason I'm not a Christian," someone says, "is because of what I've seen of Christians. Who'd want to be like them?"

The authorities in the story from Acts had a different reaction. They could see that Peter and John were uneducated, rough around the edges kind of guys. But they could also tell that they'd been hanging around Jesus. There was just something different about them. Despite their lack of education, their words were compelling. More than that, they actually healed a guy. No one could deny the power of their message when a lame guy was walking around on two perfectly good legs.

"Maybe if we tell them to stop," they thought, "Peter and John will just shut up and our problems will be solved."

But it wasn't so easy. "You have to do what you have to do," Peter and John said, "But as for us, we can't stop talking about what we've seen and heard."

Are you different? Are you different in some way because you've been with Jesus? I'm not expecting you to be healing lame people, although if you are, don't let me stop you. But is there something in your life that is different because of Jesus?

Is it the way you approach your days - or the way you get through long nights? Is it the way you see people - or the way you speak to people or the way you speak of people? Is it the work you do or the way you approach your work and your co-workers? Is it how you make your decisions about how you spend your money or how you spend your time?

What difference does it make in your life?

And what difference does it make for the people who watch you live your life?

October 27
John 4:27-38

It just wasn't done. A man speaking to a woman. A woman speaking to a man. Out in public. Neither one married to the other. It just wasn't done, but the disciples found Jesus doing just that.

None of them had the guts to ask Jesus directly but it was all they could talk about behind his back. What in the world was he thinking?

Jesus talked to them about old and new wineskins but he could have just as easily talked about old and new eyes. Old eyes can only see the way things have always been done. Old eyes can only see with the expectations of society. Old eyes look around in fear of what people will think.

But Jesus calls us to be people with new eyes. New eyes see people, not issues. New eyes are willing to break a few rules for the sake of those people. New eyes see that who God loves is more important that what people think.

Admittedly, it's easy to talk about this when we're talking about a man and a woman talking in public. It's much harder when you're debating about opening your church to the homeless on a cold winter's night. Or what to do about the immigrants - and their children - in your community. Or how you will welcome - or not welcome - the gays and lesbians in your midst. Or (fill in hot button issue here)...

They can be difficult issues. But as followers of Christ we are called to wrestle with them, not from the standpoint of what we've always done but seeking what Jesus would have us do.

It can be a scary thing to see with new eyes. But in the end, it can be as satisfying as food for the hungry.

October 28
John 4:39-42

The Samaritan woman with whom Jesus talked at the well had to run back and tell all of her friends and neighbors about this man who talked with her in public and his amazing insight into her life. Some of them believed based on her story while others were intrigued. When the man himself showed up, they asked him to stay. Being with him and hearing him for themselves sealed the deal.

How did you learn about God? Who told you about Jesus? Was it a joyful story? Was it a scary one? Who said to you, "Let me tell you about this man..."?

Whoever it was, it was only a beginning. At some point, we have to see for ourselves. At some point we have to sit down with Jesus and hear what he has to say to us.

I know, it was easier to do when he was walking around in flesh and bone. But it's no less necessary now. So how do you spend time with Jesus?

The answers will be different for all of us. For me, sometimes it's through journaling. Sometimes it's while taking a run or walking my dog. Sometimes it's while driving down the highway. Sometimes it's sitting, just sitting in a beautiful place. Sometimes it's listening to the music of the pipe organ that vibrates down into my bones or the music of a cello that reaches into my soul.

And sometimes it's just stopping long enough, stopping and being still and listening with heart and soul and mind.

How will you clear space today?

October 29
1 Thessalonians 5:1-11

Every so often I come across people for whom faith means anxiety. It's not just performance anxiety, wondering if I'm doing good enough and enough good. It's salvation anxiety. Jesus is coming and it's going to be awful, they're told. Jesus is coming and are you absolutely sure you're going to be on the right side of the lines? Texts like today's text are sometimes trotted out as a way of encouraging that fear. You just never know... they're told.

But what if? What if there was a different way of looking at this text? You're already children of the light, he says, so you have no need to fear the night. Be awake and pay attention. As I read the text now, I hear a call to mindfulness. Be present. Be awake.

You know, it's too easy to sleepwalk through some days. We can drive to the office or to school or to the store without even thinking about where to turn. We go through our day while we're a thousand miles away.

But as God's people, we're called to pay attention. Be present. Be awake. The writer of Thessalonians said it was because Jesus was coming at any time. Jesus said it was because he is there with us at the most unexpected times.

Be present. Stay awake. Not because Jesus is coming, but because when two or three of us are gathered, he's there as well. Because he shows up the in guise of a hungry woman or abandoned child. Because he's behind bars or in the cancer ward.

At least for today... be present.

Stay awake.

October 30
John 18:15-27

They are like actors on the opposite sides of a stage, unaware of each other and yet mirroring each other. The spotlight, shifts between them, spotlighting the contrast between them.

Out of fear, Peter hides his true self. He denies even knowing the man who has changed his life. Jesus, who has everything in the world to fear, refuses to hide. "Everything's out in the open," he tells his inquisitors. "Do with it what you will."

Fear. No fear.

Hiding. Speaking out.

Denying. Claiming.

At the time, it seems like such a good idea to listen to our fears. Our fear is only trying to protect us. After all, fear is one of our earliest and most basic human emotions. Fear kept our ancestors from trying to give the bear a bear hug. But for most of us, fear has morphed from a basic evolutionary gift to an out of control dictator, like a science experiment gotten out of hand.

Like Peter, fear keeps us from being who we really are, from following the paths we're called to follow, from living the life that may be more challenging than what fear would choose but is infinitely more satisfying.

Fear keeps us small. Fear whispers that we have to be careful or else it will be the end of us.

It's a lie, for when we step past that fear, we find that what we thought was the end was in fact a beginning.

So what do you do with your fear?

October 31
John 12:1-8

It was a painful time, finally realizing that I was too old for Halloween. I used to love getting dressed up - one year I was the stereotypical hobo in my father's old clothes. One year I wore the clown outfit that my mother so gladly made for me. But the best part was the candy.

One neighbor gave out homemade popcorn balls, sweet and crunchy all at the same time. (Once the campaign started against such homemade treats, I learned to eat them before I got home.) Once home I dumped out my plastic pumpkin, eagerly separating out the good candy and my favorite candy from the pieces that were good for nothing. Normally my parents didn't buy huge bags full of candy for me, but this was Halloween.

So what was a normal situation for Jesus? He certainly told some of his followers to sell everything they had and give it to the poor. And yet in today's text when Mary is chastised for not spending her money on the poor instead of on such frivolous things like perfumed ointment, Jesus rises to her defense.

"The poor will always be with you," he says, "the need will always be there. But I'm not always going to be here." I have to wonder if the human side of Jesus so deeply needed such an unselfish gift of caring as he contemplated the days ahead.

The most pressing needs of every day are not the same. One size doesn't fit all. It isn't black and white. One day you may be called to do this one thing. And on another day, while the original need is still there, your calling may lead you to something else.

But whether we are doing this thing or that, may we follow Mary's example. May all we do be done with extravagant love.

November 1
Judges 16:15-22

I was fascinated by the old family Bible at my grandmother's house. Over a hundred years old, it had thick and heavy covers and a family record inside. Scrawled in spidery scripts were the names and dates of my ancestors, stretching back into a time I couldn't imagine. I was also fascinated by the detailed engravings that accompanied some of the stories.

The story of Samson had such an engraving. Even as a child, it seemed to me to be heart breaking. Blinded, mocked and humiliated, Samson struggles in this strange new world. As fascinated as I was, the story seemed as remote to me as some of those ancestors.

Until I started thinking about it as I prepared to write this devotion. The story is more common that we realize.

We lose touch with that which gives us strength. Maybe we forget the things we know to be true about ourselves and our lives. We lose connections with the habits and people that build us up day by day. Through carelessness and impatience we let go of them. Or, like a swimmer in a rushing river, waters of grief or crisis pulls us away from the grasp of all that holds us together.

Like Samson, we find ourselves lost in a world where we cannot see the old signposts. The strength we once depended upon is gone. Unlike Samson, we have a chance to move forward.

A lot of times in my work as a counselor I am really helping people remember the things they've forgotten, to reconnect with the strength with which they'd lost touch. As followers of a God who is ever bringing about new creations we always have a chance to write new endings.

What about you? Have you lost touch with your strength or your hope or your vision... or your gifts? Today ask God to help you find the way back.

November 2
Judges 16:23-31

What a sad ending. The only option Samson can imagine for himself is to die and to take as many Philistines with him.

The fact is that Samson had never been the most subtle or discerning of judges. In fact, his life reads a bit like an MTV reality show. When he sees a woman he wanted (a Philistine at that) he throws a bit of a tantrum until his parents agree. When he gets angry he wrecks havoc, destroying land or animals or both. He never misses a chance to flex his muscles. He falls for another woman named Delilah who eventually hounds him into betraying the secret of his strength. We're told he judged Israel for twenty years but not much more is said on that score.

In the end, his epitaph is both true and haunting: He killed more in his death than he'd killed in his life. What a way to sum up a life.

His birth had been foretold by an angel but violence and lust were the passions that drove his life. There would come another boy whose birth was also promised by an angel. But this boy's life would be driven by love, so much so that they wound up calling him not a judge but the Prince of Peace.

What drives your life?

November 3
Luke 11:37-44

How do you decide which parts of the Bible to follow? Some argue that if you neglect any part you're on a slippery slope to believing nothing but whatever is your passing fancy. I don't know about you but I don't follow all of scripture. I personally don't eat shellfish but I have no issue with my friends who do. I've seen some teenagers stoned but I've never stoned one for being disrespectful. And my closet is full of clothes made with more than one kind of thread.

The Pharisees who confronted Jesus were proud for keeping every rule and regulation. They did all of the right things. They followed every single law.

And they missed the big picture, the one that talked about doing justice and loving mercy and walking humbly with God.

It's much easier when you have rules for everything. You always know where you stand. It's not always easy to know what it means to do justice. Sometimes loving mercy more means loving getting our way a little less. And loving God opens us up to all kinds of things like loving enemies, going second miles and sometimes leaving familiar places for a strange land.

How do we decide if something is of God? Day after day we have to face situations that those ancient Pharisees never dreamed of. How do we know what to do? How do we know what it means to be faithful in such situations?

We can try to make the Bible into a book of rules. Or we can seek to know where the mercy, justice and kindness are in any given situation. And if we need help with that we have the example of Jesus.

You'll find him sitting over there with the hookers, the AIDS patients and all the other unclean folks whom religious people wouldn't touch.

November 4
Psalm 103

I can't read this psalm without thinking of the song, "Bless the Lord," from Godspell. "Oh, bless the Lord, my soul," one of the singers starts out, the music strolling and rolling along. The rest of the cast chimes in to name God's blessings, "He will not always chide. He will with patience wait." As they sing, the song starts building. The beat gets faster and more intense. The song suddenly explodes into a dance of joy, "Bless the Lord, bless the lord, bless the lord" until it reaches the big, exuberant finish. "Oh bless the Lord, my soul!" It is both exhausting and wonderful.

I grew up in a tradition where one of the first prerequisites for praying was getting still. Bow your head, close your eyes... and DON'T MOVE! Reading this psalm, and indeed, looking at God's blessings in my own life, I wish that sometimes we could dance our prayers. When I saw this scene in Godspell, something in my soul said, Yes! I want that kind of joy. I want to let my gratitude for God's blessings in my life to run all the way though my soul and on out into my body.

Today, let yourself really feel your prayers. Let yourself dance with gratitude. And if you can't quite dance, let yourself feel the wave of it wash over you, body and soul.

November 5
2 Samuel 18:31-33

Losing a child is a special kind of grief. Losing a parent can be hard and you may miss them for the rest of your life. But you never really expected them to be there for the rest of your life. Losing a sibling is also hard. They are the only ones who shared with you the experience of your childhood in your family. But losing a child means something is out of order in the universe. In the order of things, children bury their parents, not the other way around. This is true even when the loss was through miscarriage or stillbirth.

A parent remembers all of the milestones their child didn't get to celebrate, whether it was first grade or getting a drivers license or going to college or getting married. A parent remembers all of the birthdays that have gone uncelebrated. In today's text, King David has been fighting against his son and yet when he hears that his son has been killed, his wail can be heard through the centuries. "Absalom, my boy. I wish it had been me instead of you."

If you have lost a child, then may God's healing grace be with you each and every day, and especially strength and comfort for the hard days. If you've never had to walk that hard journey, you may know someone who has. The best gift you can give to them is to remember their child. If you knew them, share the stories you remember. If you did not, ask the parents to share their stories. Many parents fear that lives cut short will be forgotten.

Today as you pray, pray for all of the parents who grieve, who cry out for their own Absalom.

November 6
John 20:24-30

I always felt like Thomas got a bad rap. Forever he is known as "doubting Thomas" but how many of us would have done the same? He knew Jesus was dead. Buried. Gone. When people started coming back with stories of a Jesus up and walking around, how could he not doubt? Sometimes hopeful hearts see what they wish to see. Thomas said he couldn't believe it until he saw for himself. Until he felt the scars with his own hands.

And that's exactly what Jesus gives him. "Here, Thomas - you need to feel the scars? Here are my hands. Go ahead... touch those ugly scars. There's one in my side as well. You can touch it."

He gives Thomas what he needs and then invites him to believe. Thomas isn't cast out from the disciples for not believing sooner. He doesn't shame him. If Thomas needs to feel the scars for himself then that's what Jesus offers him.

What holds you back from being able to trust God? What keeps you from living in the fullness of a resurrection people? Tell him. Tell Jesus what's holding you back. Tell Jesus what gets in your way. Not in a magical thinking kind of way, thinking you can make Jesus do your bidding.

No, tell him because only as you're honest about where you are can Jesus meet you there. Maybe not in the way you thought or envisioned but in the end, none of that matters.

And if you yourself doubt, just listen to Thomas and the story he can't stop telling about scars and skin and life.

November 7
1 John 3:18-24

Love is a verb.

The writer of I John makes no bones about the face that love isn't primarily a warm and fuzzy feeling in our hearts. Love is what we do. Love is in the choice we make and the actions we take.

And there's the rub of it. I can talk all day long about how much I love God and even how much I love other people. But that doesn't count for as much as my actions. I make a choice as to how I treat people. I make a choice as to how I spend my time and my money. I make a choice as to whether or not I spread that rumor, oppose that proposed law that I believe is unjust, or the groups I support.

I make a choice as to whether or not to speak up for a person or a group who is being discriminated against. I make a choice as to whether or not to send that card to someone who is hurting or grieving or who deserves my thanks and appreciation. I make a choice as to how I walk in this world, whether I walk in fear or anger or greed or kindness. I make a choice as to whether I will be brave enough to speak up and wise enough to keep silence.

Love – or lack thereof - is played out in at least a dozen choices a day. But all of our choices stem from one choice. Loving God. Loving neighbor. I can choose the tough, demanding, giving, joyful way of love.

I don't always do it right. Some days I seldom do. But thanks be to God, there is always the next choice to be made.

What choices are you making?

November 8
Jeremiah 29:1-10

The prophets reassured the people of Israel that there was no way God would let Babylon defeat them. But it happened and now they were in exile. Some of those same prophets were busy reassuring people that there was no need to get really unpacked because they wouldn't be there long. This would be but a blip.

Like he's done before, Jeremiah crashes the part of pretend prophets. Don't listen to them, Jeremiah says. Settle down and make a home here because you're going to be here a long time. Plant your gardens. Plan your weddings. Decorate the nursery. This is where your life is going to be taking place.

It's tempting to listen to the people who tell us what we want to hear. That cheesecake has no calories. It isn't that bad. You don't drink that much. God wouldn't expect you to do that.

It's tempting to think we can take a detour around the hard places in the journey. It's nice to think that we can avoid the consequences of our choices. It'd be nice to be able to avoid having to confront something in ourselves that we'd rather not acknowledge. When we're in exile, it's nice to think that it's just a bad dream and in the morning we'll wake up and be home again.

Except we aren't. And those things don't magically go away. Sometimes clients will ask me how long this will take, how long before the grief is bearable or the depression is gone. How long before the relationship is restored. And I have to say that I cannot say.

Allow yourself to see the reality of your situation. For that reality isn't the last word. Tomorrow's text continues the story.

November 9
Jeremiah 29:11-14

A lot of people love this text. What's not to love? God has plans for us, plans for good stuff, not bad. Plans that are shot full of hope.

Reading it in context makes it even more powerful. Jeremiah has just engaged in some reality therapy, telling the exiles that they're not going home any time soon. It was a bitter word to hear.

But right on the heels of those hard words come this promise. God has not forgotten about them. God hasn't abandoned them. Even in exile, God is holding a future for them. Even though the people got themselves into this mess by turning their back on God, God will not repay them in the same manner. "You call on me and I'm here," God says. "I will bring you home again."

When you find yourself in your own exile (and I'm certain everyone lands there sooner or later), remember these words. Even in the midst of hard truth, God reaches out with arms of love to embrace us. Even when we feel lost, God does not forget us. Even when we feel far from home (physical home or spiritual home or both) God doesn't lose track of us.

No matter what hard things you face, God doesn't forget about you. No matter what hard truths about yourself or your life you have to accept, God doesn't forget about you. No matter how badly you've screwed up or turned away or taken the wrong road, God doesn't give up on you.

I know the plans I have for you, God says, and they are such plans. Plans for good things. Travel plans for coming home. Call on me and I'm here. Come looking for me and you'll find me.

Always.

Forever.

No matter what.

November 10
Luke 19:1-10

Being vertically challenged myself, I've always loved Zaccheus. I've spent my life being ushered to the front row of group pictures, sitting on the front row of the choir and having to hem clothes already made for short people.

When I served as an interim pastor, the pulpit in that church had been made for a tall man. That first Sunday they could hear my sermon – they just couldn't see me. The second Sunday they'd provided a wooden drink crate for me to stand on. That was fine, until one of my heels went through a space in-between the slats and I nearly fell from grace (or at least, the Coke crate) during the sermon. The next Sunday the crate had been covered with plywood and a scrap of carpet, with the addition of a helpful carrying handle. So, I sympathize with Zaccheus climbing up the sycamore tree.

In many ways, it's Zaccheus who takes the initiative in this story and Jesus who responds to him. He takes the initiative to put himself in a place where he can really see this Jesus, and Jesus responds by inviting himself home for dinner. Jesus doesn't ask Zaccheus to right his accounts; Zaccheus volunteers to do it.

Where do you need to take the initiative in your life of faith? Maybe there's an avenue your soul has been longing to explore and to seek, but you've been telling yourself that you're too busy or maybe you're too scared to leave a spiritual comfort zone. Is it time to right a few accounts of your own and begin cleaning up a few messes you've been trying to ignore? Maybe it's time to put yourself out there, to reach out to a friend, an enemy or a stranger. Maybe it's time to take the initiative to be really honest with God and not merely nice. Are you willing to risk taking the next step?

Sometimes it's a little child who leads us.

And sometimes it's just a short person.

November 11
1 Thessalonians 3:6-13

Time magazine carried the article on how all of the old people had ruined Facebook. If you don't know it, Facebook is an internet site by which people can connect and keep up with each other. Originally geared towards kids, more and more "grown ups" started finding their way onto the site. As one woman noted, it was actually better for older folks. We've lived more places and had more friends with whom we've lost contact. We can take advantage of the chance to reconnect. For me, it became a way to reconnect joyfully with people whom I loved, from whom I learned and with whom I laughed.

Oddly enough, that's what I thought about when I read today's text. Timothy has just arrived with the news of the good people of Thessalonica, and the news seems to be mostly good. Paul celebrates their faith and indulges in some brotherly pride. How can we thank God enough for you? You bring us joy.

Who are the people in your life who bring you joy, the people whom you may not see very often but who inspire you nonetheless? Maybe it's someone who mentored you , a youth leader or a pastor who played an important role in your life. Maybe it's a friend who finds a way to live faithfully and with such joy that you cannot help but be lifted up. Or maybe it's the kid who was in your Sunday School class or handbell choir, the one who always seemed to be causing trouble or who had such a rough road to walk. But walk it they did, and here they are, all grown up and wonderful.

Whose life of faith brings you joy? Thank God for them. And then, if you are very brave, ask God how you might be such a person for others.

November 12
John 21:15-19

I was the world's easiest child to discipline. All I needed was the threat of disappointing my parents. (Once when I was a small child, my father spoke to me harshly regarding some infraction and I burst into tears. He went into the other room and teared up himself and neither one of us did that again.)

Have you ever disappointed someone? Have you ever said those words that you'd give anything if you could take back? Have you ever done that thing that you'd give your right arm to undo?

Peter knew about that. Three times he was given a chance to stand up for Jesus in his dark hour of literal trial. Three times he declared that he didn't even know the man. It surely must have been a bitter memory for him.

Now the night is over and it's a fresh morning on the beach. Jesus doesn't confront Peter about his betrayal but instead asks him, "Do you love me?" Three times. Three times a do over, three chances to declare what he should have said all along.

But Jesus doesn't stop with just asking Simon Peter to reverse himself. He gives him a job to do. He trusts Peter again and in so doing entrusts him with an important job.

"Feed my sheep."

Have you ever felt like you let God down? Maybe you forgot about all of those promises that you made in the heat of the moment. Maybe you turned your back on what you knew God was calling you to do. Maybe you just let God drift away, out of sight and out of mind.

Here's some good news for you. Jesus is waiting on the beach with a nice fire going and a good piece of fish to share. More than that, Jesus is waiting to restore things. "Do you love me?" He's going to ask. And you can tell the truth this time. Just don't be surprised if he gives you a job to do as well.

November 13
John 1:1-18

"And the Word became flesh, and dwelt among us."

It was one of the great scandals of the early Christian church, this notion of incarnation, the idea that God had chosen to take on the flesh and blood-ness of our lives. Many religions taught that earthly, fleshy stuff was lower on the spiritual scale. One should aspire to rise above earthly desires. And yet, here's God, walking around with his stomach rumbling.

It puzzles me why, if we believe in the incarnation and celebrate the incarnation, so many Christians are so uncomfortable with their own bodies. Traditionally, we've spent a lot of energy trying to corral those terrible bodily desires that might just get out of control. We didn't pay attention to our Jewish brothers and sisters who understand that desire can be part of God's gift to us (how's that for irony?).

One of the saints of the church, Julian of Norwich, used to say a prayer of gratitude when she had a bowel movement, for it was a reflection of the perfect working of her body. (Some of you will be able to relate to this more readily than others.) And yet it seems to me that many Christians I meet today would rather pretend that we just don't have bodies.

We starve them or stuff them. We give them too much work and too little play. We go for days and weeks and months – and maybe even more – without appreciating the marvel of their make-up.

As I recovered from a fractured pelvis, people asked me what the doctors were doing to help me heal. The answer was, not much. They told me not to put weight on one side. They gave me medicine to prevent blood clots while I'm off my feet. They tracked my progress.

Other than that, it was all my body's doing. My bones knew how to heal themselves. And frankly, I think that's pretty miraculous.

Today, take some time to appreciate your body. It doesn't matter if you don't like its size or shape. It doesn't matter if there are things that are wrong with it. Today, appreciate all that is right with it. Send messages of love and appreciation to it. And give thanks to God, who not only created the wonder of our bodies but then decided to join us in having one.

November 14
Isaiah 58:6-14

"I know every little girl thinks her father can do anything," I said. "But mine actually could."

He was something of a renaissance man, creating a successful career as an ad man, but was also a gifted painter, a craftsman who both designed and built beautiful furniture, a sailor, a golfer, a writer, a sports car racer... he had many things of which to be proud.

But one of the things he was proudest of was his support of Operation Smile, a group that repairs the cleft palates of children in third world countries. The wall above his desk in his office at home was plastered with family pictures. Among those photographs were pictures of children who'd been helped.

"Look at this," he'd say, his voice full of wonder. "This child will have a whole new chance at life."

My father was a faithful member of his church, showing up every Sunday for Bible study and worship for as long as his health permitted. But he understood that the flip side of that faithfulness was caring for God's children.

Isaiah understood that kind of faithfulness. He reminded the children of Israel that being faithful was all about helping free the captives, whether they were imprisoned by hunger, injustice or oppression or poverty. Things like fasting had been intended as a means to an end of focusing hearts on God. Israel mistook it for the end itself.

As hard as it may be for some of us to fast, it is much harder still to address issues of injustice and poverty and hunger.

Where do you get the ends and the means confused?

November 15
1 Samuel 16:14-23

She told me of her work, part of the healing team of the hospital. She wasn't a doctor or nurse or physical therapist. She was a harpist, and each week she brought her harp into the intensive care unit to play for the patients. The music soothed them and helped them.

I guess we could call David the very first music therapist, for it was his harp playing that soothed King Saul, giving him relief from what he called demons and from what we would call mental illness. David's music calmed his spirit.

Music is a powerful force. Groups who sing for Alzheimer patients report that people who couldn't tell you who they were or where they were will sing along on every song or hymn, singing word for word. Even after everything else is erased from the brain, it seems that music remains. Too often we treat music as an option when in fact, it seems to be a necessity for us living well and living fully.

Cultivate the gift of music in your life and in your community. If you can sing, then by all means sing. And if you cannot carry a tune in a bucket and have the rhythm of a stone, you can still listen.

Listen to music that uplifts you and inspires you.

Listen to music that makes you want to dance.

Listen to music that makes you want to pray.

November 16
John 14:15-25

The story is told that when Jesus was crucified the temple veil was split in two, that veil that kept the holy separate from the people. In a way today's text is also about the splitting of a veil. Jesus promises that after his work is done, the curtains that cloud our eyes will be lifted. We will be able to see how we are all connected, Jesus to God and Jesus to us and us to God. The believers will see, not because we're in some secret society, but because we've let go of the illusions that kept us blind.

We are a part of Jesus and he is a part of us, and if it all sounds a bit mystical, then maybe because it is. Jesus himself goes round and round trying to explain it. Maybe it's something that has to be seen rather than said, something we feel in our souls more than we can say with our mouths.

We see who we belong to and who is a part of us and in that moment following Jesus' commandments isn't about following the rules that we don't really like. It's what we gladly do because we love him and want to be more like him, to live in a way that people know we're kin. We don't have to gird up our loins to follow this way. We just have to open our heart.

Jesus belongs to God and we belong to Jesus and he belongs to us. I think that's about enough wonder for one day.

November 17
Hosea 2:16-23

The family therapist Virginia Satir believed that when we were able to act out something physically we got it at a deeper level than just talking about it. Hosea would have been her prize pupil. He didn't just talk about God's judgments and Israel's faithlessness; he acted it out through his life.

Under God's direction, he took a prostitute as a wife. Among his children were "Not pitied" and "Not my people." (If ever two kids were destined for therapy...) God was writing the message in bold letters: Israel had been faithless, going after other gods. So God was done with them.

Except that wasn't the end of the story.

Even though God had every reason to do otherwise, God doesn't give up on Israel. The day will come when God will embrace them, when "Not my people" gets a new name of "Absolutely my people."

I suspect that there's not a one of us who, in ways large or small, hasn't had a time of turning our backs on God. We know God is calling us to speak but we stay silent out of fear. We know God is calling us to act but we stay put out of fear of the unknown or fear of failure. God is calling us to give but we hold back out of fear of scarcity.

God's forgiveness doesn't come cheaply, nor is it a ticket to do what we jolly well please because there's a get out of jail free card at the end. Instead, it is the life-changing embrace of love that welcomes us when we've no reason to expect it. We cannot fail deeply enough for God to give us up.

We are indeed God's people, God's children.

And that is blessing enough for today.

November 18
Luke 6:27-38

As I write this, in the United States we are living in a bitterly partisan time. Members of Congress aren't challenging each other to duels, but it's not so far removed from that. If a butterfly flaps his wings and causes a tidal wave on the other side of the world, you can bet that Republican and Democratic pundits will be making the Sunday talk shows to expound as to why the other party is to blame for said butterfly. I'll admit that my own political passions can get pretty heated at times.

Of course, this doesn't even begin to touch the political passions inside the Church. Churches split up and people take sides and sometimes even sue each other. Members of a body refuse to speak to each other because they are so certain that the other one is wrong.

Then comes Jesus with this tough bit of instruction. Love your enemies. Do good to those who hate you. Bless those who curse you. Pray for those who abuse you.

Gee whiz, Jesus, where's the fun in that?

The point isn't that our prayers will magically transport the other person over to our side. The point is that when we follow this path, it changes us. Sometimes enemies start looking less like enemies and more like just people with whom we disagree.

Today think about someone for whom you need to pray (mostly because you need to do it) and then ask for God's help in doing just that.

November 19
Colossians 2:1-6

It's an old habit to which I've lately returned. Each morning as I hang out with my cat I make a list of five things for which I'm grateful from the previous day as well as five people whom I appreciate. On some days there are specific events for which I'm grateful, like time with a friend or being able to work out a problem. Other days I look around and take the time to appreciate what I often take for granted: my home, my work, my friends and family (including the four legged ones), my church, the gift of being able to sing in a choir, the gift of being able to run and move my body.

Giving thanks becomes in and of itself a gift. Some days it's like a navigator finding that North Star and re-ordering course. I may be too busy or not busy enough. I may have problems to solve and issues to tackle. I may have relationships to mend or to tend.

But beneath it all and beyond it all, I am blessed. On any given day I have a hundred things for which to be thankful. I suspect, so do you.

What would happen if you took a gratitude challenge? Every night before going to sleep or every morning upon rising, what would happen if you looked for things for which to be grateful?

I dare you to try.

November 20
Mark 1:32-39

The to-do list was pretty full for Jesus. He filled his day healing and casting out demons. And yet, when morning came, he was up early ("a great while before day") to go off by himself and pray.

There is something important about taking a pause in the beginning of the day, a break between our sleeping and our ceaseless doing. If you're like me, you can find a hundred excuses as to why it's impossible. If you have children at home you have even more reasons.

But when there is a clear intention to find a way, a way can be found. Sometimes it's not the perfect way. Sometimes good things have to be sacrificed to better things. Because I need a certain number of hours of sleep in order to function well, my early rising has meant that I go to bed early. I have to give up pointless channel surfing – either I record the show or it probably doesn't get watched. But I've found that life can go on.

The point is that Jesus knew that in order to do his work and face his days he needed time alone with God. Why do we think we can get away without it?

November 21
Luke 21:1-4

God,
I feel ashamed to come to you
    with so little
        but this penny or two is all that I have
            in threadbare pockets.
            What good could it do?
God,
I feel ashamed to come to you
    with so little
        but this moment or two are all that can be squeezed
            from a day with too many demands
            and not enough hours.
God,
I feel ashamed to come to you
    with so little
        but great things seem to be beyond me
        and this small, stupid, commonplace act
            seems to be all I have to offer.
God,
I feel ashamed to come to you
    with so little understanding
    that your ways are not my ways
    and my judgments are not yours.
            Whatever is in my hands
            whatever is in my pockets
            whatever is in my heart
                may I give it to you.

November 22
Psalm 26

I've learned that there's a very powerful two-word phrase (other than "I do.") It's "right now." Not as in, "I want that report RIGHT NOW!" The way I encourage clients to use it is in adding it on to the very real and very negative thing they are feeling. Right now I feel like I don't have a friend in the world. Right now I feel hopeless. Those feelings may be very real feelings but when you add "right now" to them it opens the door to the possibility that you may feel differently at some other time. Right now I feel this way... but tomorrow may be different.

The psalmist had their own version of right now. Things aren't so good now but once upon a time they were. Once upon a time they were, and I trust they shall be again. Once I laughed and will laugh again. Such is a prayer of faith and of trust.

If you read this in a time of delight, then enjoy and give thanks for such a time. But if you're struggling, hold tight to this psalm. Once I laughed... and I will laugh again.

By God's grace.

So be it.

November 23
Matthew 13:31-35

I don't know much about the cultivation of mustard seeds but I do know a little bit about yeast. Back in the days when my days weren't quite so scheduled I used to love to make bread.

One of the things a baker learns early on is not to overwork the bread. Dough that has been kneaded too many times will produce bread that's tough instead of soft. You have to knead it in order to help get things started... and then you leave it alone. You place it in a warm place, cover it with a cloth... and leave it alone.

You don't have to stand over the dough to supervise its rising. Checking on it every five minutes to see if it's started rising yet is actually counterproductive. You kneed the dough, create the right conditions for its success... and then leave it alone.

What a great image for the work of God's kingdom. We do the things that are ours to do. We work to create a climate and condition where grace may flow. And then we trust God's Spirit to keep working even when we cannot see the work happening.

Do what you can. Create safe spaces and inviting places. And let God work.

You don't have to do it all. You cannot do it all. Indeed, you get in the way when you try to do it all. Part of our work is trusting that the kingdom we cannot yet see is in fact still alive and growing in our midst.

What do you need to do today? What do you need not to do?

November 24
Philippians 4:4-7

After my mother died, my sister-in-law passed along a prayer to me. Some years before she and my brother had been through a particularly difficult time with work and family concerns.

One day she opened a letter from my mom. There was no note inside, just a copy of a prayer. The prayer was a request either to change the situation at hand or to give the pray-er the strength to get through it. The prayer was a gift to them… as it was to me.

We do Paul an injustice if we read his words to the Philippians as an encouragement to just pretend that hard things aren't hard and scary things aren't scary. Talk to God about them, Paul writes, and then trust God with it. For you, trusting God may mean following God's leading to allow yourself to get help and support for whatever you're facing. It may mean that God leads you to make some hard choices. The situation may change or you may simply have the grace and the strength for getting through it.

But down deep the river of joy still flows. It's there, Paul says. Dip into it. Stick your toe in. Dive right in if you dare. For there is a peace that goes beyond our ability to explain that will hold you up and carry you through.

November 25
Matthew 23: 37-39

I've not seen it in real life myself but I've seen it many times on television shows. An animal gives birth to a batch of children - puppies or kittens or even chickens. The mother curves her body protectively around her young ones. A hen spreads her wings over her baby chicks. It is both a protective and nurturing act.

In a tender and touching passage, Jesus uses the image to describe himself. He's been railing against the Pharisees and their hypocrisy, and there's no way to read his words without imagining him yelling them. "Woe to you!" he shouts. You brood of vipers... you are going straight to hell.

Suddenly it's as if his anger is spent and he nearly weeps for the pain and compassion of it. Jerusalem, he laments, what are we to do with you? You keep killing God's messengers.

Oh, my people... if you would but allow it I would wrap you up in my arms, I'd encircle you like a momma hen gathering in her chicks. (Jesus the Momma Hen is one advent carol that is yet to be written.)

I wonder how many times he says it to us... Oh, my people.. my sisters... my brothers... I wanted to wrap you up in my love. I wanted to hold you in the safety of my Spirit. I wanted to bring you into my own heart.

The Pharisees, at least some of them, pushed Jesus away. What will you do?

Jesus the Momma Hen is waiting.

November 26
John 3:16-21

Sometimes the most familiar verses are the hardest. If we can quote any scripture at all, many of us can quote John 3:16. For some of us, it may unfortunately conjure up a guy in a rainbow colored wig at a football game holding it up on a sign before it stirs theological reflection. (I always wondered if anyone actually saw that and thought, "A crazy guy in a rainbow wig - I want to be a part of THAT religion!")

The point is that God isn't mad at us. God isn't angry with us. God yearns for us so much that God sent a part of God's own self. The most intimate, the most valuable gift possible – God's own son.

There is no length to which God will not go for your sake... and mine. God will go all out and all in just to bring us close. God will do whatever it takes to open the door. God won't drag us through it. We have to make that choice ourselves. But God will hold it open for us as long as it takes.

God isn't mad with us. Not only that, God loves us more than we can say.

Today take some time to talk with this God who loves you that much. There's nothing you have to hide and nothing you have to fear. In God, there is only love for you.

November 27
Luke 1:5-25

So there was Zechariah going about his priestly duties. Imagine his surprise when an angel showed up. Not only that, but an angel who tells him that even though he and his wife are getting along in years, they're going to have a son. Surely he knew the stories of Abraham and Sarah but he didn't expect to be living them.

There God goes again, bringing new life where there was no reasonable hope of it. There God goes again, re-igniting a dream that had long been given up. No wonder Zechariah left the Temple unable to talk. What could he have said had he been able to speak? They would have thought he'd gone mad.

What have you given up on? Personally, I've given up on getting that growth spurt. As much as I'd love another inch or two or three, I don't think it's coming my way. But I can live with that.

What have you given up on God being able to do in your life? What have you told yourself you'll never do or be or have? God still has a way of working surprises.

Open your heart to God, even those places that seem dead to you. Talk together about God's dream for you and your dream for yourself.

Then be willing to be surprised.

November 28
Exodus 1:15-22

Thank you, God, for the disobedient among us.
Thank you for the ones wise enough to see injustice
    and brave enough to confront it
    in the service of doing your will.
Thank you for people brave enough
    to sit down on buses
    and at lunch counters.
Thank you for those brave enough
    to stand up for those
    who are being bullied
    and not given a fair shake or fair chance
        even when it costs them their own standing.
Thank you for those clever enough
    to find their way around and though
    systems that oppress.

God,
    let us not be blinded by convenience or custom.
Give us the eyes to see where your pathway lies
    and the courage to follow
    even when it means breaking the rules.

November 29
Exodus 2:1-12

Not to put too fine of a point on it, but it was the women who made it all possible.

First was Moses' mother. She scrambled and struggled to find a way to protect her baby boy. She hid him for the first three months, heart racing every time he cried at the wrong time. Finally it was all too much. She knew she couldn't keep hiding him – he was bound to be discovered and if he was discovered he'd be killed. Putting him into the river was a risky move with no guarantee of success but it was the only option she had left.

Her tears mixed in with the reeds as she wove his basket. Perhaps he'd drown or be eaten by a wild animal or be found and killed on the spot. But maybe he'd be rescued. The odds were slim but they were the only odds she had. Later she'd never know how she found the strength to let that basket go into the water.

Her daughter stood close by because good or bad, she had to know what happened to the boy. It was her daughter who was quick thinking, stepping forward to volunteer her own mother as a nurse.

Finally there is Pharaoh's daughter. She recognizes the boy as belonging to the Hebrews, a child who should have been killed. But she cannot resist his tiny hands and big eyes. She welcomes him as her own and gives him a home.

They are the warm-up act before the big show. And yet, without them there would have been no Moses to lead Israel to freedom.

Today give thanks for those unseen people who by their faithfulness make miracles possible. Who knows – you may even be one of them.

November 30
Ephesians 2:1-10

The other Sunday our worship included the singing of one of the hymn texts that I've written. I wrote it a number of years ago but I still remember the care with which I worked. I thought about the subject - how to frame it and develop it. What meter would I use? What was the rhyming scheme going to be? What tune would work best for this hymn? I looked for just the right words, just the right phrases. I made sure that it not only worked on the page but it worked when I sang it.

As we sat down after singing I turned to the woman next to me and said, "I do like that hymn." The comment came not out of a boastful spirit but out of a full heart. Like many craftsmen, I delighted in my creation. I delighted in hearing a sanctuary filled with people singing these words not out of misplaced ego but out of that delight. It made me so happy to see one of my creations fulfilling its purpose.

In Greek one of the words for beautiful denotes something that is beautiful because it so clearly and fully fulfills the purpose for which it was made. I was happy because, in that respect, my hymn felt beautiful to me.

In Ephesians we get the picture that we are the craft which Jesus is creating. May we be beautiful as we live out our own purposes and fulfill that for which our lives were created.

December 1
2 Kings 4:1-7

Manna in the wilderness.
Oil for a widow's debts.
Bread and fish for a crowd.
  When it seems as though there is nothing
  and nowhere to turn
  and we are left with empty bellies
   or unimaginable futures
God steps in
 and there is enough.
 Enough.
 Just enough.

God, we enter a season in which
 much that surrounds us
  screams more...
   have more
   give more
   do more
   eat more.

In such a time, God, remind us of the grace of enough.
And in our own times of scarcity
  of money
  or of time
  or of hope,
 remind us of the grace of enough.

December 2
Colossians 4:2-6

I almost missed it.

As I read and re-read this passage and contemplated its meaning and its meaning for me and whoever might be reading this, I almost missed it. Paul asks the people to pray for him. Nothing unusual there. But pay attention to what he asks them to pray for.

Paul doesn't ask for prayers for release from prison. He asks that a door might be opened to do God's work where he is.

I'm no expert on first century penal systems but I have to think that Paul's accommodations weren't overly comfortable. Even if they were, this peripatetic preacher was being kept in one place. And yet, Paul doesn't ask for prayers for release. He asks that other kinds of doors might be opened, that he might know how best to speak of the grace that changed his life.

We pray often for God to change the circumstances of our lives and I believe it is not an unfaithful prayer to make. But how many times do we pray to find grace and to find God and to find a way of serving where we are?

Wherever you are today, ask for the courage and wisdom to pray such a prayer. Where you are physically. Where you are emotionally. Where you are financially. Where you are spiritually.

Even here, ask God to use you.

December 3
Isaiah 55:12-23

She shared with me her "favorite verse." "And it came to pass..." I told her my favorite was from Ecclesiastes: "Of making many books there is no end and the reading of them is much weariness of the flesh." (I discovered that verse in seminary during a time in which it was particularly appropriate.) Had I thought about it, since we were standing in the midst of a church reception, I could have said today's text: "Eat what is good and delight yourself in fatness." Now there's a text for the holiday season.

The "meat" of today's text, of course, is God's invitation to the people. Stop eating the things that don't fill you up. Stop spending your money on things that don't satisfy you. You've got everything you could want, everything you'll ever need right here. Let me fill you.

For what are you hungry? Where do you have that holy itch? You know the one I'm talking about. It's like standing in front of the open refrigerator, wanting something but you don't know what, hoping it will jump out and call your name. Sometimes our spirits do a lot of refrigerator gazing.

In what place does your heart feel empty? In what direction does your spirit long? What are you missing? What are you craving?

What are you waiting for? God is right here, waiting, wanting willing to give you delight.

What are you waiting for? Open yourself up to God.

December 4
Luke 1:26-38

Today's text has been a favorite subject for artists through the ages. Usually they paint a radiant Gabriel hovering over a calm and serene Mary, her beautiful alabaster skin testifying to the fact that she didn't get outdoors much. Mary, looking sometimes a bit older than the young girl she probably was. She always looks completely unperturbed to be discussing her life with an angel.

Maybe they were all painting the end of the text, because the beginning presents a very different picture. At first, Mary was scared. And after all, who can really blame her? It's one thing to read about angels. It's another thing altogether to have one showing up on your doorstep, not to mention one bearing sonogram pictures you didn't know you needed.

Then Mary was confused. None of this made sense to her. Whatever her dreams were for her upcoming life with Joseph,

raising the Messiah had not been a part of the plan. She gives voice to her confusion and doubts. "How can this be?"

Only after the fear and doubt and confusion comes the acceptance. "Let it be to me." I'm willing. I don't know that I understand it all, but I'm willing.

If we only look at the third scene in this story, we get a terribly distorted picture. We think of ourselves somehow less than faithful if we also find ourselves face to face with fear, if our souls are confused and our hearts are filled with doubt. Those places are not the end points of our journeys, but sometimes we have to travel through them nonetheless.

Wherever you are in your faith, today let that simply be where you are. No judgment. No beating yourself up for not being better or stronger or whatever it is you think you are lacking.

Accept where you are then ask for God's help in taking the next small step.

December 5
Psalm 144

"Who are we that God should even pay attention to us?" the psalmist asks. And in the next breath the psalmists asks this cosmic God for some very specific help. "Rescue me!"

It is the eternal tension of our faith. Who are we that God should be mindful of us? We are as small as ants when compared to God's grandeur. The God who had the power to create all of creation surely has more important things to consider than our petty lives. And yet, not only does God take notice of us, God cares about us.

My mom used to say that as we grew up, her favorite time of the day was when she heard us coming in the back door from school. "Hey mom – guess what happened today!" As impossible as it is to comprehend, this God of all creation is also like a parent, waiting for us to walk in the door and say, "Hey mom, hey dad – guess what happened!" This God wants us to reach out for help, to open up our hearts with all of the good, bad and indifferent desires in them.

Standing in the midst of Advent, we remember that it's true. God loved us so much and cared so much about our lives that

God took on the limitations of our flesh to walk among us as one of us.

Today, allow yourself to feel the awe of this God who is beyond our ability to understand fully or to grasp completely. Then allow yourself to talk freely with this God who knows us right well and yet loves us completely.

December 6
Micah 4:1-7

Usually when I read this verse, I focus on the "swords into plowshares" part of it. And why wouldn't I? It's a beautiful, hopeful, challenging picture of a time when the weapons of war will be transformed into the tools of farming, the taking of life replaced by the nourishing of life.

But today I am drawn to the verses near the close of this section. God will gather up the exiles and God will put the lame on sure footing. I've known only a few physical exiles — my Cuban born Spanish teacher, the Bosnian families we helped resettle. I've known a lot more spiritual exiles.

They are the people who feel cut off from the spiritual homes who raised them. They no longer share the same beliefs but they no longer know where home is. Or they're the ones who have been driven out from their spiritual homes because of what they've done or who they are. They've been told they are no longer welcome.

And then there are the exiles who simply wandered away. Life got too rough or their spirit took too many bruises or their soul filled with too many questions and they wandered away from places that once felt like home. They are surprised to find themselves in the wilderness but are not at all certain if they could even find home again.

Do you know them? Maybe you are one of them. If so, hear these words of the prophet. God doesn't forget about you, no matter how far you are from the faith that once was so certain. No matter how cut off you feel from God's family. God doesn't forget about you. The day will come – maybe soon and maybe in time – when God will lead you to the address with your name on it.

December 7
Luke 1:39-45

And blessed is she who believed...
Is Elizabeth speaking of Mary... or of herself? She has been singing a hymn of blessing for this young woman who is carrying the love of the world in her body. But somehow I think Elizabeth is at least partially thinking of herself. Her hand over her belly, she's felt the baby kick and she cannot help but smile. We're told that Zechariah couldn't believe the news that he was going to be a dad. We're not told how Elizabeth reacted. But as the boy grew within her, so did her sweet joy.

Sometimes it takes nine months – or more – for God's promises to grow to fruition. And sometimes when they get here, they don't look exactly like we thought they would. (Did Elizabeth anticipate the whole honey and locust diet?) But blessed are they... blessed are you when you believe that God's promises to you will not be barren. Birthing day will come... in some time and in some fashion. Birthing day will come.

Are there places in your life that feel empty... barren... hopeless? Maybe everybody sees it, like the people who knew Elizabeth had no children. Or maybe you keep it hidden well so that no one would guess. Or maybe life is pretty darn good... but there's a little rumbling in your soul that there may yet be the next step on your journey.

God has made promises to you, too. Promises that God is not yet done with you, nor done with your life. Promises that God is still working in you and through you. Promises that God is still about birthing new things.

Blessed is she.... Blessed are you who believes that there will be more.

December 8
Isaiah 55:1-8

Hesitantly, you peer into the banquet hall. When the host approaches you, you try to get away without being noticed, but he calls out to you.

"Hey you – yes, you. Come on in. The party has started and the buffet is spread and it's all good stuff."

He notices the grease splattered bag that you're half-hiding. "Hey you – yes, you. Why are you bothering with that fast food that will never satisfy you? Sink your teeth into this food that's filling, good for body and soul."

Cautiously, you follow him into the party. He hands you a plate, and for a while you stand by the buffet, overwhelmed by the delicious choices. It is all so strange to you, so much more than you could have dreamed. Then you start to smile, to grin and soon you even start to laugh.

This is where you belonged. All along, you never knew, you never knew such a party existed and certainly never knew you were included. But now you're here, discovering that your name's been on the guest list all along.

You belong. You have a place at the feast of God. Regardless of the size of your bank accounts, at this party you discover how very rich you are. Your plate is piled high with wonder and your glass is overflowing with love. It reaches way down into your bones, giving you strength. It stretches your spirit out until it's bigger than you ever dreamed possible.

God wants for you a life that matters. God invites you to a life not only of service but also of joy, for indeed, they are frequently one and the same.

Hey you – yes you. The party has started. Come on in...

December 9
Isaiah 55:6-13

After my grandfather died, my mother's doctor reminded her that she was going to have to take a more parental role with my grandmother. After all, my grandmother was the kind of woman who'd never driven a car or written a check (not so unusual in those days.) So my adult mother began talking with her mother, telling her what they needed to do and what they were going to do.

My grandmother finally interrupted her.

"I don't know who you think you are," she said, "but I am still your mother."

I thought of that story as I read today's text. Lest Israel become too familiar with the almighty, God makes it clear. "I don't know who you think you are, but I am still your God. I'm still thinking thoughts you can't begin to hold in your head.

It's a creative tension that we're called to hold. On the one hand, God becomes intimately familiar, taking on the same bodies we have and sharing in our same experiences. God speaks of being as close as our next breath.

And yet, God is still God. We may know of God and we may know God, but we cannot completely know God. There is always something just beyond our grasp, something too big for us to take in.

Therefore, we are called to act and to speak with a certain humility when it comes to God. We know what we know but we also know that knowledge is partial. "This is what I believe God is saying to me,'" we may say with certainty... but we do well in being cautious about making absolute pronouncements about what God is thinking.

For all we know of God, we know only in part. As you go through your day, ask God to help you keep your mind and your spirit open to learning more, understanding more. Ask God to help you keep the balance between speaking the truth of your faith experience with both confidence and humility.

December 10
Luke 1:46-56

When we first meet Mary, she is troubled and filled with questions. Out of the blue, her world is being turned upside down. She's just a girl, just another girl making her way through life never expecting to find herself talking with angels or pregnant with God's son.

Seeing her today, it's clear that something has happened. Something more than just finding herself pregnant. Something more than discovering her old cousin Elizabeth to be pregnant as well, as amazing as both of those facts are. Mary is no longer troubled or filled with questions. Now Mary stands straight and speaks with a clear prophetic voice. She speaks of the world being turned upside down and finds a song of praise in those words.

What made the difference? The only thing that the text tells us is that she said yes. She allowed herself to become the person God intended for her to be. Standing in the truth of who God created her to be she was free to speak the truth of what God was doing in the world.

Let's face it — we're not going to be faced with the same decision that Mary faced. And yet, we are.

God may not be asking us to give birth to and raise up God in the flesh. But God is asking us to be who we were created to be, to do that which we are called to do. What that looks like in each of our lives will be as different as our fingerprints.

I don't know what that means for you. Some days I'm not sure even of what it means for me. But I do know that when we are able to say yes to God, when we step into the lives that God created us to live then we are freed to stand tall, to speak clearly and boldly.

It is then that we find our own true voice.

December 11
Luke 1:57-80

The stories of Advent are filled with unexpected twists and turns. There's a much too old woman becoming pregnant. There's a priest who loses his voice and a baby name that is seemingly out of the blue. There's a brand new father who regains his speech and cannot help but sing. Elizabeth and Zechariah's friends cannot help but wonder what in the world is going on.

The stories of Advent are filled with unexpected twists and turns. Too familiar with routine, we sometimes miss the surprising shock of them. We know the story – we know how it goes and how it ends. We even know some Christmas carols by heart. We can almost quote the Luke 2 version of the Nativity because it's in "A Charlie Brown Christmas."

But what if…

What if God still wanted to surprise us? What if God wasn't done with the unexpected, with unexpected gifts and unexpected callings and finding new songs with voices we didn't know we had?

It's two weeks until Christmas. You may be overwhelmed with shopping or cooking or travel plans or dreading old family dramas. You may be burdened by worries about how to pay for things or grief for the empty places at your table. But in the midst of the bustle and busy, keep your eyes open. In the midst of the memories and questions, keep your minds open. In the midst of all that is good in this season and all that is commercial and all that is just a little too much, keep your hearts open.

For God has been known to do unexpected things.

Even with the likes of us.

December 12
Isaiah 40:1-11

Being a choir geek, on my iPod I have a section for choral music, mostly anthems I've sung and love to sing. (Being an alto, it's sometimes surprising to hear what the actual melody sounds like.) One of my favorites is an African-American spiritual, *The Storm is Passing Over*. When I hear the opening words ("Take courage my soul, and let us journey on") they never fail to lift me up and encourage me.

Today's text is that kind of song. Israel is in exile with soul and spirit bruised and battered. "Speak tenderly to her," God says. A calming, soothing voice for the one who is in shock, the one who is hurt, the one who has just been through a terrible thing. The song is all about hard things becoming easier. Curvy roads becoming straight shots. Tall mountains becoming gentle hills. Deep valleys being flattened out. The exile was absolutely shattering for Israel on every level – physical and emotional but especially spiritual.

Today's song reminds them that their brokenness isn't the final chapter. They may feel lost but they are still held in God's hand. Everything they believed may be called into question but God is still there.

This season may be a comfort for you as familiar music and traditions wrap you round like a favorite blanket. This season might be a joy for you as you delight in the celebrations. This season might be a struggle for you as you measure it against the abundance or the ease of Christmases past. This season might be an ache for you as you feel the emptiness- the empty place at the table or the empty place in your own soul.

Whatever the case, take courage my soul and let us journey on. For God goes before us and with us... and we are not alone. The way may yet be made straight and the deep places will be lifted up. And God will speak tenderly to us, to each of us, with exactly the words we need to hear.

December 13
1 John 4:13-25

As we walk through the gospels the message comes a hundred different ways. You don't have to be scared. Don't be so scared. Fear not. It comes to Mary while she's conversing with an angel. It comes to shepherds who have their evening interrupted. It comes to disciples in the midst of a storm. It comes to bewildered and perplexed friends of Jesus who only want to finish burying him well. Don't be so scared.

And now it comes near the end of the story. Perhaps written at the end of the first Christian century, the message is clear. Our way is the way of love and not fear.

Even though we may have a quite sophisticated theology, deep inside some of us are still driven (at least occasionally) by that demon god who tells us that we are not good enough or we haven't done enough. Instead of hearing the angel songs of joy we hear all of the voices of those who told us there was something wrong with what we believed or how we lived - a judgment rooted not in the gospel but in habit, fear or prejudice. Fear is a weed that starts small but quickly spreads if left unchecked.

It's not about fear, the writer of 1 John says. Our way is the way of love. This is how you know you're on the way, by your love. This is how you know you're worshiping the God revealed in Jesus and not some shabby fake. We know because there is love there.

Love may challenge and love may correct but love will never shame. Love may call us out to uncomfortable places but love will never cast us aside. Love may demand but will never demean. Love will never ask us to dim our light lest we shine too brightly. Love will never ask us to be less than we were created to be.

By this we know God. By this we follow Jesus. By this we serve one another.

Love.

Not fear.

December 14
2 Kings 4:8-10

Some years ago it seemed that "hospitality" was the hot topic for Christian publishing. Books and Bible studies sprung up to reassure (mostly women) Christians that hospitality was indeed a spiritual gift and to teach them how to exercise it.

That's a study this wealthy woman didn't need. When Elisha the visiting prophet was in town she and her husband would treat him to dinner. She finally told her husband that she thought Elisha was the real deal and that she wanted to give him a place to stay while he was in town.

She would have done Martha Stewart proud – a bed, a lamp, a table and a chair. It was everything a visiting prophet would have needed. I can only imagine how good it felt to Elisha to have this home away from home.

We all need to receive – and to offer such a gift, spiritually if not materially (although if that is a material gift you have to offer, blessings upon you. Create warm and welcoming spaces for your guests.) We all need people in our lives who create a space in which we can just relax. We can just be.

One of the best gifts we can offer to each other is the gift of space in which we can be who we are, how we are in any given moment. If you're not a member of the clergy, I'll let you in on a little secret: ministers need it most of all. (Here's a radical thought: Invite your minister to dinner and don't ask them to say the blessing.)

Today think about the ways in which you can offer such hospitality to another. Think about places in which you might receive it.

December 15
2 Kings 4:11-17

Elisha was grateful for this bit of hospitality so he decides to reward his hostess. There's only one problem: he can't get her to ask for anything. Everything is just fine, as far as she's concerned. She doesn't need Elisha to do anything for her. Really, she's fine.

Finally it's Elisha's servant who speaks up on her behalf. She doesn't have a son and her husband is quite old so the prospects aren't looking good. This, of course, was more than an empty nest matter. Children were the only safety net for them as they grew older.

So Elisha tells her that she's going to have a son. Her response? "Don't lie to me." You can almost feel the disappointment in her. She's done nothing but offer this man hospitality and he chooses to repay her by cruelly mocking her. It was her heart's desire that had been put upon a shelf and there was no good reason to believe it could be otherwise. Nowhere in our text does she say to him, "I believe."

Martha Stewart or not, we may be closer to this woman than we know. How many times has God pulled up a chair beside us, rested a head in a hand and said. "So, what do you need me to do for you?" There are a hundred answers we'd like to give but what we really say is, "Nothing. I'm fine." Life is okay and okay is good enough.

"No, really," God says. "What do you need?"

This text reminds me of two things. One is that although not every prayer is answered in the way that we think we want, we may yet ask God for what we need. It's okay to ask. Secondly, God may yet do things in our lives that we are completely sure are impossible.

If you don't think that's true, just ask this woman who quite unexpectedly had to find room not only for a visiting prophet but also for a nursery, all done up in baby blue.

December 16
2 Kings 4:18-31

Yesterday we ended with the cry of an unexpected baby. Today we begin with the anguished cry of an angry and terrified mother. The little boy came and grew until one day he complained of a very bad headache… and then he said no more.

His mother is a mix of faith ("It will be all right"), anxiety ("Urge the animal on and do not hold back") and anger. You can hear the emotion in her voice even after all these years. "Did I not say' Do not mislead me'?" She was given a son but now he has been taken away. She's not going to leave without Elisha coming with her.

I often hear people talk about what they "should" be feeling. They should be thankful. They should be grateful. They shouldn't be angry. They shouldn't be upset. I hear people upset with themselves because their feelings aren't neat and simple and covered by checking one and only one box.

Life's a lot messier than that. Even the Christian life. Especially the Christian life. In one breath we're begging God to hear us and in another breath we're raging at God for not doing what we wanted or needed or not saving the person we loved.

None of these things are signs that our faith is lacking or that our devotion should be found wanting. It is a sign that our faith gets lived out in the midst of our messy lives.

Talk with God today about your messy life. If you're angry, have at it. If you're frustrated and confused, let it rip. If you want to believe or to trust or to find a hope that's bigger than what lies before you but you don't know that you can, tell God about it.

God's not company. God's family, and we don't have to straighten up our lives before we can invite God in.

December 17
2 Kings 4:32-37

The story we've been following of Elisha and the Shummanite woman has a happy ending after all. Elisha does a kind of full body CPR on the dead boy. He does it once, walks around a bit then does a second round. The boy sneezes seven times and opens his eyes to life.

As you recall from yesterday, this is the woman who didn't hide her anger and frustration from Elisha. She let the prophet have it. And still he healed her boy.

What feels dead in your life? Maybe nothing. If so, give thanks and go your way. Or maybe what is dead is what needs to be gone because it doesn't belong in your life now - or maybe it never did.

But there may be something dead that you long to have living again. A hope. A dream. A possibility that doesn't seem quite possible. Or a relationship that doesn't seem relatable anymore.

Maybe it's a faith that you're too embarrassed to admit feels too musty and dusty and cramped. It's Advent and we're supposed to be all spiritual but sometimes we feel more desert than devotion.

Whatever the case, be as bold as this Shummanite woman. Yell at God if need be then ask of God what you will. It may take a while. There may be sneezes involved. And if you ask God to breathe life in your life, it may look wildly different than what you'd planned.

Still, there's life to be had.

So what needs a new breath in your life?

December 18
Isaiah 42:1-9

I have been a part of more commencement ceremonies than I care to remember. Some, if not most, of the speeches have been somewhat forgettable. The one speech that sticks with me was from my high school graduation.

Our speaker was Mary Garber, a local sportswriter who was far ahead of her time. But Garber wasn't just known as a pioneering woman who broke through gender barriers. She was also known as a writer who'd write about anybody, no matter their skin color or economic standing. One of the things that I remember Garber talking about was some of the forgotten lines on our newly minted high school diplomas: "rights and responsibilities." As high school graduates we had a certain standing. But that standing carried with it responsibilities.

Not so many days ago we were reminded of God's great love for the people of Israel, comforting them and reaching out to them. Today's text reminds us that this salvation carries with it responsibilities. They are to be a light. They are to be about the work of liberation, and freedom not just for themselves. They are to be gift for the world.

So it is with us. God may have – and probably has – carried you through a difficult time or two. For all of us, God has certainly echoed the same words of love, care and compassion. But the story doesn't stop there. God both holds us and sends us out.

There is a purpose for your life, a purpose for all of our lives. In ways as individual as our fingerprints, we are called to be about God's work of doing justice.

What does it mean for you to do justice today?

December 19
Jeremiah 31:27-34

Knee deep in Advent as we are, it's hard to read these words and not think of Jesus. No longer will God's law be cast in stone, the prophet Isaiah proclaims, but it will be written on our very hearts. And now we celebrate that Jesus came to be God's heart among us.

What is it that you know? What do you know down deep in your heart? What do you know about who God is and who God is in your life? What do you know about who you are to God?

Some things may pop quickly to the surface like candy in a Pez dispenser. Measure them against what Jesus said and did. Are they consistent with what Jesus taught about grace or are they founded on a vague and global guilt? Do they ring with the truth of Jesus' command to love God and others and ourselves or are they distorted by old and angry judgments?

Go down deeper. What is it that you know? Go beyond the obvious and what they taught you in Sunday School was the right answer. What do you know, really know in your heart? If you bump up against not knowing, don't despair. Be willing to sit with it, to hold it gently. Instead of rushing for an easy answer, be willing to say, "I don't know." Such courage is often the beginning of faith.

Today in the midst of all that must be bought or wrapped or baked, let yourself take a few minutes to sit. In the midst of all of the places you must go, take a moment to go into your own heart.

God wants to leave a message for you there.

December 20
Isaiah 60:1-7

It doesn't take much imagination to imagine that one of the consequences of the Babylonian exile was families being torn apart. Some are taken away because of the skills they can offer while others remain in their shattered homes. They certainly have no say in whether they stay or whether they go. For those who stay, poverty replaces plenty. So much has been destroyed and the best of what they have has been taken away.

So it is that the prophet gives a vision of a time when these things will be reversed. Children will return home. Plenty will replace poverty. All of the delights that had been denied them in defeat will now flow with abundance.

One of the great themes of Advent is the theme of hope. Unto you a child is born and unto the world a light has come. This hope is based in a God who keeps writing the next chapter. God keeps opening the book. God never says to us, "You're done."

These may be words that you need right now, or they may be words that you need to share. God knows what darkness is like and God is still about bringing light. God knows the exiles we've found ourselves in and God is still about bringing us home. God knows about all we have lost along the way and God is still about restoring our souls.

Pick yourself up, for your light has come.

Get up and shine, for God is come and God is with us.

No matter where you've been or what you've been through, the invitation is still for you: Get up and shine.

December 21
Isaiah 61:1-4

It's getting near Christmas time as you read this, but as I'm writing it's hurricane season. A storm has just slashed its way up the east coast and everywhere you turn you can see pictures of the devastation. Houses, roads and bridges have all been washed away by the raging water. Old trees have crashed under the force of the wind. In some communities, whole neighborhoods are in ruins.

Isaiah's audience certainly knew what that was like. Their temple was destroyed. Their country defeated. Everything they held dear in this life was turned upside down.

So when Isaiah speaks of the coming Messiah, he doesn't speak of the soldier who will conquer but the builder who will restore. Those who mourn will be comforted. Those who are in one prison or another will be freed. That which was destroyed shall be rebuilt.

It's almost Christmas and for some of you the delight is in every breath you breathe in. If so, give thanks and celebrate. Others of you, however, may be thinking more of ruins than good tidings. Your heart is too heavy for what has gone out of your life to feel very joyful about what is about to come.

It doesn't matter if you're wandering around in the mess you made of your own life. It doesn't matter is someone made the mess for you and left you with the remains. It doesn't matter is no one is to blame but it is just something that happens, like terrible accidents and diseases that rob and kill.

If you think that maybe you'd be better off skipping Christmas this year, well friend, you're exactly who this is for. Not the Christmas that's presents and bows and white lights on the house. It's the Christmas that's the God who comes to us as a restoration specialist, who cleans up the broken pieces of our lives and builds them back. The one who sets us free from all that has held us captive, even our pasts. The one who heals the wounded places in us. You're why he's here.

If you think you don't belong at this Christmas feast, think again. Read Isaiah's comforting words that are meant for Israel – and for you. And if you are able to sing carols with gusto, bake cookies with abandon and have the best gosh darn tree on the block, then pay attention. Pay attention to someone who may be trying to blend into the woodwork, someone who needs to hear that this good news is for them.

December 22
Acts 3:1-10

He thought he might get a few coins, maybe enough for a meal here or there. He gave up the hope of that much when they said their pockets were empty. Another handful of nothing.

A handful of nothing that became a lifetime of everything. A lifetime for walking and dancing and jumping in the air, unable to keep the smile from his face and the God-praise from his lips.

Look at us, Peter said and for this man, the world would never look the same.

Look at me, Jesus says as he stops by our way. In one moment we're disappointed because we're not getting what we thought we needed. But then a handful of nothing becomes a lifetime of everything and we walk and we dance and we cannot keep the thanks from our lips.

Lest you think this story doesn't apply to you, listen to the stories of Advent again. We just thought we were getting a God who'd set things right and if we were good, who'd bring us along. Instead we got a God who will come along right with us, spending nine helpless, developing months in the body of a woman, just as we do. Emerging helpless and vulnerable and utterly dependent, just as we do. Growing and learning and getting skinned knees and growth spurts, just like we do. Hurting, frustrated, angry... just like we are. Suffering, humiliated, dying in ways, God willing, we will not fully know.

We just wanted a God who would listen to our life. We got a God who was willing to live our life.

How can we not walk and leap and dance and praise such a God?

December 23
Psalm 150

You don't have to worry about waking the baby.
He's not quite here yet.
But my Lord, he's coming.
    My Lord, he's almost here.
and if that psalmist had cause
    to blow trumpets and bang cymbals,
    well then,
        he just didn't know.
Didn't know how much more cause for celebration
there'd be.
    Praise the Lord who rules over all creation.
    Praise the Lord who chooses to come stay at our house,
      take on our address
      live in our same kind of skin.
Praise God who is so great
  and so absurd
  and so filled with love
      that the Almighty becomes tiny,
        the all powerful becomes helpless,
        the Word becomes flesh.

He's not quite here yet.
But my Lord, he is coming

and what a wonder it is.

Praise the Lord
  and give it all you've got.
With the fullness of your heart and breath
  and brain and soul...
      praise the Lord.

He's not here yet,
  bu my Lord, he's coming.

December 24
Matthew 1:18-25

What do you dream? Tonight you may have visions of sugarplums dancing in your heads or nightmares of some assembly required.

Sometimes my dreams are magical flights of fancy that leave me laughing with their absurdity. Honestly, I think my imagination just wants to go for a joy ride some nights. Other nights my dreams are clearly conveying a message – something I need to look at in my life or some reassurance that I need to hear.

How do you know when to listen to a dream, when to sit up and pay attention? More to the point, how did Joseph know that it was right to ignore all of the rules and everything he'd been taught? How did Joseph make peace with not only not condemning this woman but also marrying her?

Somehow he knew it was the right thing. Somehow the dream was edged with God's dream, and that was enough to give him courage. Can you imagine the conversation he and Mary must have had?

Tonight you may dream of sugarplums... or of family reunions or of that long awaited gift or you may have nightmares about the neighbor's dog eating the turkey. But as you go to sleep on this night... on each night... be open to the possibility that your dreams may be edged with God's dream.

December 25
Luke 2:1-7

The angels will come soon enough, filling the sky with light and sound. The bewildered, believing shepherds will show up before you know it. The grand scenes of the Christmas pageant will play out with all of their glorias and alleluias.

But for now it is the quiet hours, or as quiet as things get with a donkey to lead and accommodations to negotiate and a woman in labor. Once the family is settled in, once the baby comes, it's a time for a new family just to be. Did they talk about the road that got them here, talk of angel visions and dreams? Did they count the fingers and toes of their baby son? Did he have hair? Were they a bit scared as they held these fragile few pounds of flesh? Did Mary have to tell Joseph to support his head? Did he cry a lot? Did first time mom and first time baby get the hang of the nursing thing right off or were there a few awkward times?

Today we throw a birthday party for a God who came as a baby, a real baby and not a role playing one. A baby who'd have to learn to sit up and crawl and whose gums would hurt when his teeth came through. A baby who'd have to learn toilet training and how to feed himself. A God who is on this night utterly helpless and vulnerable and seemingly incapable of saving himself, much less the world.

Today we throw a birthday party for a God who became one

of us all the way through. For some of you it will be a day that begins early and ends late, a day filled with people and noise and stuff to do. But sometime today, even for just a moment, take a moment to be still and quiet. For God's son has been born and you are God's child as well... so your brother is here.

Take a moment and breathe in deeply the wonder of a God whose love is so big that God would choose to become so small.

December 26
Luke 2:8-20

So now it's time to send out the birth announcements but there seems to be something wrong with the address list. You'd think the announcement of the birth of God's son would go first to the rabbis and chief priests. You'd think the angels would find the people who, in modern PR language, had a platform. The people who had influence. The people who had position. The people who could spread the word through official channels.

Something's wrong with the advance planning because none of those people get the first announcements. No, the angelic messengers show up with shepherds, the people nobody cared about (except maybe the sheep.)

The king is born not in a palace but in a stable. His birth is first announced not to the religious leaders but to a bunch of nobodies.

Maybe this announcement was a statement about the topsy-turvy nature of this gospel, of the messiah who came to preach good news to the poor. And maybe angels came to the shepherds because they were the ones who were open enough to listen.

The priests and religious leaders thought they had it all figured out. They knew how Messiah was going to come, and it certainly wasn't like this. They had no room in their priestly hearts for God's surprise.

May we never suppose that we know God so well that we miss the sound of angels celebrating an event we never imagined happening.

December 27
Matthew 2:1-12

For all of their wisdom, they are incredibly naive. Like a bumbling detective they happily show up at the palace of the king to ask about the birth of the new king. They may have been wise in the way of the stars but politically astute they were not.

When the king tells them to find the child "so I can worship him too" they ignore the ominous music in the sound track and go happily and eagerly on their way. They follow a star and give this newborn gifts found in no Babies R Us store. Fortunately, they have the good sense to heed the dream that directs them to go home by another way and avoid Herod altogether.

Angels announce the birth to shepherds... and Iranian (modern day Persia) wise men are the first to see the news in the stars. Not the Jewish leaders. Not the people who were supposed to be looking for a Messiah's arrival. From the very beginning the gospels make it clear that the old boundaries are being broken and old walls of division are coming down.

So why do we so often miss the point? Why do we spend so much time and energy on who is in the circle of God' favorites? Why do we keep insisting that the world must be divided between us and them, between our kind of people and those people. God so loved the world...

God, in the midst of our celebrations of Christmas help us not to miss the point of it.

December 28
Matthew 2:13-23

It doesn't take long. It doesn't take long for the shadows of evil to break into this scene of light and joy.

Evil. How else do you describe a man who is willing to wipe out the lives of untold children just so none of them will grow up to challenge his power. After all of our celebrations of joy, this text hits hard as we try to imagine (or try not to imagine, as our stomachs and hearts will allow) the anguish of mothers and fathers seeing their sons slaughtered.

From the beginning, Jesus is on the run. A kind of Moses in reverse, he flees to Egypt for the sake of his safety and to wait for the death of King Herod. It doesn't take long for that warm and fuzzy Christmas feeling to leave.

What kind of world do you return to after the holidays? Maybe you're already there. Who knows what the headlines will read on the day you read this. I hope that it's good news.

But if it's not, consider this good news. Not only was God willing to become flesh and become one of us, God was willing to engage the battle with evil from the beginning. Entrusted to the faithful and wise care of his parents, Jesus didn't come into a world that was sunshine and roses and rainbows and unicorns. He came into a world of unnecessary suffering and cold-hearted murder.

We live in a world chock-full of wonder, as bright as sunshine shining on fresh snow. But we also live in a world in which very bad things happen to very good people.

In Christ, God was not afraid to come into all of the corners of all of our world.

December 29

Esther 4:9-17

For various reasons, certain people were conspiring to manipulate the king into issuing an order for all of the Jews to be killed. The king, by the way, was unaware that his own queen Esther was Jewish. When her foster father, Mordecai, heard the news he went into deep grieving.

Esther sends a message to ask what's wrong and Mordecai reports back the terrible developments. He asks her to go to the king on their behalf.

At first Esther is unwilling. She cannot see the king without being called and it's been over a month since he called for her. If she goes to him unbidden the penalty is death.

"If we die," Mordecai warns her, "don't think you'll escape. And besides," he adds, "maybe this is why you're in this place at this time." For such a time as this.

Mordecai is persuasive. Esther risks her own death in order to speak up and instead of the Jews being killed, the conspirator who'd started the ball rolling is put to death.

For such a time as this. We seldom see such moments coming. You were just living your life and all of a sudden the moment is here. The moment to speak out. The moment to take action. The moment to start something. The moment to end something.

I don't know when your moment will come nor mine. But I pray that when it does we will have the wisdom and vision to recognize it for what it is as well as the courage to do what must be done.

For such a time as this. Is there a moment before you now?

December 30
Isaiah 11:1-10

Perhaps it's just the day in which I write. It's rainy and gloomy and cannot decide if it will tease us with spring (as it has no business doing in January) or behave like proper winter. Perhaps it's just the time in which I write, a time in which brutality and violence seem to have become a staple of our news.

Whatever the cause, what struck me as I read this familiar passage today was the utter lack of violence. Sure, we begin with the whole picture of judgment, a winnowing out of the wicked, a lifting up of the poor.

And then we are treated to this great scene of peace. The hunter and the hunted lie down together. Animals that normally would be tearing each other apart are snuggling up together. The symbol of danger, a deadly snake, is now harmless. Everything is safe enough for a small, trusting child to be in the middle of it.

Listen, I can't even get my dogs and my cat to stay in the same room together without fireworks (mostly instigated by the cat.) I cannot imagine a lion and lamb hanging out together with no bloodshed.

It's as incongruous as the creator of heavens and the earth coming to earth as a small and helpless infant.

Obviously, this day is not yet here. The kingdom that has come in the birth of Jesus is yet still on its way. But in the meantime...

In the meantime, can we as Christians not commit ourselves to working for peace? Can we not do what we can to reduce the amount of violence in this world, whether it's addressing national policy or the ways in which we interact with each other?

God's kingdom has come. God's kingdom is coming.

Are you willing to accept the challenge and the invitation to live as a kingdom person?

December 31
Psalm 23

When I began as the first editor of *Reflections* daily devotional magazine (Smyth and Helwys) I had to make many decisions. One of those decisions involved how I'd pick out the texts for each issue. I decided that the text for December 31 of each year would be the 23rd psalm. I can think of no more complete text for the hinge point of our years. Whether we have been beside still waters or walking through dark valleys, God has been and will be with us.

One year we asked the children in our Sunday School class to illustrate this psalm. Young Andrew drew a picture of someone walking along, two dogs on leash following behind: goodness and mercy. I will never read nor hear this psalm again without thinking of goodness and mercy happily trotting behind me.

Take some time today or tomorrow to think about your year. What have been the valleys and where have the dark places been? Where has God surprised you? Where did it feel like God abandoned you? When have you feasted on God's grace? When have you been aware of goodness and mercy faithfully following you?

Take some time today or tomorrow to think about the upcoming year. What's your hope for this year? What's your dream? Are you willing to commit to your own spiritual growth? What needs to change? What question needs to be asked?

The road of a new year stretches before us and we do not know where it will lead nor what it will ask of us. All we can know for sure is that there is a God who goes with us through every turn of the journey, guiding, holding, prodding, loving.

Amen.

And amen.

Thanks to....

James M. Pitts who, when he was the Associate Chaplain at Furman and I was but a freshman, suggested that I might write some prayers for campus worship. Thanks, Jim, for getting things started and then opening many doors along the way.

My friends who invariably greet me with the question, "What are you writing now?" and thus remind me that I should be doing just that.

Carolyn Ashburn who, out of the blue and in the midst of choir rehearsal volunteered to proof this manuscript. Any errors that slipped through are entirely my own fault and not hers.

The good people of College Park Baptist Church (Greensboro, NC) and Knollwood Baptist Church (Winston-Salem, NC), both of whom welcomed me as member, sister, friend, and colleague. I have been greatly blessed over these last few years to be a part of these two congregations who share a commitment to telling, singing and living out in the world the good news of God's grace, and who worship God with heart. And soul. And mind.

About the author

Peggy Haymes is a minister of many things, including working as Licensed Professional Counselor as well as a hospital chaplain. The founder of the online site, Heart Callings, she enjoys running and biking, cheering for her favorite teams, and hanging out with her cat and dogs She has received a number of awards, including the Richard Furman Award given by Furman university in recognition of her ministry contributions.

Other books by Peggy Haymes

Be Thou Present: Prayers, Hymns and Litanies for Christian Worship

Heart Prayers

Didn't See It Coming: How I faced bouncing off a Buick and other assorted stuff

heart prayers 2

I Don't Remember Signing Up for This Class: a life of darkness, light and suprising hope

If you have enjoyed any of my books, would you do me the favor of leaving a review at www.amazon.com? Thank you!

You can contact Peggy at
Peggy@PeggyHaymes.com

Heart Callings

Your Path To Spiritual, Intentional Living

At www.HeartCallings.com you'll find:

Callings blog

*Spirit, Mind and Hear*t podcast

The Journey to Good Enough
(online course for releasing your inner critic and need
to be perfect.)

Heart Callings membership site
(starting in 2017). Membership includes monthly
master class and weekly insights/tools from the worlds
of psychology and spirituality.